Hospitality Generics

Student's Book

TVET FIRST

NQF Level 3
B van Niekerk
J H van Niekerk

TROUPANT · PUBLISHERS
TROUPANT

IN PARTNERSHIP WITH
macmillan
education

TVET First: Hospitality Generics NQF Level 3 Student's Book
TVET First

First published 2007

Published by
Macmillan South Africa (Pty) Ltd
Private Bag X19, Northlands, 2116, Gauteng,
South Africa

Typeset in Palatino 11pt
Cover design by BrandTalk , a subsidiary of African
Access

Acknowledgements
Mr. Hannes De Bruyn, Gautengpics for photographs (www.gautengpics.co.za)
ABSA Card Division, Pretoria, for paypoint guidelines and information.
Saint George Hotel, Rietvleidam, Pretoria, Gauteng.
Elephant Springs Avuxeni Hotel, Bela Bela, Limpopo.
Mr. Leon Gouws, HDM Productions, Secunda for illustrations & information on lifting heavy objects.
THETA for use of information from Learner's Guides.

ISBN-13: 9781770172159
e-ISBN: 9781431020799
WIP: 0280Y000

While every effort has been made to trace the copyright holders and obtain copyright permission
from them, in some cases this has proved impossible due to logistic and time constraints. Any
copyright holder who becomes aware of infringement on our side is invited to contact the
publisher.

Note: Any reference to Further Education and Training (FET) in this book should be taken to
mean Technical and Vocational Education and Training (TVET).

To order any of these books, contact Macmillan Customer Services at:
Tel: (011) 731 3300
Fax: (011) 731 3535
E-mail: customerservices@macmillan.co.za

Printed and bound by Pinetown Printers

Contents

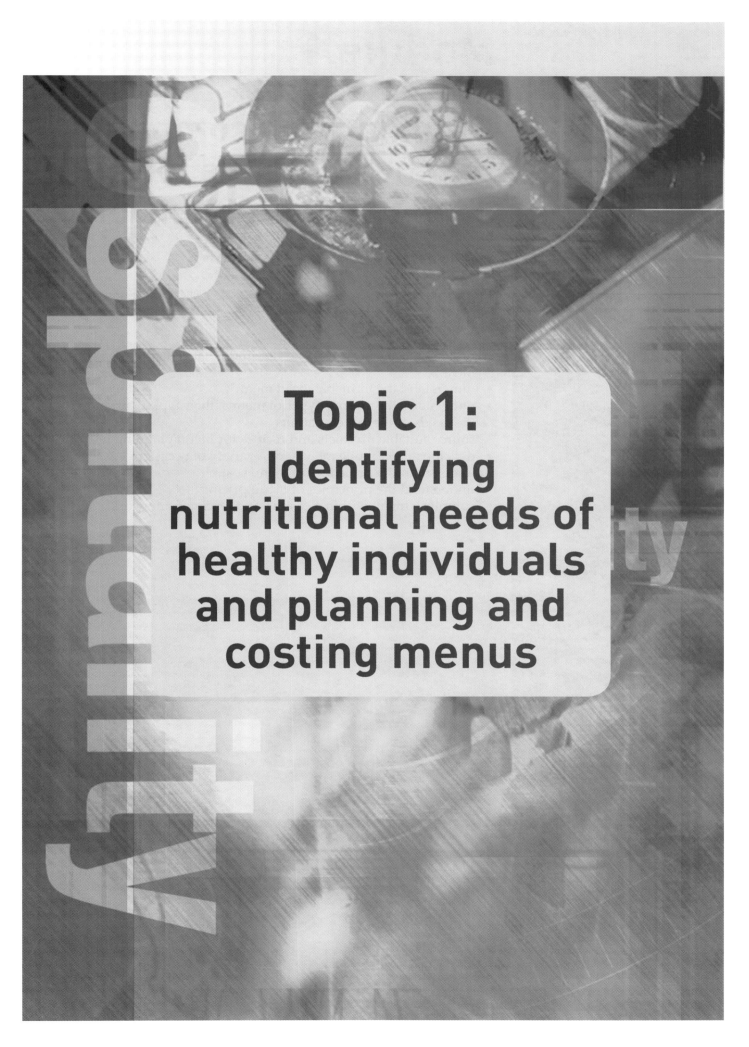

Topic 1:
Identifying nutritional needs of healthy individuals and planning and costing menus

Module 1

Planning and compiling balanced menus for a variety of occasions or establishments

Overview

The student should be able to ...

- understand the basic food groups and what constitutes a nutritious meal
- understand the term 'balanced menu'
- understand the various types of menus, their typical structures and the needs of the target markets
- source suitable products and recipes for menu planning purposes
- develop and compile menus for a variety of occasions
- understand the principles of menu costing
- understand the principles of menu pricing
- compile a menu within a costing and pricing framework

Unit 1:

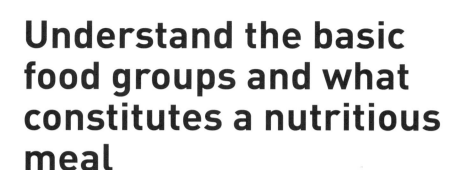

Understand the basic food groups and what constitutes a nutritious meal

Nutrition is the study of how food is utilised by the body. Food is composed of nutrients, which are chemical compounds needed for survival. Some of these are essential nutrients that cannot be made in the body and must be supplied by food or supplements. Examples of essential nutrients are minerals, such as iron and calcium, vitamins, and certain amino acids that combine to form protein. Without an external source of these essential nutrients, good health cannot be maintained by the body. There are other nutrients that are equally important for survival, but these can be synthesised in the body, provided that the raw materials are available. Examples of this type of nutrient are the fatty substance, lecithin, and the nonessential amino acids.

There are six major nutrient groups, and they are as follows:

1. Proteins
2. Carbohydrates
3. Fats
4. Vitamins
5. Minerals
6. Water

To live a healthy and balanced life the body needs a certain minimum of these nutrients on a daily basis. In order to receive an adequate supply of all the essential nutrients, it is important to eat a variety of foods.

The Basic Food Groups

As knowledge and technology developed over the years the classification of basic food groups developed from an original three basic food group to the current approach based on the food guide pyramid. In this book the basic four food groups and the food guide pyramid will be discussed.

The Basic Four Food Groups

The Basic Four Food Groups was developed as a convenient method for ensuring that this goal is met. It divides foods into four groups based on their nutrient content and recommends the number of servings from each group.

The four food groups plan

Words & terms

Nutritious meal:
A Nutritious meal strives to provide food from each of the food groups in a balanced combination.

Nutrients:
Chemicals compounds found in food needed for human survival, classified into six major groups: proteins, carbohydrates, fats, vitamins, minerals and water.

Food Groups:
Generally accepted way of distinguishing foods into certain dietary groups.

Food group	Servings per day	Serving size

Milk and milk products
    Calcium, vitamin D,
    riboflavin, vitamin A,
    protein
	Children: 3-4
	Adults: 2
		250ml milk
		30g cheese
		250ml yoghurt

Meats, fish, poultry, eggs, nuts, legumes Protein, iron, B vitamins	2 or more	60g – 90g cooked beef, pork, poultry, lamb, fish, 2 eggs 250ml cooked legumes 60g peanut butter

Fruits and vegetables
    Vitamin A, vitamin C, iron,
    fibre
	4 or more	125ml fruit or vegetables,
		1 piece fruit
		125ml fruit juice

Grains
    Carbohydrates, B vitamins
    Iron, some protein, fibre if
    Whole grain
	4 or more	1 slice whole grain or enriched bread,
		30g cereal
		125ml cooked grain

The food guide pyramid

The pyramid is a visual representation of the dietary guidelines. It reminds us to use plant foods as the foundation of meals. Our diets should be based on breads and grains, with lots of fruits and vegetables added. A moderate amount of meats and other high protein foods, as well as several servings of milk and dairy products ensures that the vitamins and minerals needed for good health are consumed. Another important part of understanding the food guide pyramid is to look carefully at portion sizes in order to evaluate how many servings are being consumed.

Did you know?

Dietary guidelines
The dietary guidelines are a set of recommendations designed for healthy people aged two years and older. These guidelines emphasise the relationship between healthy eating and physical activity, as well as the importance of eating a wide variety of healthy foods. The guidelines recommend that diets follow the pattern of the food guide pyramid
Energy allowance
Energy allowance is the amount of energy (kilojoules) allowed per person, according to his/her age, height, weight and activity level, as recommended by the RDA.
RDA
The Recommended Dietary Allowances (RDA) specify levels of kilojoules (energy allowance) and selected nutrients for specific ages to maintain health and to support the dietary guidelines.

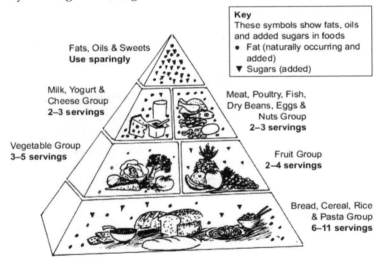

The food pyramid not only ensures that the right nutrients are included in the diet, but also that the recommended energy allowance is not exceeded. Every day, foods should be selected from the following food groups:

Bread, cereal, rice and pasta: 6-11 servings per day
Vegetables: 3-5 servings per day
Fruit: 2-4 servings per day
Milk, yoghurt and cheese: 2-3 servings per day
Meat, poultry, fish, dry beans, eggs and nuts: 2-3 servings per day
Fats, oils and sweets: use sparingly

Serving sizes in each food group

Food group	One serving equals
Bread, cereal, rice and pasta	1 small roll, biscuit or muffin 1 slice of bread ½ hamburger bun or English muffin ½ cup of cooked cereal ½ cup of cooked rice ½ cup of cooked pasta
Vegetables Fruit	¾ cup of vegetable juice 1 cup of leafy raw vegetables, such as spinach or lettuce ½ cup of chopped raw or cooked vegetables ¼ cup dried fruit 1 medium-sized melon wedge ½ cup of strawberries ¾ cup of juice 1 whole apple, banana or orange ½ cup of chopped, cooked or canned fruit ¼ cup of dried fruit
Milk, yoghurt and cheese	1 cup of milk 30g of cheese (enough thinly-sliced cheese to cover a piece of bread) 1 small tub (175ml) of yoghurt
Meat, poultry, fish	60-90 grams of cooked lean meat or fish (the size of a cassette tape) 90 grams cooked chicken, without skin (the size of a chicken leg, thigh or breast) 2 cooked eggs 1 cup of cooked dry beans 4 tablespoons of peanut butter

The fruit and vegetable group

Fruit and vegetables are probably the most important group when it comes to good health. Fruit and vegetables are naturally rich in nutrients that ensure good health such as beta-carotene, vitamins A and C (powerful antioxidants), minerals, dietary fibre (wonderful for regularity and reducing the energy content of the diet), and bioflavonoids (protective against many diseases).

Because fruit and vegetables contain so many nutrients that help protect the body against disease, they should be eaten in large quantities Five or more portions a day should be eaten.

The grain and cereal group

This food group is also called the carbohydrate or starchy food group. Carbohydrates provide energy to the body for our daily activities - the bulk of each meal should, therefore, contain a carbohydrate-rich food, for example, unsifted maize meal, mabela or oats porridge, or high-fibre cereal, plus wholewheat toast for breakfast, wholewheat sandwiches for lunch and food like jacket potatoes, brown rice, pasta, samp, or boiled crushed wheat for dinner.

The cereal and grain group is the best source of B vitamins, vitamin E, essential minerals and trace elements (zinc, copper, selenium, magnesium, potassium), and dietary fibre – all nutrients that help protect us against heart disease, many different kinds of cancer, diabetes and obesity.

Two or more portions of the cereal and grain group should be eaten at each meal. It is important to select as far as possible only unprocessed or minimally processed starches and grains to ensure the best benefits for the body.

Milk and dairy group

Food in this group is an excellent source of calcium. Human beings need a sufficient supply of calcium to ensure they develop strong bones and teeth during childhood and adolescence and maintain this strength throughout their lives to prevent osteoporosis.

Milk, yoghurt, maas, and cheese are all excellent sources of calcium. One glass of milk can supply 300mg or more of calcium to the body. This represents a third of the Recommended Daily Allowance (RDA) which is 1000mg of calcium/day for adults, especially women.

Meat, fish and eggs

Meat, fish and eggs, are rich in high-quality protein, vitamins, minerals and essential fatty acids.

- High-quality protein

This food group is derived from animals - the richest sources of complete high-quality, protein.

Proteins consist of building blocks, called amino acids. Essential amino acids cannot be manufactured within the human body and must, therefore, form part of the food we eat. During periods of rapid growth within the body, such as pregnancy, lactation, infancy, childhood, the teenage years, and when one is recovering from illness, our bodies require high-quality protein in larger quantities to rebuild body tissues.

Some plant foods also contain protein, but for periods of rapid body growth plant proteins are not sufficient - one has to eat really large quantities of plant foods to obtain the same amount of protein that is contained in one egg or a small portion of meat or fish. Infants and young children just don't have the capacity to eat sufficient plant protein. They need protein derived from animals, such as those found in milk, cheese, eggs, meat or fish.

- Vitamins

Meat, fish and eggs are generally good sources of B vitamins, including niacin, riboflavin, vitamin B12, and pantothenic acid. If you do not eat any animal-based foods, including eggs and milk or cheese, you run the risk of developing vitamin B12 deficiency, which can result in iron deficiency.

- Minerals

Meat, fish and egg yolk are the richest sources of bio-available iron for human consumption. Iron is important for healthy blood and for

preventing iron-deficiency anaemia, which is one of the most common deficiency diseases in the world today. The iron in meat, fish and eggs is more easily absorbed and utilised in the human body than iron found in plant foods. In addition to iron, the meat, fish and egg group also contains other important minerals such as zinc and phosphorus, which are required to keep the immune and nervous systems healthy.

Essential fatty acids

Essential fatty acids – nutrients that the body cannot manufacture – have to be obtained from food. Fatty acids, especially omega-3, are important for the body to ensure normal development of the brain, nervous system and eyes in younger children. Research has shown that Western diets tend to be deficient in omega-3 fatty acids, much needed to boost immunity and prevent heart disease. Fish like salmon, mackerel and other fatty fish are excellent sources of the omega-3 fatty acids and should form part of the diet.

Guidelines

Guidelines for eating meat, fish and eggs

- Red meat should be eaten once or twice a week only - not every day and definitely not at two or more meals a day.
- Utilise white meat like chicken, turkey or ostrich to replace red meat.
- Select the leanest cuts of meat to reduce your fat intake.
- Remove all visible fat from meat and don't eat the skin of the chicken.
- Replace meat with fish as often as possible.
- The SA Heart Foundation recommends that anyone with cholesterol or heart problems should not eat more than four eggs a week.
- Prepare foods without adding fat - grill meat, discard dripping, steam and bake fish, boil or poach eggs.
- Have regular meatless meals – use pasta or legumes (dry beans, peas and lentils, Toppers and textured vegetable protein dishes).
- Avoid eating too much smoked, cured or charred meat, as these methods of preservation and preparation promote cancer .
- When you prepare meals combine plant and animal protein foods for the greatest benefit.
- Avoid excessive saturated fat intake by adding dry beans to stew, or stretch mince with cubed soy protein.

Fat group

The human body needs fat as part of the diet, but we should not eat too much. Some fats are good for us, while others are bad for human consumption.

- How much fat?

This food group can raise the level of both the total amount of fat, and the amount of saturated fat, we consume.

A great deal of research has been carried out to determine the role that fat plays in a whole range of degenerative diseases, such as heart disease, cancer, obesity and diabetes. The basic message from this research is that human beings should be careful not to eat too much fat as a whole, and to cut down specifically on the amount of saturated fat in their diets. Most people should reduce their intake of fats like margarine and salad oils to 1-2 tablespoons a day.

- Different types of fat

Fats can be divided into various categories, depending on their chemical composition and the effect they have on health. Not all fats are equal.

Fats are divided into four main classes:

- saturated
- monounsaturated
- polyunsaturated
- essential fatty acids

According to their effect on the body and health, some fats are worse than others. In this regard fats can be divided into 'bad' and 'good' fats:

Saturated fats

Generally speaking, saturated fats and cholesterol, are regarded as the 'bad fats'. These fats are found in animal products (cream, butter, lard, bacon fat, meat fat, chicken skin), and also in plant fats that have been saturated by a process called hydrogenation, for example, hard or brick margarines.

Limit the intake of foods that contain hard, saturated fats such as brick margarine, pies and other baked goods that don't specify what kind of fat has been used in the recipe.

Mono- and polyunsaturated fats

Mono- and polyunsaturated fats, which are found in sunflower, safflower, canola and olive oils, soft or tub margarines and nuts, are regarded as 'good fats'.

The ideal is to replace as much saturated fat in the diet as possible with monounsaturated and polyunsaturated fats and oils. These fats and oils help reduce the risk of heart disease and cancer. However, when consumed in large quantities they could raise the total fat content of the diet significantly. When selecting 1-2 tablespoons of fat a day, choose margarine with a high poly- or monounsaturated fat content (read the labels), and use olive or sunflower oil over salad.

Essential fats

We need to obtain the important fatty acids the body cannot produce from our diets. These are the essential fatty acids, i.e. omega-6 and omega-3. As modern-day Western diets contain quite a lot of omega-6 (derived from the soft margarines and salad oils mentioned above), we need to concentrate on eating food that contains sufficient omega-3. Fish, flax, canola and soybean oils are rich sources of this fatty acid. At least one teaspoon of these oils per day is recommended as part of the diet.

Did you know?

All South Africans at risk of dying young, says new report

According to a new report commissioned by the Heart and Stroke Foundation South Africa and undertaken by the Medical Research Council, South Africans are at risk of premature death due to heart disease, despite dramatic variations in age, gender, race and standard of living.

The report, entitled Heart Disease in South Africa, reveals that risk factors such as stress, obesity, inactive lifestyle, poor nutrition, smoking, hypertension, diabetes and high blood cholesterol are present across all demographic sectors.

Currently about 195 South Africans – or 13 minibus loads – die each day from heart disease.

Get active

Moderate physical activity like brisk walking, swimming, dancing or participating in non-competitive sports for just 30 minutes per day can reduce your risk of heart attack to half that of an inactive person and give you three times the chance of surviving such an attack.

Watch your diet

Good dietary choices are key. Opt for a prudent, varied eating pattern with reduced total fat intake, particularly saturated fats from animal products. Eat more fruit and vegetables and reduce your overall salt intake.

Heart and Stroke Foundation SA on 0860 22 32 22 or visit www.heartfoundation.co.za.

Unit 2:

Balanced menu

A menu is said to be balanced if all four main food groups are proportioned in it

When designing a menu, take into account the various factors that affect the design (type & style of establishment, target market, food habits & preferences of customers, production & service constraints, equipment, personnel and availability of ingredients, etc.). In addition, the dishes offered must provide a balanced meal. This does not only refer to the nutritional balance, but also to other factors such as the following:

- The predominant colour of each course should be different.
- A commodity should not appear as a major component in more than one course.
- Avoid making delicate flavours with stronger ones.
- Methods of cooking should vary between one course and the nex
- The texture of dishes and within dishes should be varied.

Words & terms

Balanced menu:
Menu that contains food from all four main food groups in correct proportions

Balanced meal:
A meal that has a nutritional balance from the four main food groups

In the workplace

South African cuisine

For the more daring diner, South Africa offers culinary challenges from crocodile sirloins to fried caterpillars to sheep heads. All three are reputed to be delicious. For the not-quite-so-brave, there are a myriad of indigenous delicacies such as biltong (dried, salted meat), bobotie (a much-improved version of Shepherd's pie) and boerewors (hand-made farm sausages, grilled on an open flame).

Those who prefer to play it altogether safe will find that most eateries offer a familiar global menu – anything from hamburgers to sushi to pad thai to spaghetti bolognaise. And you can drink the water.

On a single street in a Johannesburg suburb, one finds Italian restaurants, two or three varieties of Chinese cookery, Japanese, Moroccan, French, Portuguese and Indian food, both Tandoor and Gujarati. Not far away are Congolese restaurants, Greek, even Brazilian and Korean establishments, and, everywhere, fusion, displaying the fantasies of creative chefs.

It's not much different in the other major centres, such as Cape Town or Durban. Restaurant guides that categorise eateries by national style list close to two dozen, including Vietnamese and Swiss.

Those in search of authentic South African cuisine have to look harder for those few establishments that specialise in it – like the justly famous Gramadoelas in central Johannesburg, Wandie's Place in Soweto, the Africa Café in central Cape Town or smaller restaurants in that city's Bo-Kaap, in Khayelitsha and Langa.

SouthAfrica.info *The all-in-one official guide and web portal to South Africa*, Barbara Ludman.

Did you know?

Nutritional status of children in South Africa

Food, or the lack of it, is one of the factors affecting the nutritional status of children in South Africa. The Department of Health (DOH) in South Africa is embarking on a multi-faceted program to address malnutrition (nutrient deficiencies), that is rife amongst children aged 1 - 9. One of these is the National Food Fortification Program which recommends fortifying wheat, maize flour and retail sugar, three of the five most commonly consumed food vehicles as reported by the National Food Consumption Survey.

The National Food Consumption Survey reported that for South African children as a whole, the average dietary nutrient intake of energy, calcium, iron, zinc, selenium, vitamin A, vitamin D, vitamin C, vitamin E, riboflavin, niacin, and vitamin B6 was less than 67% of the Recommended Dietary Allowances (RDA), and in many cases below 50% of the Recommended Dietary Allowances.

Unit 3:

Menu styles

There are several kinds of menus

Table d'hôte menu or set-price menu

- This is a menu offering a meal consisting of two or three courses at a set price.
- The menu may offer a choice of dishes for all courses, but is usually limited to two, three or four.
- This type of menu is often used in small hotels, canteens, hostels, functions and old age homes where limited facilities and cooking skills are available for food preparation.

À la carte menu (see Annexure A)

- This is a menu where all the dishes are individually priced and individually added to the bill at the end of the meal.
- Customers compile their own meal, which may consist of one, two or more courses.
- A true à la carte dish should be cooked to the customer's specific order.
- Customers usually have to wait for the meal to be prepared.
- This type of menu is suitable for restaurants, steak houses and coffee shops.

Buffet menus

- A buffet is a display of a variety of food consisting of many different dishes.
- The food selection is displayed in a specific area of the room.
- Customers or guests serve themselves from the display.
- The buffet is usually an all inclusive price - eat as much as you like.
- This menu style is often used for functions or family-type restaurants.

Cocktail menu (See Annexure B)

- This menu consists of light snack-type foods, such as sausages rolls, canapés etc.
- The cocktail menu is usually presented in buffet style on different platters.
- The cocktail menu is usually charged per person.
- A cocktail menu is used for cocktail parties or lights meals.

Du jour menus

Plat du jour menu (*Dish of the day*)

- Plat du jour menu items are offered with an à la carte or table d'hôte menu.

Did you know?

The buffet menu is especially popular when groups from different cultures eat together.

Menus
The menu is a means of communicating with guests to
- tell them what is offered
- let them know about the preparation styles currently in fashion
- tempt them to try something they may not have thought of trying
- encourage conversation about your menu and style of food

It should therefore
- accommodate a wide range of dietary needs and culinary preferences
- accommodate the current trends in dining. For example, there is an increasing trend towards healthy eating, while heavily sauced food has fallen out of favour
- be sufficiently innovative to appeal to the most adventurous eaters, while accommodating the more conservative ones
- give enough information to enable guests to make an informed choice

- The dishes are offered separately in addition to the usual menu.
- Although the dish of the day items can be any course on the menu, they tend to be mostly special offer main courses.
- Dish of the day items are priced separately from the à la carte or table d'hôte menu.
- The dish of the day is normally a ready-to-serve dish.

Carte du Jour menu (*Card of the day*)

- This menu offers a number of usually seasonal dishes.
- These items are not offered on other menus of the establishment.
- Some restaurants offer the carte du jour instead of the table d'hôte menu.
- If offered with an à la carte menu, items from this menu are priced separately and are usually more expensive than other items.

Photograph courtesy of Gautengpics

Cyclical menus

- The cyclical menu is compiled to cover a given period (the cycle) of time, for example, two weeks, eight weeks, one month, etc. The duration of the cycle is determined by the season, type of food service operation and management policy.
- The cyclical menu consists of a number of set daily menus used by the particular establishment for a specific period. Normally the menus are repeated once the cycle is completed.
- Cyclical menus are typically utilised by establishments like industrial catering restaurants, cafeterias, canteens, hostels, hospitals, etc. where food is provided on a mass scale and at low cost for the benefit of consumers.

Selective menus

The selective menu offers two or more choices in each menu category. The exact number of options offered varies according to the different types of food service establishments.

Various types of menus

Breakfast

Breakfast menus can be divided into **two** main categories:

Continental breakfast
The continental breakfast or café complet is a simple meal and includes fruit, cereals, yoghurts, juices, pastries, breads, jams, preserves, and tea or coffee. It can also include cold meats and cheese.

English or full breakfast
The English breakfast consists of several courses and is more complex. An English breakfast consists of all of the items offered with a

continental breakfast plus eggs, steak, bacon, two types of sausage, kidneys or liver, etc.

It is commonly found that hotels combine these two types of breakfast on one menu in order to simplify menu organisation and presentation. This guest can see what is available and then make his/her selection. The guest is then billed according to the selection made.

Photograph courtesy of Gautengpics

The customer or guest having breakfast is often in a hurry – usually on the way to work, a meeting or leaving for the airport. This has to be taken into consideration when developing, offering, presenting and serving a breakfast menu.

Points to consider when compiling a breakfast menu:

- As large a variety as possible should be offered, bearing in mind that it is better to offer a smaller number of well-prepared dishes than a large number of hurriedly prepared ones.
- A choice of plain foods such as boiled eggs or poached haddock should be available for the person who may not require a fried breakfast.
- Breakfast menus may be table d'hôte or à la carte.

Examples of food for a breakfast menu

- Fruits: grapefruit, orange, melon, apple etc.
- Fruit juices: cocktail, apple, guava, orange etc.
- Stewed fruit: prunes, fruit salad, apples, pears, etc.
- Selection of yoghurt
- Cereals: porridge, cornflakes, All Bran flakes, muesli, etc.
- Eggs: fried, boiled, poached, scrambled, omelettes, etc.
- Fish: grilled herrings, or kippers, fried sole, fish cakes, smoked haddock, kedgeree.
- Meats (hot): fried or grilled bacon, sausages, kidneys, calf's liver with tomatoes, mushrooms or sauté potatoes or potato cakes
- Meats (cold): ham, bacon, pressed beef with sauté potatoes
- Preserves: marmalade, jams, honey
- Beverages: tea, coffee, hot chocolate
- Bread: rolls, croissants, toast, pancakes, waffles

Photograph courtesy of Gautengpics

Luncheon menus

Customers' requirements for lunch vary considerably according to the type of establishment and the preferences of the customer. Menus must be carefully compiled if they are to be successful, for example, pub lunches, business lunches, etc.

Different types of luncheon menus

Set price menu

- normally a three-course menu with ideally a choice for each course.
- The variety offered is usually determined by the skills of the caterer offering what can be afforded within the selling price. In some cases this may be a simple choice between two dishes, in others four or five.
- The above menu with an option for the customer to choose and pay for either one (main course) or two courses.

- A varied list of dishes each priced individually so that the customer can make up his/her own menu of whatever number of dishes required.

Buffet

This may be all cold or all hot dishes, or a combination of both, either to be served or organised on a self-service basis. Depending on the time of year and location, barbecue dishes may be considered.

Special party, which may be either

- set menu with no choice
- set menu with a limited choice such as soup or melon, main course, choice of two sweets
- served or self-service buffet

The critical success factor with this type of menu is to offer only a variety of courses and dishes within each course that can be satisfactorily prepared, cooked and served normally within a lunch hour.

Photograph courtesy of Gautengpics

Foods to select from for a luncheon menu

Traditional luncheon menus, both set price and à la carte, may be compiled from the following foods: (Kinton, Ceserani & Foskett, 1992)

- fruit cocktails, fruits and fruit juice
- shellfish, shellfish cocktails
- smoked fish or meat: salmon, trout, mackerel, ham, salami
- hors-d'oeuvre: assorted or simple items. Light salads with a vegetable, fish, meat or game content
- soup: consommé with simple garnish, cold in summer and hot in winter; vegetable soups, creamed soup (mushroom), chicken, minestrone, Scotch broth, etc.
- pasta: spaghetti, macaroni, ravioli, cannelloni, gnocchi, noodles, risotto, pizza and quiche
- eggs: when served for a luncheon menu egg dishes are usually garnished: scrambled, poached, soft boiled, en cocotte, sur le plat, omelette

Photograph courtesy of Gautengpics

- fish: nearly all kinds of fish can be served, but without complicated garnishes. They are usually steamed, poached, grilled, deep or shallow fried; dishes to include various fish in light sauces

Main courses:

- brown stews of meat
- braised steaks, braised beef
- goulash, braised oxtail, salamis of game
- hot pot, Irish stew
- meat pies, chicken pies
- tripe, sautéed kidneys
- Vienna and Hamburg steaks, hamburgers
- sausages, minced meat, chicken à la king
- fried lamb, veal or pork cutlets or fillets
- fried steaks (entrecote, tournedos, fillets, etc.)
- veal escalopes
- vol-au-vent of chicken
- pilaff, kebab, chicken cutlets
- vegetarian and ethnic dishes
    - roasts: beef, pork, veal, lamb, mutton, chicken

Grills:

- steaks (chateaubriand, fillet, tournedos, point, rump, porterhouse, entrecote)
- cutlets (single, double)
- chops (loin, chump)
- kidneys, mixed grill
- chicken, chicken legs, kebabs

Cold buffet:

- salmon, lobster, crab
- pâté or terrine
- beef, ham, tongue, lamb
- turkey, chicken, chicken pies, raised pies
- vegetarian dishes
- salads, simple or compound, mixed salad leaves tossed in a light oil with lemon juice or vinegar dressing topped with baked goats cheese, fresh asparagus, fried chicken livers, fried wild or cultivated mushrooms, a poached or soft boiled egg removed from the shell

Photograph courtesy of Gautengpics

Vegetables

Potatoes

Sweets:

- steamed puddings
- milk puddings
- fruit (salad, stewed, flans, pies, fritters)
- egg custard sweets (baked, bread and butter, cream)

Photograph courtesy of Gautengpics

- bavarois, savarin, baba
- charlottes, profiteroles, gateaux
- pastries
- various ices and sorbets

Savouries: simple savouries may also be served, for example, Welsh rarebit

Cheese: a good selection of cheese; biscuits, celery and radishes

Dessert: fresh fruit of all kinds and nuts.

Coffee or tea

A vegetarian lunch menu may be offered as an alternative to or as part of the à la carte or table d'hôte menus.

Dinner menus

Both table d'hôte and à la cart menus are suitable for dinner menus. The type and variety offered usually depend on the size of the establishment and capabilities of the staff in preparing the dishes.

The number of courses on special party menus may be from three upwards. The reason for the party or occasion is very important for the host. The compilation of the menu is extremely important, calling for expert knowledge and wise judgement on the part of the caterer.

The following are some traditional and classical dishes that may be served with light contemporary style dishes: (Kinton, Ceserani & Foskett,1992)

Photograph courtesy of Gautengpics

- Cocktail: fruit and shellfish
- Fruit
- Delicacies: caviar, oyster, snails, potted shrimps, prawns, foie gras
- Smoked fish and meat
- Hors d'oeuvre
- Salads: small dressed salad served simply, sprinkled with chopped fresh herbs or topped with hot pieces of lightly fried scallops, wild mushrooms or chicken livers; or cold crab, lobster, prawns, crayfish, etc.
- Soup: clear and consommé-based, petite marmite, shellfish bisques and cream soups, etc; cold soups include vichyssoise and consommé
- Fish: poached, shallow poached, baked, shellfish, fried, grilled, cold and combinations of several fish in delicately flavoured sauces
- Main courses:
  - light dishes which may be small and garnished
  - sauté of chicken, tournedos, noisettes or cutlets of lamb
  - saddle of hare, filet mignon, vol-au-vent
  - pot roasted chicken with mushrooms
  - pheasant in casserole
  - braised ham, tongue, duck pheasant, pigeon

- roast
- saddle of lamb or veal, fillet or sirloin of beef
- poultry or game such as chicken, turkey, duck, goose, partridge, pheasant, wild duck, venison, saddle of hare

Grills

- steak (chateaubriand, fillet, tournedos, rump, sirloin)
- lamb (chops, cutlets or kidneys)
- chicken (kebabs)

Vegetables

Potatoes

Sorbet: lightly frozen water ice flavoured with fruit, liqueur or champagne, sometimes served during, a meal of several sources with the intention of refreshing the palate before proceeding with the remainder of the meal; a sorbet or a small assortment of sorbets may also be served as a dessert

Cold dish: such dishes as chicken in aspic or mousse of foie gras or ham may be served.

Vegetarian dishes: should be a regular feature on menus

Sweets:

- light sweets (soufflés, pancakes)
- cold, iced soufflé, bombes, coupes with fruit such as peaches, strawberries, raspberries, sorbet, posset, syllabub, mousse, bavarois
- sweetmeats also known as friandises, mignardises or frivolities (these are different names for very small pastries, sweets, biscuits also known as 'petit fours')

Coffee or tea

Savoury: any hot savouries prepared in neat, small portions may be used on dinner menus

Cheese: all varieties may be offered

Dessert all dessert fruits and nuts may be served

Banquet menus

When compiling banquet menus, consider the following important points:

The food (usually for a large number of people) must be prepared and presented so that it can be served fairly quickly. Heavily garnished dishes should be avoided.

Keep in mind that a large number of dishes may have to be dressed at the same time. Some types of food deteriorate quickly and do not maintain their crisp & freshly prepared appearance when in storage, (even a short time on a hot plate) especially deep-fried foods.

Photograph courtesy of Gautengpics

Tea menus

Tea menus vary considerably, with establishments becoming known for specifically this type of menu among patrons. An upper-class hotel will usually offer a dainty menu.

For example:

- sandwiches (smoked salmon, ham tongue, egg, tomato, cucumber) made with white or brown bread
- bread and butter (white, brown, fruit loaf)
- scones with clotted cream
- jams, honey, lemon curd
- small pastries, assorted gateaux
- fruit salad and cream, ices
- tea (Indian, China, Russian, iced, fruit, herb)

Photograph courtesy of Gautengpics

Commercial hotels, public restaurants and canteens offer simple snacks, cooked meals and high teas.

For example:

- assorted sandwiches
- buttered buns, scones, tea cakes, Scotch pancakes, waffles, sausage rolls, assorted bread and butter, various jams, toasted tea-cakes, scones, crumpets, buns.
- eggs (boiled, poached, fried, omelettes)
- fried fish; grilled meats; roast poultry
- cold meats and salads
- assorted pastries; gateaux
- various ices, coupes, sundaes
- tea, orange and lemon squash

Photograph courtesy of Gautengpics

Menus in French

Specialised restaurants, typically those of the chef-proprietor type still aim for the gourmet market by catering in the French style. French language used on a menu may puzzle customers, but the menu items are normally explained to guests by the restaurant waiters. The French menu remains meaningful to the trained chef and may continue to be of value and convenience. French is not imposed on the menu for pretension but in recognition of the contribution that French practitioners have made in developing professional cookery, and it further conveniently codifies dishes.

To avoid embarrassment to the establishment menu writing in French must conform to the correct French grammatical codes, specifically use of plurals, gender and correct spelling.

- If the whole menu is in French, each dish should use the correct French spelling.
- If the menu is in English each dish should be spelt according to its country of origin or the generally accepted English equivalent.

Cheese and wine

The core and most important items of a cheese and wine party are obviously the cheese, the wine and the bread. A variety of other snacks may also be served.

Cheese

- A variety of flavour, texture and appearance of the cheese served and presented is essential.
- A variety of five to six types of cheese should be arranged on each board.
- Little name flags may be used to indicate the different types of cheese.

Bread

- A variety of crackers or bread is normally served.
- The bread & crackers should not be on the same boards as the cheese but be arranged in batches close to the cheese boards, dips and spreads.

Wine

The event or party organiser will usually decide on the types and quantities of wine to be included – from red wines, white wines, port, aperitifs and sherry.

- Dry wines and semi-sweet wines are usually served, with some aperitifs, dry and semi-dry sherry and port.
- Apple juice, grape juice or other fruit juices should also be available for guests who do not use alcoholic beverages.

Other food that can be served at a cheese and wine function:

- Fresh fruit in a variety of offerings together with vegetable combinations of crisp salad leaves, radishes, gherkins, olives, celery sticks, carrot sticks, fresh chives, parsley, cucumber slices, apple cubes, bunches of grapes, pineapple rings, etc. are commonly served
- Miniature 'sosaties' or kebabs made from cheese cubes and coloured onion pickles
- Mixed dried fruit and nuts are essential items to be included
- Tasty dips in a variety of flavours for the biscuits, potato crisps, or other snacks, such as cocktail sausages must be available
- Patés to eat with the bread are essential for a successful function

Coffee shops or bistros

A coffee shop or bistro is generally considered a family-type restaurant, for example, Maxi's. Some coffee shops, however, are not aimed at the family market but may be classified as a more exclusive type of foodservice institution, for example, Burgundy's, Seattle Coffee shops within Exclusive books, House of Coffees, etc. They offer table service as well as self-service in the form of salad bars, breakfast bars and dessert bars. Family restaurants usually offer breakfast, lunch and dinner.

The food preparation staff is usually limited in number as well as culinary skills. The bulk of the menu dishes are prepared to order, either from basics (as with the sandwiches and breakfast items that give the menu much of its variety), or from frozen or chilled prepared foods that are then processed to order. The production process is generally very similar to that of the typical fast-food preparation process.

The table and general service customers receive is limited and not as elaborate as in up-market restaurants. The limited number of courses offered helps to simplify the service required. Platters, sandwiches and salads are the main items on the menu.

Photograph courtesy of Gautengpics

Normally breakfast is the most important meal offered for some operations and a significant one for all the others. Customers looking for a snack while shopping and taking a coffee break are an important source of business, particularly for family restaurants that have an in-house bakery on their premises. no better advertising than the smell of freshly baked bread & pastries.

See Annexure C for examples of menus

Unit 4:

Suitable products and recipes for menu planning

It is an interesting challenge to develop and produce a new dish. It is not easy to develop a totally new dish, but many an interesting dish has been made by varying available ingredients and creating new combinations. Exotic or unusual commodities may be used to provide a different flavour or an eye-catching garnish. Many chefs use ideas from the cooking of other countries to develop new ideas as a basis for a new dish.

Any new dish must appeal both to the eye and the palate. This can be done without necessarily using expensive or unusual ingredients – a variety of interesting dishes can be prepared by using locally available fresh produce in season.

To ensure continued success and sales of the dish it is important to follow good kitchen practice, apply the basic rules appropriate to each selected method of preparation, cooking and storage. The key success factor for any new recipe is to repeat it accurately each time the dish is made and consistently deliver the same quality product. This aspect is achieved with great success in food service franchises around the world, for example, McDonalds, Wimpy, Kentucky Fried Chicken (KFC), etc.

Did you know?

The Role of Food in Various Cultures

Cultural traditions relate to food in its role as an everyday source of sustenance and its role in rituals and ceremonial practices. Based on the roles food plays in different cultures, Kaufman-Kurzrock have devised five categories:

- Food versus non-food (what is considered edible)
- Sacred versus non-sacred food
- Medicinal food
- Social food
- Food with an oppositional pair (yin-yang: cold-hot, for example)

There may be differences in these roles based on variations within any cultural group. For example, an elder of Lebanese descent who is Christian may eat pork while a Lebanese elder who is Muslim will not.

Factors affecting menu planning

When planning menus for a food service business, note important factors not only of the demographics of the target market, but also its nutritional requirements, food habits and preferences as well as the style of the operation.

The target market

A profile of the clientele for which menus are being planned will include

- age
- sex
- state of health and activity
- cultural and economic environment
- nutritional requirements, and
- preferences

Photograph courtesy of Gautengpics

Nutritional requirements

Meeting the nutritional requirements of individuals in the group to be served is important in meal planning. This is critical for foodservice operations that are responsible for providing the total daily nutritive requirements for hostels, hospitals, old-age homes, etc.

Food habits and preferences / type of customers

The customers of foodservice operations are generally composed of individuals from different cultural, ethnic and economic backgrounds, most of whom have definite food likes and dislikes.

- Nutritional

There is an increasing trend towards healthy natural eating styles and menus.

- Medical

It is important to cater for diabetic, gluten intolerant and dairy intolerant customers.

- Type of customer:

The variety of customer needs can be illustrated by the following examples of customer groups: 21st birthday party, senior citizens' function, conference, football players' get-together after an international match, visiting overseas students' dinner and a mayor's banquet. All need personal consideration and special menus to meet their needs.

- Religious rules if applicable:

If the restaurant has a large Jewish or Muslim clientele, the menu should also accommodate kosher or halaal requirements.

- Ethnic/Cultural

Ethnic menus specialise in the food of a particular country or region.
For example: African, Chinese, Indian, kosher, Afro-Caribbean, Greek,
Portuguese, etc.

- Meat or non-meat preferences:

The menu must be able to accommodate vegetarians.

Did you know?

Food, Culture and Religion

Food is an important part of religious observance and spiritual ritual for many different faiths, including Christianity, Judaism, Islam, Hinduism and Buddhism. The role of food in cultural practices and religious beliefs is complex and varies among individuals and communities. The following article is not all-encompassing. It is an introduction to a diverse and complex topic, and includes some of the ways in which various religious groups include food as a vital part of their faith.

Christianity
The various faiths of Christianity include Roman Catholic, Orthodox and Protestant. The regulations governing food differ from one to the next, including some faiths that don't advocate any restrictions.

Judaism
Judaism can be Liberal or Orthodox, based on the degree of adherence to the Jewish laws. 'Kashrut' refers to the laws pertaining to food in the Jewish religion. 'Kosher' means that a food is permitted or 'clean', while anything 'unclean' (such as pork and shellfish) is strictly forbidden. The Jewish 'food laws' originated more than 2,000 years ago and contribute to a formal code of behaviour that reinforces the identity of a Jewish community. Food forms an integral part of religion in life for a practising Jew.

Islam
Regulations surrounding food are called 'halal'. Prohibited foods are called 'haram'. It is thought that the Creator turns a deaf ear to a Muslim who eats haram foods.

Hinduism
People who practise the Hindu religion don't eat meat from animals. They also avoid foods that may have caused pain to animals during manufacture. Depending on the level of adherence to this belief, in many cases beef is forbidden, while pork is sometimes restricted or avoided.

Buddhism
The dietary rules of Buddhism, which is more of a life philosophy than a religious doctrine, depend on which branch of Buddhism is practised and in what country.

Style of the operation

The style of the foodservice operation describes the type of food offered,
the internal arrangement and setting, the décor, location, etc.

A foodservice operation style influences menu items in the following ways:

- **Suitability of an establishment in an area:** for example, a fine dining restaurant situated in an affluent residential district or a self-service restaurant in a downtown inner-city area
- **Target market:** the type of people catered for influences menu choices. The spending power of the target market is one of the most important considerations. How much is the customerable and willing to pay for food?

- **Customer requirements:** It is the customer not the chef who selects menu items, so analysis of the preferences and popularity of dishes offered is critical. Unpopular dishes must be removed from the menu. Consider customer demands, such as traditional dishes and modern trends in food fashions.
- **Competition in the local area:** It is important to know what is offered by competitors in terms of style of food, price and quality.

Production and service constraints:

The menu offered must take into consideration the factors affecting the actual production of the dish, for example, kitchen equipment, staff skills, raw materials required and storage, capacity to prepare a number of different orders at the same time. All these are limiting factors and constraints that must be accommodated to ensure customer satisfaction and return of repeat business. The lifeblood of any business is sales, and sales can be achieved more easily by satisfied customers returning because they enjoy the food.

Photograph courtesy of Gautengpics

Amount of money available

When starting to plan any menus, you must know the amount of money available per meal. This amount is usually based on anticipated income from the sales of food in commercial types of establishments (coffee shops, restaurants, hotels, etc.) or the available budget in non-commercial institutions (old-age homes, hostels, etc).

For the commercial business this anticipated income must cover the cost of the raw ingredients to be used, the cost of the production labour and general business-operating expenses as well as allowing for a reasonable profit. Unless fair prices are charged, repeat business may not occur and the caterer may go out of business.

Photograph courtesy of Gautengpics

Non-profit types of operations like old age homes, hospitals, worker canteens, etc. have to operate within an available budget per meal. The other costs listed for the commercial operation are covered from other budgetary sources. Only the food ingredients have to be taken into account for meal planning.

Equipment and physical facilities

The menu of the day must be planned in accordance with the establishment's skilled staff, work space and number and capacity of small and large available equipment in order to produce the required meals/dishes.

Photograph courtesy of Gautengpics

Personnel

The number and specific culinary skills of employees are critical factors to consider when determining the variety and complexity of dishes offered on the menu.

Availability of foods

The location of the fresh produce market and/or other sources of food ingredients may have a limiting effect on the menu, especially fresh foods, for example, an exclusive game lodge/hotel/guest house a long distance from town may not be able to quickly secure alternative ingredients if required. A sound knowledge of fresh fruit & vegetables per season enables the menu planner to include them on the menu while they are at their peak quality and available at affordable prices. The regularity of deliveries and the types & storage space available must also be taken into account.

Service

The style of serving food to customers will influence food item selection and choices on the menu. Some food items are more suited for seated service, for instance, soup is not suitable at a cocktail party, as guests usually stand and enjoy cocktail-type snacks while talking to one another. The distance between the place of preparation and the place of distribution/serving should be taken into consideration, as well as the time elapsing between the completion of preparation and service. No customer enjoys cold food that should be consumed hot.

Time

In some foodservice establishments the time the guest occupies a seat is of importance. The menu should be adjusted to facilitate increased turnover (minimum time per customer per seat). To achieve this, the menu could include more quick-to-prepare or pre-prepared items.

Food characteristics and combinations

In the menu-planning process how the food will look on the plate when served must be visualised: the tray or cafeteria counter, the combinations of food presented, how the flavours will combine, whether there is contrast in texture, shape and consistency. The meal must look and smell attractive to the customer. In other words, menu planning must include an overview of the final menu and each item as it is to be served.

Choice of dishes

- Time and season of the year

The prevailing temperature in, as well as outside, the establishment should be taken into account when menus are planned: certain dishes suitable for cold weather may not be acceptable in mid-summer and vice versa. The venue may have tables inside and outside creating different environments within one establishment.

- Time of the day

Whether for breakfast, brunch, lunch, tea, high tea, dinner, supper, snack or special function, the menu must suit the time of day. Often menus will indicate items that are only available up to a certain time, for example, breakfast served only till 11:00 or pub lunch menu only available up to 15:00, etc.

• Sensible nutritional balance

A selection of dishes with varying nutritional contents allows customers to make their own choices according to their needs. Some people need/prefer a full meal while others may want only a light meal or snack type of dish.

• No repetition of commodities

Try to avoid repeating basic ingredients, for example, mushrooms, tomatoes, peas, bacon on one menu. The basic ingredient used in one course should not form the basis of any other course on the same menu.

• No repetition of flavours

When using strong seasoning like onions, garlic or herbs (thyme, sage, bay-leaf) do not repeat the use in more than one course.

• No repetition of colours

The colour of the food is important in order to give the plate an appetising appearance. Avoid repetition of colour. At least one or two colourful foods should be included in each menu offering; for example, a green vegetable adds colour to an otherwise colourless combination of boiled fish and creamed potatoes. Garnishing can also be used very effectively to add colour to a plate.

• Texture of courses

Texture refers to the structure of foods and can best be detected by the feel of foods in the mouth. Crisp, soft, smooth and chewy are adjectives describing food texture. Ensure variations are offered on the menu - food should not all be soft or all crisp. Create a balance of textures, even within a single dish.

• Sauces

If different sauces are served on one menu, the foundation ingredient of each sauce should vary. For example, reduced stock, demi-glace, velouté, cream, butter-thickened sauce, yoghurt, etc.

• Consistency

This is the way foods adhere together, their degree of firmness, density or viscosity and may be described as firm, thick, thin or gelatinous. Serving two creamed foods on a plate is unattractive.

• Shape

Shape of food plays a big part in eye appeal. One way to add interest to the menu is to vary the way in which vegetables are cut, for example, carrots cut into julienne strips or circles, cubed or shredded, green beans served whole, cut or French cut.

• Flavour combinations

Flavour combinations are important in menu planning. In addition to the basic flavours of sweet, sour, bitter and salty, vegetables may be thought of as strong and mild flavoured; chilli or other food as spicy or highly seasoned.

Certain food combinations complement one another, such as turkey and cranberries, roast beef and horseradish sauce, or pork and applesauce.

• Variety in preparation

Variety in preparation should be considered in menu planning and two foods prepared in the same way should not be included in the same meal. Variety may be introduced by marinating or stir-frying foods in addition to the traditional fried, broiled, baked, braised or steamed methods. Food may be further varied by serving it creamed, buttered or escalloped, or by adding a variety of sauces.

Photograph courtesy of Gautengpics

Did you know?

SA cuisine: glossary of terms

Take milk with your rooibos? Fancy some pap with your wors? Brave enough to try some skop or mashonzha? Brush up on your culinary vocabulary with this quick list of indigenous South African food terms and what they mean.

South Africa is home to numerous ethnic and racial groups, many of them migrant communities, all of whom have contributed to the country's rich cultural mix.

The resultant kaleidoscope – the famous "rainbow" – applies not only to the people but to the food, for one finds in South Africa the most extraordinary range of cuisines. The glossary below represents ethnic dishes of particular groups, many since adopted by other groups and no longer the preserve of the group of origin. The list is far from exhaustive, representing only a sample of the full South African menu:

Achaar	Imported to South Africa by migrant Indians, achaar is a salad made of mango and oil; it comes spiced. Eaten in excess, it could trigger an offensive smell of the armpits.
Amanqina	A hoof of a cow, pig or sheep. It is boiled, then spiced for taste. It is very delicious but sticky.
Biltong	Dried and salted raw meat similar to the beef jerky made in the USA. An older Afrikaner delicacy, can be made of ostrich, beef, kudu or any other red meat.
Bobotie	Of Malay origin, made with minced meat and curried spices. An egg sauce is poured on top of this and it is then baked.
Boerewors	A traditional spicy South African sausage made of beef or lamb. Popular at open-air braais (barbecues), where it is grilled over charcoal.
Chakalaka	A salad of Indian / Malay origin made of onion, garlic, ginger, green pepper, carrots and cauliflower spiced with chillies and curry.
Chotlo	A delicacy of the Tswana people, this is meat cut into extremely small pieces with the bones removed. The meat is first boiled, then ground before being put back into the pot and stirred until it becomes very fine. A treat for the toothless.
Frikkadel	Traditional South African meat balls. Made from tomatoes, onion, minced beef and other ingredients, and shaped into round balls.
Gherkin	A small pickled cucumber, often sliced thinly and used in salads or on hamburgers.
Koeksusters	Traditional Afrikaner, plaited dough cakes. They are syrupy, sweet and sticky.
Mala	Intestines, especially those of chicken. They are thoroughly cleaned, cooked in boiled water, then fried. Eaten with pap (see below).
Maotwana	Legs of a chicken boiled to remove the hard skin. Thoroughly washed, salted, then fried. Often served to children because of their low cost.
Mashonzha	Worms, similar to caterpillars in appearance. These establish their habitat in and around

	mopani trees found in the Lowveld areas of Mpumalanga and the Northern Province. Popular with the Shangaans, Vendas and Bapedi of the Northern Province.
Mogodu	Tripe, thoroughly cleaned then boiled for two to three hours. Once softened, allowed to simmer before being served with pap (see below).
Morogo	Wild spinach, the most popular being thepe; delicious when boiled, softened and served with stiff porridge
Pap	Boiled corn meal, often served with sous - a sauce, usually featuring tomato and onions.
Rooibos tea	A popular South African herbal tea made in the Cape from the Cyclopia genistoides bush. Rooibos is an Afrikaans word meaning "red bush". Rooibos has no caffeine and less tannin than tea.
Samoosa	A small, spicy, triangular-shaped pie that has been deep-fried in oil. Made by the Indian and Malay communities, samoosas are popular with South Africans in general.
Serobe	A dish of the Tswana people. Thoroughly washed, then boiled mixture of tripe, intestines and lungs. They are cut into small pieces with a pair of scissors before being spiced to add taste.
Snoek	This is a popular and tasty fish, caught off the Cape coast and often eaten smoked. If you're lucky, you may get to experience a snoek braai - a real South African treat.
Skop	Head of a cow, sheep or goat. The head is first scrubbed with a sharp instrument like a razor to remove skin and unwanted parts like ears and the nose are then cut out. The head is then boiled and allowed to simmer. Favoured by African men.
Ting	A dish favoured by the Tswanas in both South Africa and Botswana. It is a sour porridge made of sorghum – great soft porridge for breakfast!
Umngqusho	A delicacy among the Xhosa people, this is samp (maize kernels) mixed with beans. It is boiled over three hours then mixed with beans. Salt and oil are then added and the dish allowed to simmer

SouthAfrica.info The all-in-one official guide and web portal to South Africa.

Assessment activity 1:

Compile the following menus according to the principles given above:

- A three-course table d'hôte menu with two choices in each course
- A three-course set menu for a 21st birthday party
- A breakfast menu for a small hotel.

Photographs courtesy of Gautengpics

Unit 5:

Suitable products and recipes for menu-planning purposes

Developing new recipes

Test various combinations and cooking methods. As recipes are being tested, keep notes of the following:

- ingredients used and quantities
- cooking methods
- finishing methods

A dish may have to be tried out a number of times before a successful product is achieved.

Following are ways of testing a dish:

Colleagues - throughout the development testing phase, involve colleagues (both in and out of the kitchen)

Guests - test dishes by offering them as specials and requesting specific feedback from guests.

Staff - involve staff in the testing process, monitoring and supervising their activities. Ask for their suggestions for improving the recipes, and test these. Make recipe adjustments as necessary.

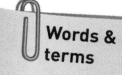

Words & terms

Standard recipe:

A standard recipe is a formula for producing a particular dish of a specified quantity and quality.

? Did you know? ?

South African cooking origins

East meets West: that's how the cuisine of South Africa can be described, where Indian curries meet British meat pies and Dutch cookies meet Indonesian chutney. The origins and development of South African culinary tradition are as diverse as the peoples who make up the population of South Africa, a potpourri of African, Eastern and Western foods and flavours. Early African tribes planted millet and sorghum, and indeed, they still do. Millet makes quite a nice traditional beer, as does sorghum, which can also be used for an excellent porridge. The Dutch brought with them dishes and customs that prevail to this day – cooked vegetables served with butter and nutmeg, pancakes, waffles, biscuits. The Malay slaves brought their cuisine, perhaps the best-known of all South African cooking styles. Most Cape homes employed Malay cooks who adapted traditional Eastern recipes using local ingredients and in the process developed those aspects of South African cooking which can truly be said to be unique – the combination of sweet and spicy in meat and fish dishes, the addition of appetizing side dishes and accompaniments like sambals and chutneys. The variety of curries, atjars, samoosas and beryani are a delight to the South African palate.

Lacking the amenities of town life, early settlers perfected cooking over the coals and in outdoor ovens, producing marvelously tasty and nutritious meat dishes, stews and breads from home-grown produce, the wealth of veld plants and abundant game. When the Cape became British in the nineteenth century, British immigrants settled the eastern part of the colony. They and other settlers during this century – German and Portuguese among them – introduced their own traditional dishes and cooking methods. From this variety of influences, traditional South African cooking evolved. Such a rich heritage is rightly cherished for itself.

Standard recipes

A standard recipe is a formula for producing a particular dish of a specified quality and quantity. It shows the exact quantities and qualities of the ingredients together with the sequence of preparation and service. It enables the kitchen to control costs and quality.

The objectives of a standard recipe are as follows:

- The quantities and qualities of ingredients to be used – a purchase specification
- The yield obtainable from the recipe
- The food cost per portion
- The nutritional value of a particular dish
- To facilitate
  - menu planning
  - purchasing and internal requisitioning
  - food preparation and production
  - portion control

In the workplace

The standard recipe is the basis of success of the many food and restaurant chains or franchises that are in operation – Kentucky Fried Chicken (KFC), WIMPY, SPUR, McDonalds, Ocean Basket, Something Fishy, Greenfields, Burgundy's, etc. People know that a dish ordered in Cape Town will taste, look and cost the same as when ordered in Polokwane, Ethikweni or Johannesburg.

Launching the menu

Set the date for when the new recipe/menu is to be launched. To do this, consider *production planning*, or *volume forecasting* of the volume of sales for an establishment for a specified time period, for example, for a day/week/month.

The aims and objectives of production planning are as follows:

- Facilitate food cost control
  - Facilitate stock purchasing
  - Reduce the problem for leftover food/wastage/insufficient food
  - Gear production on demand by forecasting number of meals to be served for a period of seven days and customer specifics

Once the final menu has been 'put to bed', it is useful to launch it. This may include the following (and is usually coordinated by senior management):

- Advertising
- Inviting the press
- Inviting loyal guests

Always be open to feedback and suggestions from guests. Keep a record of their input. If several guests give the same type of feedback, try to accommodate this. Develop and compile menus for a variety of occasions

Take note of how the franchise operations launch new menus or dishes: national TV advertising campaigns offering a 'special' (especially in school holidays and during festive seasons), big newspaper advertisements, flyers at robots, in post boxes, etc. A substantial amount of money is invested in making people aware of the new dish to attract them to come and try it. To make it successful, planning, testing, ensuring availability and quality control are needed before the launch. This process may take months before the dish is finally approved and launched.

Unit 6:

Menu costing and menu pricing

It is important to know the exact cost of each process and every item produced, so a system of cost analysis and cost information is essential.

The advantages of an efficient costing system

- It discloses the net profit made by each section of the organisation and shows the cost of each meal produced.
- It will reveal possible sources of economy and can result in more effective use of stores, labour, materials, etc.
- Costing provides information necessary for the formation of a sound price policy.
- Cost records provide and facilitate the speedy quotations for all special functions, e.g. special parties, wedding receptions, etc.
- It enables the caterer to keep to a budget.

No one costing system will automatically suit every catering business, but the following guidelines may be helpful:

- The co-operation of all departments is essential
- The costing system should be adapted to the business and not vice versa. If the accepted procedure in an establishment is altered to fit a costing system then there is danger of causing resentment among the staff and as a result losing their co-operation.
- Clear instructions in writing must be given to staff who are required to keep records. The system must be made as simple as possible so that the amount of clerical labour required is kept to a minimum. An efficient mechanical calculator or computer should be provided to save time and labour.

> **Words & terms**
>
> **Menu costing:**
> Menu costing is calculating the cost of the ingredients used to prepare each of the dishes on the menu.
>
> **Menu pricing:**
> Menu pricing is the calculation of the selling price of the dishes offered on the menu

Menu costing

Menu costing refers to calculating the food cost of the ingredients used to prepare dishes on the menu. Note that the cost of staff and overheads are not included in the food cost.

To be able to calculate the food costs the following will be needed:

- Recipes (these must detail the exact volume/weight of each ingredient)
- Conversion tables (grams to millilitres or vice versa)
- Price lists (cost at which ingredients are purchased)

Example: Grilled cheese sandwiches

Recipe: total yield - 50

Bread	100 slices
Cheese	1.42kg
Margarine	454g

Price List:

Bread   (20 slices)   R5.00
Cheese   R39.99 / kg
Margarine   R10.99/kg

Step 1:

Make sure the weight or volume units that are used in the calculation are the same; if not convert. (Use the conversion table to convert g / kg to ml / L and vice versa)

Example:

In the above example the margarine in the recipe is given in grams while the price list refers to kilograms:

>   Option 1: convert 454g to 0.454kg
>   Option 2 convert 1kg to 1000g)

Step 2:

Calculate the cost of each ingredient.

Example:

20 slices of bread cost R5.00. The recipe requires 100 slices.
$100 \div 20 = 5$
100 slices cost R5.00 X 5 = <u>R25.00</u>

1 kg of cheese costs R39.99. The recipe requires 1.42kg of cheese
$1.42kg \div 1kg = 1.42$
1.42kg cheese costs R39.99 X 1.42 = <u>R56.79</u>

1 kg of margarine costs R10.99 The recipe requires 454g of margarine.
Convert to 0.454kg
$0.454kg \div 1\ kg = 0.454$
0.454kg margarine cost R10.99 X 0.454 = <u>R4.99</u>

The total food cost of grilled cheese sandwiches for 50 people is
R25.00 + R56.79 + R4.99
= <u>R86.78</u>

The food cost per person is therefore
$R86.78 \div 50$ (recipe yields 50 sandwiches)
<u>=R1.74</u>

To determine the menu cost this process has to be followed for each item/dish on the menu. Add all the item costs to determine the total menu cost.

Menu pricing

Menu pricing refers to the calculation of the selling price of the menu.

The total costs of a catering business are normally broken down into three main areas: namely,

- Food costs (actual cost of all ingredients used in recipe)
- Labour costs - (wages, holiday pay, overtime pay, pension costs, etc.)
- Overhead expenses (rent, electricity, gas, insurance, advertising, etc.)

Total costs = food costs + labour costs + overhead expenses

Therefore, the price charged for a meal must be enough to cover the cost of the food used, labour costs and overhead expenses.

A system is needed that collects and analyses costs correctly and accurately. It is important that the system be accurate, because decisions will be made on the figures generated from the system.

Food costing

Accurate food costing is helped by carrying out yield tests for commodities such as meat, fish, poultry, game and vegetables, that have as major an effect on the price of the food product. A yield test will give the amount of edible produce (EP) and the amount of waste produce (WP).

Through yield tests the amount lost during trimming and cooking, the percentage left for the intended dish, and the real cost of the commodity are shown. A standard yield for all or some of the most important commodities assists management in purchasing of ingredients by indicating which size or weight of a particular item is best to buy. The information from a yield test can also be used to check the number of portions achieved against the predicted portion numbers.

Calculate the gross profit

The annual accounts of a foodservice show the following figures:

SALES		R 200 000
Food costs	R 80 000	
All other costs	R 70 000	R 150 000
PROFIT		R 50 000

After consideration of these figures management may decide that they are satisfied with the profit and wish to achieve similar results in future. As already stated, the selling price must recover the food costs and a share of the other costs. In the above illustration, it can be seen that the food costs represent 40% of the sales. The gross profit (other costs and profit) represent 60% of the sales.

The selling price of each item can, therefore, be calculated by adding 60% gross profit to the food costs.   When calculating a selling price, two known factors are needed:

- Food costs
- Gross profit (mark-up)

Calculate selling price

If the food cost of a food item is R5.50 and the required gross profit is 60%, the selling price will be as follows:

$$\text{Selling price} = \frac{\text{Food cost}}{100 - \text{required gross profit}} \times 100$$

$$= \frac{R5.50}{(100-40)} \times 100$$

$$= R9.17$$

Assessment activity 2:

Cost the menu you compiled in Activity 1 for the 21st birthday party. Calculate the selling price of the menus if the required gross profit is 60%.

Assessment activity 3:

Your college is requested to do the catering for a business conference. The conference will be attended by sixty delegates. The banquet manager has asked you to compile menus for breakfast, lunch and dinner for which the total food cost (cost of ingredients only) will not exceed R100 in total for the three meals.

The following must be done:

- compile the menus
- source the recipes for all the menus
- cost the menus to assure that you stay within the pricing budget framework
- if necessary, you will have to reconsider your menus until they are within the allocated budget.

Present the menus, recipes and costing in a flip-file to your banquet manager.

Summary

To be able to plan and compile balanced menus for a variety of occasions or establishments there are a number of basic factors and principles that must be considered.

Nutrition is the study of how food is utilised by the body. Food is composed of nutrients, which are chemical compounds needed for survival. Some of these are essential nutrients that cannot be made in the body and must be supplied by food or supplements. To live a healthy and balanced life the body needs a certain minimum of these nutrients on a daily basis. In order to receive an adequate supply of all the essential nutrients, it is important to eat a variety of foods.

The basic four food groups were developed as a convenient method for ensuring that this goal is met. It divides foods into four groups based on their nutrient content and recommends the number of servings from each group.

- Milk and milk products - human beings need a sufficient supply of calcium
- Meats, fish, poultry, eggs, nuts, legumes - are rich in high-quality protein, vitamins, minerals and essential fatty acids

- Fruits and vegetables - fruit and vegetables contain many nutrients that help protect the body against disease; they should be eaten in large quantities
- Grains - carbohydrates provide energy to the body for our daily activities - the bulk of each meal should, therefore, contain a carbohydrate-rich food

The food pyramid not only ensures that the right nutrients are included in the diet, but also that the recommended energy allowance is not exceeded. Every day, foods should be selected from the following food groups.

Fat in the diet - the human body needs fat as part of the diet, but we should not eat too much. Some fats are good for us, while others are bad for human consumption. According to their effect on the body and health, some fats are worse than others. In this regard fats can be divided into 'bad' and 'good' fats: saturated, monounsaturated, polyunsaturated, essential fatty acids.

Balanced menu - when designing a menu, consider the various factors that affect the design (type & style of establishment, target market, customers' food habits & preferences, production & service constraints, equipment, personnel and availability of ingredients, etc.). The dishes offered must still provide a balanced meal. This does not only refer to the nutritional balance, but also to other factors.

Menu styles

- Table d'hôte menu or set-price menu
- À la carte menu
- Buffet menus
- Cocktail menu
- Du jour menus
- Cyclical menus
- Selective menus

Types of menus:

- Breakfast - continental breakfast and English/full breakfast. It is commonly found that hotels combine both types of breakfasts on one menu to make menu organisation and presentation simpler
- Luncheon – set-price menu, buffet and special party. The critical success factor for this type of menu is to offer a variety of courses and dishes within each course that can be satisfactorily prepared, cooked and served normally within a lunch hour
- Dinner menus - table d'hôte and à la carte menus are suitable for dinner menus
- Banquet menus – an important point to consider is that food prepared for a large number of people requires special care and practical considerations
- Tea menus - vary considerably, with establishments becoming known for specifically this type of menu among patrons
- Menus in French - specialised restaurants, typically those of the chef-proprietor type still aim for the gourmet market by catering in the French style

- Cheese and wine - core and most important items are obviously the cheese, the wine and the bread
- Coffee shops or bistros - generally considered family-type restaurants but some may be classified as a more exclusive type of foodservice institution

Menu planning requires suitable products and recipes and starts with any new dish that appeals both to the eye and the palate. This can be done without necessarily using expensive or unusual ingredients – a variety of interesting dishes can be prepared by using locally available fresh produce in season. To ensure continued success and sales of the dish it is important to follow good kitchen practice, apply the basic rules appropriate to each selected method of preparation, cooking and storage. The key success factor for any new recipe is that it must be repeated accurately each time the dish is made and there must be consistent delivery of the same quality product. Factors affecting menu planning in a food service business are not only those of the demographics of the target market, but also nutritional requirements, food habits and preferences as well as the style of the operation.

New recipe development requires testing various combinations and cooking methods. As recipes are being tested, keep notes of the following aspects: ingredients used and quantities; cooking methods and finishing methods.

Standard recipes are formulae for producing particular dishes of a specified quality and quantity. They show the exact quantities and qualities of the ingredients together with the sequence of preparation and service. They enable the kitchen to control costs and quality.

Menu costing refers to calculating the food cost, that is, the cost of ingredients used to prepare dishes on the menu. Note that the cost of staff and overheads are not included in the food cost.

Menu pricing refers to the calculation of the selling price of the menu. The total costs of a catering business are normally broken down into three main areas: namely,

- food costs (actual cost of all ingredients used in recipes)
- labour costs - (wages, holiday pay, overtime pay, pension costs, etc.)
- overhead expenses (rent, electricity, gas, insurance, advertising, etc.)

Food costing accuracy is helped by carrying out yield tests for commodities such as meat, fish, poultry, game and vegetables, that have a major effect on the price of the food product. A yield test will give the amount of edible produce (EP) and the amount of waste produce (WP).

Gross profit - the selling price must recover the food costs, a share of the other fixed costs and leave some profit for the owner to be a viable institution.

Topic 2:
Maintaining hygiene in food preparation and storage

Module 1

Maintaining and promoting food hygiene and safety procedures during food preparation, cooking and storage to organisational and legislative requirements

Overview

The student should be able to ...

- identify the most common food poisoning pathogens, their sources, associated illnesses and preventative measures
- describe methods to detect signs of pest infestation and actions to take if infestation is identified
- demonstrate procedures for the hygienic storage of different food types (including the defrosting of frozen foods). Understand why this is important
- describe the relationship of time and temperature when storing and cooking food
- explain the importance of following health and safety procedures when lifting heavy items for storage
- lift all heavy items in accordance with safety procedures
- adapt food hygiene procedures but maintain good practices in a variety of situations
- react appropriately to unforeseen operational problems related to food hygiene

Unit 1:

Food poisoning pathogens

Food poisoning

The general symptoms associated with food poisoning are vomiting, diarrhoea and abdominal pain. The symptoms in most cases occur between two hours and two days after consuming poisonous or contaminated food and may last from a few hours to a few days. The degree of food poisoning can vary from a mild 'upset tummy', increasing to severe pain, mild to extreme vomiting and in the advanced stage to diarrhoea, resulting in body dehydration.

There are three main causes of food poisoning:

- Bacterial food poisoning
- Chemical food poisoning
- Poisonous foods

Food poisoning caused by bacteria is the most important to a caterer and the foodservice industry in particular.

Bacterial food poisoning

This type of food poisoning is caused by harmful bacteria present in food when consumed. Bacteria can contaminate food during the raw materials & ingredients, pre-preparation stage, preparation & cooking stage, presentation stage and while food is already dished up and waiting to be served.

Salmonella group

These bacteria can be present in the intestines of animals or human beings and are excreted. Anything coming into contact *directly* or *indirectly* with the excreta may be contaminated (raw meat at the slaughter house or the unwashed hands of an infected person after visiting/using the toilet). Infected excreta from human beings or animals may contaminate rivers. When water from such infested rivers is used as drinking water the users will be infected as well. Chlorination of drinking water is effective in killing harmful bacteria.

Salmonella infection is the result of human beings or animals eating food contaminated by salmonella-infected excreta originating from human beings or animals, so completing a chain of infection. For example, if flies land on the excreta of a dog which has eaten infected meat, the flies may then go onto food in the kitchen - if that food is left out in warm conditions for a period of time. People who eat that food (which is then contaminated by the salmonella bacteria which is invisible to the human eye) could well suffer from food poisoning.

Food types most easily affected by the salmonella bacteria group are

- poultry
- meat
- eggs

Words & terms

Pathogens:
A pathogen is a biological agent that causes disease or illness to its host.

Bacteria:
A bacterium (plural: bacteria) is a unicellular microorganism. Typically a few micrometres in length, individual bacteria have a wide-range of shapes, ranging from spheres to rods to spi

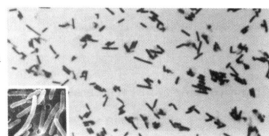

Contamination can be caused by the following:

- Insects and vermin, because salmonella is spread by droppings, feet, hairs, etc.
- The food itself
- Cross-contamination, for example, a chicken is eviscerated on a cutting board and the cutting board, knives, equipment, etc. are not properly cleaned before other food (such as cold meat) is then cut/processed on the same cutting board.
- Food can be infected by a human being who has the disease or who is a carrier (a person who does not suffer from food poisoning but who carries and passes on the bacteria/germs to others) while working in a foodservice environment.

Staphylococcus aureus

These bacteria/germs are found on human hands and other parts of the skin, or sores, spots, etc. and in the nose and throat.

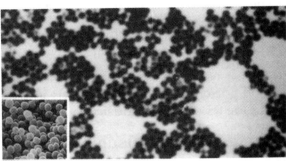

Food affected by staphylococcus aureus generally includes food which has been handled with infected hands. Hands can be infected by touching the nose, or throat (coughing over food), cuts, etc. Food items within general types of foodservice establishments that are frequently contaminated are typically brawn, pressed beef, pies and custards. This contamination takes place through food-handlers or even air-borne infection because they are ideal food types for the multiplication of the bacterium.

Clostridium perfringens

These bacteria are distributed from the intestines of humans and animals and are found in the soil. Raw meat is the main source of foods affected by clostridium perfringens. It is important to note that the spores of these bacteria can survive light cooking (that is cooking at low temperatures for a short period).

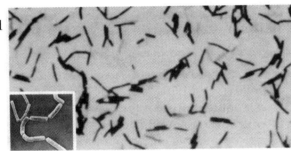

Other types of bacteria

Clostridium botulinum is another type of bacterium which causes food poisoning, but it is not commonly found.

Campylobacter bacteria are a common cause of diarrhoea. Large numbers are not required to cause illness. Poultry and meats are generally the main foods infected but adequate cooking at sufficiently high temperatures will kill the bacteria.

Bacillus cereus is found in soil where vegetables and cereals, like rice, may grow. When warm cooked food, especially rice is stored for a long period under moist conditions, the spores revert to bacteria which then multiply and produce toxins that can cause food poisoning.

Listeria bacteria are aerobic, non-sporing organisms which can cause serious food-borne disease, particularly in the elderly, the chronically sick or babies. These bacteria are found in soil, vegetables and animal feed. They can be killed by using the correct cooking procedures.

These bacteria may grow at refrigeration temperatures and in mildly acidic conditions such as those found in soft cheeses where lactic acid is present.

Prevention of food poisoning from bacteria

There are two basic approaches to prevent food poisoning that can be effectively used by everyone involved in the foodservice environment:

- prevent bacteria from multiplying
- prevent bacteria from spreading from place to place

In practice this means

- that harmful bacteria must be isolated
- the chain of infection must be broken, and
- conditions favourable to their growth must be eliminated.

It is also very important to prevent harmful bacteria being brought into the foodservice premises or getting onto food. This can only be achieved by maintaining a high standard of hygiene with regard to personnel, the entire premises, all equipment and food-handling processes.

Did you know?

Food poisoning in South Africa
Notified food poisoning cases and deaths, 2001-2005
In the past five years (2001-2005), a total of 1886 cases and 51 deaths were reported to the National Department of Health (NDoH). There was a peak in 2003 where 764 cases were reported. The number of cases that have been reported could be low because large numbers are undiagnosed/ misdiagnosed and unreported.

Provincial distribution of food poisoning, South Africa, 2001-2005
Due to under-reporting in particular provinces as opposed to others, the provincial trends should therefore be interpreted with tremendous caution. During the period 2001-2005, the majority of cases reported were from the Eastern Cape province (475) followed by KwaZulu-Natal and Limpopo, respectively. Mpumalanga reported only two cases; this may be attributed to under-reporting. In 2005, Limpopo reported the highest number of cases (126) compared to 81 cases in 2001, while in the Eastern Cape there's been a dramatic decrease in the number of cases reported since 2001.

Distribution of food poisoning by month, 2001 - 2005
The occurrence of food poisoning follows seasonal pattern, generally with a higher number of cases notified during summer months

Distribution of food poisoning by age
The majority of cases reported were among the young age (15-19 year group).
National Department of Health, Statistical Notes, Feb 2006

Chemical food poisoning

Chemicals may accidentally enter food through their use in agricultural or manufacturing processes. Some chemicals used in a production kitchen are also poisonous: disinfectants, some cleaning materials, and pesticides. These chemicals must, therefore, be used with great care and be stored in accordance with the manufacturers' instructions.

Poisonous foods

Some plants, for example, rhubarb leaves, green potatoes and certain toadstools, contain poison in sufficient quantities to cause poisoning if eaten. Occasionally a mould growing on food can produce poisonous waste material in the food.

Unit 2:

Pest infestations

Human food storage areas have a natural attraction for pests, vermin, insects, domestic animals and birds since such storage provides an easy accessible source of food. These animals and insects are carriers of certain diseases and bacteria, which could lead to food poisoning as well as loss of food supply stocks.

Rats and mice

Rats and mice constitute a serious danger of potential food and food stock infection. These rodents carry harmful bacteria on themselves and in their droppings. Rats find refuge in sewers, drains, etc. and are therefore in frequent contact with excreta. Any food, surface, etc. touched by rats can therefore be contaminated – even if they just run across a surface –as excreta are a main source of food poisoning.

Rats and mice prefer warm dark corners. They are often found in lift shafts, electrical metre cupboards, lofts, openings in walls where pipes enter/exit, under low shelves, on high shelves and under equipment like stoves, fridges, etc. These rodents enter the premises through any holes, defective drains, open doorways and in food-stuff containers.

Signs of rats and mice

- Droppings
- Smears
- Holes
- Runways
- Gnawing marks
- Grease marks on skirting boards and above pipes
- Claw marks
- Chewed boxes and packaging
- Rat odour
- Visible mice or rats

Preventative measures for infestation from rats and mice

- Frequently move and inspect food stocks to check for any signs indicating the presence of rodents.
- Do not leave scraps of food lying about, especially overnight.
- Dustbins and swill-bins should have proper tight-fitting lids.
- Prevent rubbish from accumulating outside the building.
- The premises must be kept clean and regularly inspected.

Insect infection

House flies

House flies are the most common insects that spread infection. Flies when settling on filth contaminate their legs, wings and bodies with harmful bacteria. The next object/person/food they settle on is then contaminated with such bacteria. Flies can also contaminate food with their excreta and saliva.

The best method to control flies is to eliminate their breeding places. Flies usually breed in rubbish, in warm, moist places, for example, dustbins in summer are ideal breeding grounds.

Waste control and disposal - a potential threat to food safety - is, therefore, of paramount importance. It is a source of contamination that can provide food for a variety of pests.

Cockroaches

Cockroaches like warm, moist, dark places. Their presence can be seen from their droppings and smell owing to a liquid they deposit which gives off a nauseating odour. Cockroaches can carry harmful bacteria on their bodies, depositing such bacteria on all items, surfaces, etc. with which they come in contact.

Silverfish

Silverfish are small silver-coloured insects that like to feed on starchy foods among other things. They are normally found on moist surfaces in badly ventilated areas. Simply improving ventilation will effectively help control their presence.

Beetles

Beetles are found in dark, warm places and they may carry harmful germs/bacteria as they move from place to place.

Measures to be taken to prevent insect infestation:

Insects can effectively be controlled with the correct insecticide and through fumigation of premises. Care must be taken when using insecticides as they may also cause food poisoning to humans if the insecticides come into contact with food. Foodservice establishments usually employ professional pest control companies to do this type of work. Health regulations also require regular fumigation and pest control and certification.

Cats and dogs

Domestic pets carry harmful bacteria on their coats and are not always clean in their natural habits and should, therefore, not be permitted in kitchens or on food premises. Cats especially can introduce fleas and should not be allowed access to places where food is prepared.

Birds

Birds entering through windows may contaminate food and surfaces on which food is prepared by their droppings.

Dust

Dust contains bacteria. It should not be allowed to settle on food or food preparation surfaces. Kitchens should be kept clean to prevent dust accumulation. Hands must be cleaned especially after handling dirty vegetables as these may contain dry soil and dust.

Unit 3:

Procedures for the hygienic storage of different food

Receiving deliveries of food items

All deliveries must always be checked/inspected upon arrival _before_ acceptance of goods is signed. One person must be designated and should be responsible for receiving, inspecting and signing acceptance of goods delivered.

When goods are received, it is important to check and inspect the following:

- Packaging

All packaging (cartons, boxes, tins, bottles and containers) should be well sealed with no visible signs of damage such as cracks, dents, tears, rust or water damage. Never accept goods showing any of the above signs of damage, as it is not possible to guarantee the quality (especially food safety) of the item.

- Temperature

Foods items that are frozen or refrigerated should be received in this condition. Ensure frozen foods are always kept at -15°C or below, while refrigerated goods should be below 5°C throughout the delivery cold chain. Do not accept frozen or refrigerated goods that are above these recommended temperatures. Increased bacteria growth takes place outside these temperature ranges in the product and could lead to possible food poisoning.

- Use-by dates

Check use-by dates to confirm _before_ delivery that the dates are still valid and have not expired. Ensure that the food items are used before the expiry date.

- Physical appearance of food items

Inspect and check for visible signs of colour fading or change, wilting, moisture loss, pest infestation and spoilage. Reject the delivery if any of these are present.

- General delivery vehicle cleanliness

Inspect the delivery vehicles to ensure they are hygienically clean. Dirty vehicles may contaminate deliveries of food through dust, dirt and air-borne contamination.

It is of paramount importance to store goods in the correct places (fridge, freezer, storeroom, etc.) as quickly as possible after delivery.

Maintain the cold chain with frozen and refrigerated food items as severe temperature differences affect the quality and safety of such food items, resulting in possible food poisoning.

Hygiene when storing food

Food storage areas must be kept clean and hygienic for various reasons:

- to eliminate the risk of contamination
- prevent food spoilage,
- comply with health regulations

Food storage areas need to be kept clean and hygienic to prevent or protect them from the following:

Harmful bacteria

Cross-contamination may occur when different food items come into contact with one another. This frequently occurs when food is stored unwrapped

Photograph courtesy of Gautengpics

or different items are stored in the same containers, for example, blood from raw meat products in the fridge can drip onto cooked and or other items like cold meats.

Tips

- Store different food types in different areas of the fridge, for example, cooked meat above raw meats.
- Wrap or place food items on trays or in containers.
- Clean up any spills or drips immediately with appropriate methods, especially blood spills in fridges.

Dangerous substances

Chemicals used for cleaning can contaminate food if deposits or residues from these products have not been properly removed from storage areas and/or surfaces.

In the workplace

Tips

- Never store cleaning products and chemicals in food storage areas.
- Always rinse surfaces and equipment after cleaning with clean running water to remove cleaning chemical deposits or residue.

Physical contamination

Food spoilage/damage normally occurs when bacteria are transferred from the *packaging* of one food item to another, for example, potatoes in hessian bags to fruits.

To prevent this, remove food items from cardboard boxes, paper and hessian bags and store them in clean plastic tubs or suitable food containers. Any damaged packaging should be immediately removed, contents/items inspected for damage and packaging/covering replaced with cling wrap or stored in suitable sealed food containers.

Pests & rodents

Pests and rodents are attracted by food scraps, waste and rubbish as an easy source of food for them. Food products that are stored at ground level are at risk of infestation – pests and rodents harbour and carry deadly bacteria on their legs and bodies and can transfer these bacteria to food items.

In the workplace

Tips

- Keep food covered above floor level and at correct temperatures.
- Keep areas clean and free from waste, rubbish or food scraps.

Unsuitable temperatures

Food not stored at the correct temperature will spoil and become unsuitable for human consumption. Food spoilage occurs when bacteria grow to such high levels that food poisoning becomes possible at these high levels.

In the workplace

Tips

- Frozen food should be stored in the freezer at –15°C.
- Perishable food should be refrigerated at 0°C to 5°C.
- Those foods that are dry, canned, preserved or require room temperature should be stored at 10 – 20°C.

Excessive humidity and direct sunlight

Excessive humidity (hot damp conditions) leads to sugar becoming lumpy, bread mouldy and fruit not ripening properly.

Direct sunlight can cause deterioration of coloured food ingredients as well as increased temperatures within working and storage areas.

In the workplace

Tips

- Ensure proper ventilation (either natural or mechanical) and adequate lighting (not direct sunlight) in storage areas and rooms

Unit 4:

Store different food items hygienically

All food items have recommended storage procedures that take into account

- Temperature,
- shelf life, and
- place and conditions of storage.

Time and *temperature* are the two most important factors to consider when storing food. Food items that have been prepared and are held before service as well as raw, unprocessed or partially processed food items stored at the incorrect temperatures, could spoil (bacteria growing to high risk levels) resulting in consumers/customers suffering from food poisoning.

Incorrect storage of food items also impacts on food hygiene. Food items such as chicken, eggs, pork, dairy products and sauces are all *high-risk foods* that spoil rapidly if not stored correctly. High risk food requires special care with regard to time and temperature when stored. Spoilt or contaminated high-risk foods can easily lead to cross-contamination of other foods if not stored correctly.

Hygienic storage of food items

Meat

Meat should be stored wrapped in plastic in the refrigerator at *below 5°C* or tightly wrapped and frozen:

Meat *not frozen* should be used within the following time guidelines:

- Offal, minced meat and cuts such as veal escalope are best eaten within a day.
- Chops, steak and small pieces can be left for two to three days, and large roasts for up to five days.
- Red meats keep better than white meats, and lean cuts better than fatty cuts as it is the fat that becomes rancid first, spoiling the meat.

Meat can be stored *frozen* for the following periods:

- Beef, lamb and venison can be frozen for up to a year depending on the cuts.
- Veal and pork should not be frozen for longer than eight months.

Poultry

Poultry, game birds, rabbit and hare

Stored *unfrozen*

- Poultry and small game can be stored in the refrigerator at temperatures *below 5°C* for two days.

- Goose and turkey can be stored for up to four days.

Frozen storage

- The fattier the product, the less time it can be frozen.
- As a general rule, don't freeze for longer than six months.
- To freeze a whole bird, remove the fat from the vent end and remove the giblets. Wrap the bird completely in plastic.
- Do not freeze game birds until they have been cleaned and drawn.

Fish

Stored *unfrozen*

- All fresh fish should be stored for the absolute minimum time – no more than a day or two, provided it is well wrapped in plastic.
- It is essential to ensure that fish has been gutted. Un-gutted fish will spoil more rapidly.
- Oily fish will spoil the most rapidly.

Frozen storage

- Fish may be stored frozen at temperatures *below minus-10°C* for no more than three months

Dairy products

Dairy items

- Milk and cheese should be stored in the refrigerator at all times. Milk keeps well for about a week, while cheese keeps for much longer if it is stored in an airtight container or wrapping
- Milk can be frozen for a maximum of three months.
- Cheese should not be frozen.
- Ice cream must be frozen at temperatures colder than minus10°C.

Dairy products generally freeze well, with the exception of products that have a fat content of less than 40%, for example, cream with a fat content of <40% tends to separate.

Pasteurized milk does not freeze well – the milk normally separates into fat globules and protein changes cause precipitation on thawing/defrosting. In contrast, however, *homogenised* or *pasteurised homogenised* milk does freeze well.

Blue cheeses such as Blaauwkrantz, become very crumbly if frozen.

Cream cheese does not freeze well and tends to crumble on thawing.

Vegetables and fruit

Fresh fruit and vegetables should be stored in the refrigerator as follows:

- Fruit and vegetables should be packed into suitable storage containers for that specific fruit or vegetable type.
- Store fruit and vegetables *below* other food items in the refrigerator to prevent cross-contamination stemming from the soil residue normally present on some vegetables.
- Bananas, onions and potatoes should be *stored at room temperature*.
- Wash and trim leafy vegetables (spinach, rhubarb, etc) and place in suitable containers before refrigeration.
- Potatoes, carrots and other root-type vegetables should be scrubbed in cold water to remove soil residue and then rinsed in clean, cold water.
- All other fruit and vegetables must be washed in cold water to remove soil, dust and any chemicals before storage.

Eggs

- Store in the refrigerator with the *pointed end down* to ensure that the yolk is centred.
- Store eggs for a maximum of three weeks.

Dry goods

Dry goods refer to and include food items such as flour, sugar, rice, maize meal, salt, etc.

This group of food items should be stored in *dry goods stores* as follows:

- Dry goods store rooms must be dry and cool, with good ventilation. The store must be hygienic and pest free (such as cockroaches, rats, mice, etc).
- The store must be kept clean and tidy at all times, with weekly cleaning inspections.
- Store food and drinks on pallets, shelves or in bins designed for the purpose – do not store any items on the floor.
- Any spillages must be cleaned immediately.
- Check storage, food and drink containers regularly to ensure they are not damaged, rusted, or leaking.
- Check the expiry dates on all items before storage. Do not store any items past the expiry date as this may cause a contamination risk in the store.
- Store fruit and vegetables separately from other food. Especially check fruit for mould as the mould spores are carried in the air and spread very easily.

Different storing methods

Dry storage

Dry storage is recommended for those products that are best kept at room temperature (10 – 20°C) and have a long shelf life. Examples of these products include

- preserved or dry goods,
- canned, bottled, bagged or boxed items and cakes and biscuits.

Refrigerated storage

Food items that are stored in refrigerated conditions generally have a short shelf life and are highly perishable. All food items should be kept between 0 – 5°C. Temperatures higher than 5°C generally create ideal conditions for food spoilage and high bacteria growth, resulting in possible food poisoning.

Items that require refrigerated storage include

- uncooked food such as meat
- seafood
- dairy products
- poultry
- eggs
- cooked or prepared foods
- vegetables
- some fruits

Key aspects to remember
- Refrigerators should be cleaned *and sanitised* on a regular basis especially on the inside but also on the outside. Pay particular attention to doors and door seals.
- Maintain the correct internal temperature (use internal thermometer to crosscheck temperature).
- Products stored should be raised from the refrigerator floor level on suitable shelving to allow air to circulate and cool all products.
- Cross-contamination must be prevented by allocating specific storage areas for types of food inside the refrigerator: dairy section, raw meat section, seafood section.
- Processed and prepared food should *first be cooled outside the refrigerator* as rapidly as possible to prevent food spoilage before it is stored in the refrigerator.
- Label and date all food items to facilitate correct stock rotation.
- Always observe use-by dates. Remove all items that have exceeded use-by dates to reduce the risk of contamination in the refrigerator.

Freezer storage

Highly perishable and short shelf life food products can be stored in a freezer to extend their shelf life. Freezers should be maintained at a temperature of –18°C or below.

Food items that can be frozen are

- meat
- poultry
- seafood and
- cooked or prepared foods

Items stored in paper, cardboard or tin *should not be stored in a freezer*, as defrosting will cause paper products to break down and become soggy and tins to corrode.

Key aspects to remember
- Freezers should be cleaned *and sanitised* on a regular basis.
- Ensure and monitor correct temperature of freezers. Use thermometers to crosscheck internal operating temperatures.
- All food items should be *adequately chilled prior* to freezing.
- Items to be frozen should be completely covered or wrapped in cling wrap to prevent freezer burn. Freezer burn is caused by moisture being drawn out of exposed or incorrectly wrapped items by subzero temperatures, resulting in food spoilage.
- Meat and poultry products that have been defrosted or thawed should be covered and refrigerated - *never re-freeze any defrosted or thawed item.*
- To maintain food quality, all food products should be thawed overnight in a refrigerator.
- Food items such as meat, poultry and fish products should be handled as little as possible after defrosting/thawing.
- All frozen products must be labelled and dated for proper identification, before freezing.
- Apply stock rotation techniques: FIFO (first in first out - using old stock first). This means that new stock should be stored behind old stock – *not merely packing new stocks in front of items already in storage.*

Points to remember when freezing food:

Frozen meats will not keep indefinitely. The following guidelines apply:

- Beef keeps for 9–12 months at minus 18°C.
- Veal & lamb keep for six months at minus 18°C.
- Poultry keeps for four–six months at minus 18°C.
- Pork keeps for four months at minus 18°C.
- Frozen poultry should be tightly wrapped in cling wrap and stored at minus 18°C.
- Frozen fish should be tightly and individually wrapped and stored at minus 18°C.
- Never freeze spoiled meat, poultry or seafood. Rather consult your supervisor and dispose of the spoiled item(s) in a safe manner.

Defrosting food

The correct procedures for defrosting/thawing frozen foods

- Small items such as pieces of meat and poultry, pre-cooked and reformed items of fish, meat and poultry can be cooked straight from the freezer.
- Large joints of meat and *all* frozen whole birds must be properly thawed/defrosted in the refrigerator before being cooked.
- *Never* place frozen food under warm running water as this thaws the outside faster than the inside.
- Avoid handling a thawed/defrosted item, especially meat, until it needs to be processed/ cooked as this could increase the risk of cross-contamination.

The stock rotation system (FIFO)

FIFO stands for first in – first out.

- Mark the date on all new stock and received goods.
- Goods that are newly received into stock must be packed behind or underneath stock items already in stock. This is to ensure that older stock is used first.
- Pack all stock above floor level to reduce the likelihood of pest infestation.
- The purpose of the FIFO-system is to ensure no stock is ever allowed to spoil through being in storage too long. The FIFO-system helps to reduce waste and reduce higher costs through stock loss/spoilage.

Personal hygiene when handling and storing food

Personal hygiene is an important aspect of how you take care of, and demonstrate your respect for yourself. Good personal hygiene is an important aspect of taking care of your health, and also influences how people respond to you in a working and social situation.

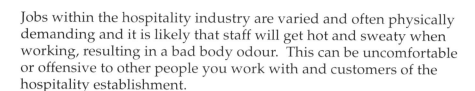

Jobs within the hospitality industry are varied and often physically demanding and it is likely that staff will get hot and sweaty when working, resulting in a bad body odour. This can be uncomfortable or offensive to other people you work with and customers of the hospitality establishment.

People who prepare food for the public have a big responsibility. This is important because the body carries bacteria on the skin and in body fluids, even when we are healthy, that can be transferred to the things we touch, especially food. The bacteria can make people ill. Companies expect employees to follow the health and hygiene procedure in terms of company policy, as well as those required by law.

Hygiene standards can be regarded as rules all staff have to abide by to ensure that their actions will not endanger any person who makes use of their services. The main aim of hygiene standards is to keep the environment clean.

General procedures to adhere to, to maintain personal hygiene:

- Wash hands after touching your face or hair.
- Wash hands thoroughly with a sanitiser after visiting the toilet.
- Wash hands regularly with soap and warm water.
- Shower or bath, use a deodorant and change underwear every day.
- Wear a clean work uniform every day.
- Clean teeth every day.
- Have neat and clean fingernails.
- Wash hair regularly.
- Wear a clean work uniform every day.
- Keep your hair tidy; if it is long you must tie it back from your face.
- Keep facial hair neat and trim.
- Avoid using strong perfumes.
- Avoid wearing too much make-up.

Appearance

- Bath or shower at least once per day to clean the body of normal bacteria and sweat to diminish body odours.
- Wash hair regularly – at least once a week, more often if working in a hot humid environment like the kitchen.
- If wearing perfume, keep the following general rules in mind:
  - Some people may be sensitive to strong-smelling perfumes especially in areas where food is being served.
  - Do not use perfume to cover up body odour.
- Wear clean uniforms and aprons for every work shift.
- Keep hair tied back. Always wear a food service hat or hairnet when doing food preparation.
- Do not wear rings or other jewellery as harmful bacteria can be concealed in jewellery.
- Keep moustaches and beards trimmed and clean. It is better to be clean shaven when working in a foodservice environment.
- Footwear should be clean and safe.

Words & terms

Personal hygiene:
Personal hygiene involves the practices that you need to perform on a regular basis to keep your body clean and healthy.

FIFO:
First In - First Out stock rotation & management system used in the food & hospitality industry

Hands

- Hands carry a lot of bacteria because hands are used for almost every activity. It is, therefore, important that hands be regularly washed before handling food, coming on duty or entering the kitchen and after each of the following activities:
  - touching or scratching any part of the body including areas such as ears, mouth, nose or hair
  - Blowing nose or using a handkerchief or tissue
  - touching dirty equipment or work surfaces
  - handling food
  - handling money
  - smoking a cigarette
  - cleaning or scraping dishes or utensils
  - eating
  - using the toilet
- Keep your hands away from your face, eyes, hair and arms while working with food.
- Keep your fingernails clean and short. Do not wear nail varnish.

Teeth

The hospitality industry is a service industry so staff are often required to talk to people or deal with customers.

Teeth that are not brushed regularly result in bad breath, tooth decay and gum disease. Teeth not properly cared for and bad breath are noticeable when talking up close to people (taking orders, explaining menus, etc.) and will affect the personal image of the staff member and the image of the hospitality establishment.

The following are basic dental and teeth care rules:

- Brush teeth every morning and evening.
- Use dental floss every day to remove food trapped between teeth. If this food is not removed it will attract bacteria that can cause tooth decay and cause bad breath.
- Use an antiseptic mouthwash to reduce harmful bacteria and freshen the breath.
- Visit a dentist at least once a year.

Health

- Cover coughs and sneezes with a suitable tissue, paper towel or handkerchief. Always turn away from food when coughing or sneezing.
- Do not work with food if you have any disease, cold, flu or infection.
- Cover any bruises, cuts or sores on the body with clean waterproof plaster or bandages.

Cuts, burns, grazes, sores or other wounds should be well covered with clean plaster or bandage because they are also breeding grounds for bacteria. If you have any wounds on your hands or other parts of your body, wash your hands each time you dress or touch the wound.

- Cuts and grazes that happen at work should be washed, treated with disinfectant and covered with a waterproof dressing. Do not handle food if you have wounds or cuts on your hands.

Unacceptable habits

- Do not smoke or chew gum while on duty.
- Do not sit on working surfaces.

Assessment activity 1:

Prepare a manual with guidelines on personal hygiene procedures and practices for new kitchen assistants.

Unit 5:

The relationship of time and temperature when storing and cooking different food items

Conditions for bacterial growth

Oxygen

Bacteria can reproduce and grow *with or without* oxygen.

Temperature

Bacteria like warm conditions, especially room temperature. Food poisoning bacteria usually only grow between 5–60° C. This temperature range is known as the *danger zone.*

Acidity

Bacteria cannot grow in high acid levels. Lemon juice and vinegar are quite often used to preserve foods to help stop bacterial contamination

Moisture

All living things need moisture to grow, especially bacteria.

Time

Given the right conditions, bacteria can reach large numbers over time. Bacteria are able to double in numbers *every 20 minutes*

Prevention of bacterial growth

To prevent microbial growth and reproduction of conditions favourable to their growth, heat, time, moisture and suitable food to grow on must be eliminated. Proper care should be taken and health and safety procedures followed during the preparation and cooking of different food items:

- It is firstly important to identify those food groups that are at high risk of bacterial contamination. Foods in which bacteria multiply rapidly are known as potentially hazardous foods.
- Some examples of potentially hazardous foods are raw and cooked meats, cooked potatoes, rice and pasta, stocks, gravies and sauces, egg products, cream and milk products.

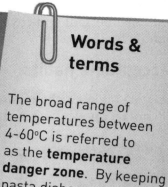

Words & terms

The broad range of temperatures between 4-60°C is referred to as the **temperature danger zone**. By keeping pasta dishes out of the temperature danger zone, the bacteria's ability to reproduce is decreased.

Did you know?

Most bacteria that cause food-borne disease multiply rapidly between 16-49°C.

It is important to keep hot food hot and cold food cold. This is known as the **time-and-temperature principle**. Potentially hazardous food should be heated or cooled quickly so that it is within the temperature danger zone as briefly as possible.

Working hygienically when preparing different food types

When preparing food items for cooking, it is necessary to work in a clean and hygienic work environment. All work surfaces, equipment and utensils should be sanitised before food is prepared and no utensil or piece of equipment should be used on two different products. For example, cross-contamination can occur when cooked beef is cut on the same chopping board straight after raw chicken has been cut. To prevent cross contamination it is necessary to use either two cutting boards or clean and sanitise the chopping board between one task and the next.

Cooking food hygienically

Different food types can be prepared by using a variety of cooking methods (deep-frying, boiling etc). Cooking not only allows the combining of flavours and makes food more edible, but *cooking is also a major factor in reducing the risk of food poisoning*.

Bacteria found in

- the soil covering vegetables,
- water that vegetables have been washed in and
- in meat and meat products

can be easily destroyed by heating or cooking at a temperature *above 75°C*. A thermometer is recommended to ensure the correct temperature is reached in the cooking process. Some foods can be boiled as a cooking method. Remember that boiling point is 100°C.

Did you know?

Some suppliers are now producing different coloured cutting boards to help eliminate cross-contamination. For example, red chopping boards for raw meats, white for chicken, green for vegetable production etc.

In the workplace

Key aspects to remember:
- Prepared food should not remain at room temperature for too long.
- Do not prepare food too long in advance – processed food contaminates easier than basic ingredients.
- Clean all food items in a separate 'food only' sink.
- Never defrost items at room temperature; place them in the refrigerator on a tray.

It is recommended that you allow enough time for food to defrost in a fridge as the temperature is below 4°C and out of the danger zone. Simply placing food on a bench allows bacteria to multiply as it defrosts in a warm environment, increasing the risk of food poisoning.

Key aspects to remember
- Serve cooked food as quickly as possible and at a recommended temperature of 63°C.
- Cook food products at 75°C and above, to kill all bacteria.
- Preheat cookery equipment to help reduce cooking time and to ensure food products do not remain in the danger zone too long.
- If holding or cooking food items in a hot box or bain-marie, make sure the temperature remains on at least 75°C.
- If cooked food is to be served later, cool rapidly and place in the refrigerator.

Unit 6:

The importance of following health and safety procedures when lifting heavy items for storage

Safe practices in lifting and storing goods

Around one in five accidents in the catering industry result from handling, lifting or carrying heavy objects. Sometimes an injury to your back is not immediately felt and only becomes apparent days or weeks later. Your employer has a duty to minimise risk of injury from manual handling by ordering smaller packages from suppliers, providing trolleys, stepladders and other mechanical devices for lifting and moving heavy objects.

It is your responsibility to observe your organisation's occupational health and safety guidelines. Any injury, i.e. strains, pulled muscles, cuts and any other accident to you or other staff member must be reported immediately in accordance with organisational requirements and legal requirements as defined in the Occupational Health and Safety Act and by the Compensation Commissioner's Office. They are there to protect you, the worker.

Did you know?

Top Seven Dangers facing Young Workers
The following table identifies the top seven dangers to young workers and the types of jobs where they are at risk.

The danger	
1. Lifting objects - overexertion causing sprains, strains, tears	Retail and grocery clerks, labourers, material handlers, shippers & receivers
2. Working on elevated levels - sprains, strains, tears, & fractures	Any job using ladders, stairs, scaffolding, or other raised areas
3. Working with knives - cuts & lacerations	Cooks, food service workers, retail clerks & shelf stockers
4. Working with hot substances/object – burns	Jobs in the hospitality & service industries
5. Using mobile equipment or motor vehicles - sprains, strains, tears, & fractures	Any job requiring driving, riding, operating, or operating near mobile equipment
6. Working with food slicers - cuts & lacerations	Deli sales clerks, cooks, food service workers & retail sales clerks in supermarkets
7. Working in proximity to running equipment or machinery - cuts, lacerations, & fractures	Labourers in manufacturing or construction, machine operators, material handlers, bakers & cooks

Guidelines to keep in mind (See Annexure D)

- Size up the load to be lifted and ask for assistance if the item is too heavy.
- Heavy goods should always be lifted with the knees bent so that the legs take the weight and the spine is protected. *Never bend forward and lift heavy objects using your back muscles.*
- Use trolleys and pallet-lifting equipment for heavy items.
- Heavy items should be stored on lower shelves to minimise handling and lifting.
- Before moving a load, plan and check your path for obstacles and danger zones such as where spillage has occurred.

Correct techniques for carrying an object (See Annexure D)

- Examine the object, and assess the situation. Ask yourself: Do you need assistance to carry the object? What is the best way to carry it?
- Get close the load; spread your feet to form a stable stance.
- Bend your knees slightly as you grab the load. Make sure *your back is straight* and shoulders level. Lift gently; do not strain yourself.
- Move slowly, keeping control of the load. Do not twist your body as you move your feet.
- When putting the object down, bend the knees slowly and *keep your back straight*.

Unit 7:

Lift all heavy items in accordance with safety procedures

(See Annexure D)

Health and safety procedures that should be followed when lifting and storing food deliveries also include the following:

- Steps or small ladders to help staff reach goods on high shelves
- The use of appropriate trolleys for transporting goods
- Storage of heavy cases, containers and jars at a convenient height to prevent any strain in lifting
- Staff wearing clean clothes at all times to prevent contamination of food
- Wearing suitable safety shoes to prevent injury to feet if a heavy item is dropped.

Adapting food hygiene procedures but maintaining good practices in a variety of situations

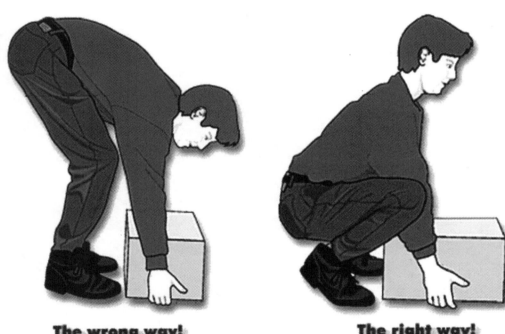

The wrong way!   The right way!

Unit 8:

Adapt food hygiene procedures but maintain good practices in a variety of situations

Food Service Legislation and Regulations as well as principles of Sanitation and Hygiene (as discussed in Hospitality Generics NQF Level 2 and Level 3) providing guidance on what aspects are critically important to maintain and ensure good Hygiene and Sanitation practices.

Every Food Service Establishment (kitchen, take-away, restaurant, etc.) has to implement the above guidelines and principles in a practical manner within that specific food service establishment. The risk involved in this process is that people may consider certain guidelines and principles as not important and implement practical procedures that in the end defies the objective of good hygiene practice e.g. not using protective clothing like hairnets in order to save costs.

Practical Guidelines for implementing Hygiene and Sanitation practices

1. Compile a detailed Operations and Procedures manual for every specific section of food production that contains the following sections:

- Personal Hygiene
- Correct Food Handling Procedures
- Food Storage
- Temperature control
- Kitchen Design and Equipment
- Cleaning and Disinfection
- Handling of waste and rubbish
- Pest Control

2. Staff must be properly trained in all aspects covered in the Operations and Procedures Manual.
3. Monitoring of implementation and procedure control.
4. Annual review and revision of the manual.

Words & terms

Food safety control:
This can be defined as a mandatory regulatory activity of enforcement by the relevant health authority to provide consumer protection and to ensure that all foods during production, handling, storage, processing, and distribution are safe and fit for human consumption and conform to safety requirements as prescribed by law.

Health Act Regulation:
A food handler shall wear overalls that are in a clean and sound condition and should only be used for one work shift, and be washed after every such work shift. The overall must be kept in a changing room, central storeroom or locker when not in use.

Health Act Regulation:
Unpacked food shall not be handled by any person who has not washed his hands thoroughly with soap and water or cleaned them in another effective manner.

Keeping record

Record all information

- Keep records of all formal quality monitoring actions and the results thereof.
- Comply with all HACCP (Hazard Analysis Critical Control Point) documentation requirements if they apply in your kitchen.
- Keep records of all maintenance requests so that you can follow up on any problems.
- Keep records of any discussions you have with suppliers relating to problems with their quality, delivery and service.

Did you know?

Managing the cold chain

Pick 'n Pay has spent the last 18 months reinventing itself by introducing 450 new items in its fresh range to compete with the Woolworths-type convenience foods. The one area where Woolworths is supreme is in the area of cold chain management, with guaranteed shelf life dates. From its distribution centres to its delivery trucks, to its back-of-the store receiving areas and finally into the display fridges, the temperature of perishable goods – and their surrounds – is very strictly monitored. If the cold chain is broken, even slightly, the food does not make it anywhere near the till points. The other supermarket groups are rather less pedantic about temperature control. Pick 'n Pay, CEO, Nick Badminton admitted that the company was "looking deeply" at their cold chain, "especially that last 100m to the shelf". No more will it be acceptable for goods to be taken off trucks and left sitting in the distribution area for up to an hour – it will be taken straight into a temperature controlled receiving area. Receiving managers will check the temperatures inside refrigerated delivery trucks, and the goods themselves, to ensure they comply. "Already at our distribution centres, if a refrigerated truck has been turned off, the goods are rejected."

Pretoria news, Consumer Watch by Wendy Knowler, 14 November 2007

Unit 9:

Unforeseen operational problems related to food hygiene

Delivery problems

Food deliveries that do not comply with

- exact standards in terms of quality, packaging
- use-by date and
- internal temperature

must not be accepted, but be returned to the supplier immediately upon delivery.

If delivery problems pertaining to the above aspects persist over a period of time, consider changing to more reliable suppliers to reduce waste and shortages.

Faulty fridge or freezer

Whenever you become aware of a faulty freezer or fridge, bring it to the attention of the maintenance manager immediately so that repairs can be done before food spoilage can occur.

If there are problems with any refrigeration equipment, keep the doors closed as long as possible to prevent internal temperature loss.

Broken packaging

Any items delivered in damaged packaging must not be accepted and must be returned upon delivery. Common sense should be used in this respect in conjunction with the type of food item under consideration.

Receiving frozen food that has thawed

Procedures must be in place for checking the temperature of frozen foods on delivery at the establishment. Delivery vehicles are subject to legislation and food should be at the correct temperatures when delivered. If frozen food is not at the correct temperature upon delivery, it must be returned. The risk of food contamination and food poisoning with accepting thawed food items is extremely high. The cold chain must be maintained up to the point of final storage at the correct temperature within your food establishment.

Assessment activity 2:

Develop a simple poster instructing kitchen staff on the cleaning of kitchen equipment.

Summary

Maintain and promote food hygiene and safety procedures during food preparation, cooking and storage to organisational and legislative requirements.

Food poisoning pathogens cause food poisoning and the general symptoms associated with food poisoning are vomiting, diarrhoea and abdominal pain.

Bacterial food poisoning – is caused by harmful bacteria present in food when consumed

- salmonella group
- staphylococcus aureus
- clostridium perfringens
- other types of bacteria - clostridium botulinum, campylobacter bacteria, bacillus cereus, listeria bacteria

Prevention of food poisoning from bacteria can be done with two basic approaches that can be effectively used by everyone involved in the food service environment:

- prevent bacteria from multiplying
- prevent bacteria from spreading from place to place

Chemical food poisoning may occur when chemicals accidentally enter food through their use in agricultural or manufacturing processes.

Poisonous foods refer to some plants (for example, rhubarb leaves, green potatoes and certain toadstools) that contain poison in sufficient quantities to cause poisoning if eaten.

Pest infestations may occur in human food storage areas as these have a natural attraction for pests, vermin, insects, domestic animals and birds since such storage provides an easy accessible source of food. These animals and insects are carriers of certain diseases and bacteria, which could lead to food poisoning as well as loss of food supply stocks.

Insect infection can cause food poisoning through insects like house flies, silverfish, cockroaches, beetles, etc. Insects can effectively be controlled with the correct insecticide and through fumigation of premises.

Other possible sources of food poisoning

- *Cats and Dogs* - pets carry harmful bacteria on their coats and are not always clean in their natural habits and should, therefore, not be permitted in kitchens or on food premises.

- *Birds* - entering through windows may contaminate food and surfaces on which food is prepared.

- *Dust* - contains bacteria and must not be allowed to settle on food or food preparation surfaces.

Hygiene is of paramount importance when storing food. Food storage areas must be kept clean and hygienic for various reasons: (a) to eliminate the risk of contamination, (b) prevent food spoilage and (c) comply with health regulations.

Food storage areas need to be kept clean and hygienic to prevent or protect them from the following: physical contamination; dangerous substances; physical contamination; pests & rodents; unsuitable temperatures; excessive humidity and direct sunlight. Store food items hygienically, according to recommended storage procedures that take into account temperature, shelf life, and place and conditions of storage.

Time and temperature are the two most important factors to consider when storing food

Hygienic storage of food items

- *Meat-* should be stored wrapped in plastic in the refrigerator at *below 5°C* or tightly wrapped and frozen.
- *Poultry, game birds, rabbit, hare and fish* each require specific storage methods.
- *Dairy products* generally freeze well, with the exception of products that have a fat content of less than 40%,
- *Vegetables and fruit* should be stored in the refrigerator.
- *Eggs* must be stored in the refrigerator with the *pointed end down* to make sure that the yolk is centred.
- *Dry goods* (flour, sugar, rice, maize meal, salt, etc.) should be stored in *dry goods stores*

Storage methods:

- *Dry storage* is recommended for those products that are best kept at room temperature (10 – 20°C) and have a long shelf life.
- *Refrigerated storage* items generally have a short shelf life and are highly perishable and should be kept between 0–5°C.
- *Freezer storage* is for highly perishable and short shelf life food products to extend their shelf life and should be maintained at temperatures of –18°C or below.

Defrosting food – there are specific correct procedures for defrosting/ thawing frozen foods

The stock rotation system - FIFO stands for first in-first out

Personal hygiene when handling and storing food is an important aspect of how you take care of, and demonstrate your respect for yourself. Good personal hygiene is an important aspect of taking care of your health, and also influences how people respond to you in a working and social situation.

The temperature danger zone is the broad range of temperatures between 4-60°C. By keeping dishes out of the temperature danger zone, the bacteria's ability to reproduce is decreased.

Conditions for bacterial growth that need to be monitored are oxygen, temperature, acidity, moisture and time.

Prevention of bacterial growth can be done by eliminating microbial growth and reproduction of the conditions favourable to their growth – heat, time, moisture and suitable food to grow on.

Working hygienically when preparing different food types is of critical importance.

Cooking food hygienically by using a variety of cooking methods (deep-frying, boiling etc.) is also a major factor in reducing the risk of food poisoning.

Safe practices should always be followed in lifting and storing goods. Lift all heavy items in accordance with safety procedures.

Unforeseen operational problems related to food hygiene are

- delivery problems
- faulty fridge or freezer
- broken packaging
- receiving frozen food that has thawed

Topic 3:
Operating a payment point and processing payments

Module 1

Preparing, operating payment points, processing payments efficiently and performing cashing-up and handing-over procedures

Overview

The student should be able to ...

- understand and demonstrate procedures for the set-up, operation and cashing up of a payment point
- understand the issues of security when operating a payment point including the prevention of unauthorised access
- deal with customers in a polite and friendly way. Understand how operational issues impact on customer service
- deal with unexpected operational situations while maintaining standards of customer service

Did you know?

Debit and credit cards offer cheapest means of transacting

With so much concern about bank charges, it's not a bad idea to do a bit of research to work out your cheapest way of transacting. According to James Fowle, Pricing Consultant at First National Bank (FNB), "Consumers have many options when it comes to using banking services. More traditional forms of bank usage, like withdrawing cash inside a branch of a bank, are generally the most expensive. Technology has allowed banks to offer certain cheaper methods of transacting, but it's in the customer's hands to make the correct choices."

Disciplined use of a credit card is certainly a good option. "If you don't use the credit facility that the credit card offers - in other words, if you pay the balance owing by due date – you are effectively transacting for free. While there is a membership fee for having a credit card, there is no fee per transaction. If you earn eBucks on your credit card this could also compensate for the membership fee. So, if you buy all your groceries and pay for all your monthly services, including the telephone account, rates and electricity, and so on, with your credit card, you can effectively limit your bank charges per month. Of course, if you use any other bank

services as well, you'd have to factor those charges in to the total you're spending."

A debit card is another way of keeping your bank charges down. Debit cards offer similar functionality to credit cards, in terms of their wide acceptance at retail outlets and for other payment needs, but don't carry the risk of getting into any difficulty with credit if you're not disciplined where this is concerned.

"FNB has made a real effort to keep charges down. Our fee for using a debit card at a till inside a shop to pay for your purchases is the cheapest available - at only R1,50 per transaction, no matter how much you're spending," Fowle explains. "So, let's say you do a weekly grocery shop and use your FNB debit card to pay for the trolley of goods, you'll incur a charge of less than R10 each month."

FNB customers can also draw cash at the till in certain shops. There is a nominal charge for this per transaction, far cheaper than the traditional ways of accessing cash from your account.

"Do your homework and research the choices available," Fowle advises. "If you keep your bank charges down on your regular, daily transacting, your total charges each month won't be that high."

Procedures for the setting-up, operating and cashing up of a payment point

Operating a payment point

Preparation

Guidelines

It is important to prepare the payment point for operation and complete a proper hand-over at the end of the shift or closure for the business day.

Below are guidelines for preparation of the pay point for service:

- The supporting computer must be on and operational, as well as the network connections. Also check the power supply for the pay point machine.
- The operator must log in with the correct user ID and secret password.
- Verify that the cash float is correct and in place in the cash drawer, checking as well that there is sufficient change for the shift.
- The float count sheet must be signed as proof of this verification.
- During the shift it is important to check change constantly, so that it does not run out at a critical time. Order well in advance so that customers do not need to wait for change.
- Change is normally requested on a 'change requisition' form. Mark the change required on the prepared sheet, rounding it to the nearest R10.00.
- Prepare the correct amount in notes before calling for change from the duty manager or cash-up supervisor.
- Ensure the duty manager or cash-up officer checks the amount of cash handed over, and signs for the receipt of it.
- Check the change requested before placing it in the till drawer.

Supplies

Audit rolls, receipt rolls and customer bills

The paper receipt till roll and the speed-point roll have an indicator near the end to indicate that the roll is nearly finished – it is usually a pink/red line on the paper. Once this is noticed, ensure that the roll is replaced immediately. Do not wait until the roll is completely finished.

Stationery

Ensure that the payment point has sufficient supplies of the relevant stationery:

- minimum of two company pens in good working condition and loaded stapler
- printer stationery
- speed-point stationery
- pre-list
- credit card vouchers (Visa/MasterCard; American Express; Diners Club)

Sufficient change

Impact on customer

Constantly check the available change throughout the shift. Additional change must be requested in good time to prevent a shortage at a critical time.

When there is not sufficient change at the pay point customers may become annoyed because

- they often have to wait long periods until the cashier sorts out the change problem
- it is an indication of a poorly managed organisation and lack of training of staff
- the image projected is that the company does not care about the customer's most valuable commodity - time

Making customers/guests unhappy because of a simple thing like change has a direct effect on repeat business and company profits.

Procedure for ordering change

- Use the correct 'change requisition' form.
- Tick the boxes of change required and the amount of change required, rounding the total off to the nearest R10-00.
- Prepare the correct amount in notes before calling for change from the duty manager or cash-up supervisor.
- Ensure the duty manager or cash-up officer checks the amount of cash handed over, and signs for the receipt of it.
- Check the change requested before placing it in the till drawer.

Operating a payment point

- Scan the item or enter the correct amount into the till point.
- State the total amount due in a friendly way to the customer.
- When the guest/customer gives you the money, say thank you politely.
- Post the required amount on the computer to the miscellaneous folios as per company procedures and associated pay point procedures.
- Put the money in the drawer and count out any change. Count out the change for the customer/guest, and say thank you, asking if there is anything else you can do for him/her.
- If the guest requires no further assistance, wish him/her a pleasant day.

When cross-border transactions are illegal

The growth of the internet distribution channel has increased the volume of cross-border transactions. In some cases, laws governing the sale of certain goods and services in the merchant outlet jurisdiction may differ from those in the cardholder's jurisdiction. As a result, there is increased risk that some merchants, while acting in accordance with the laws of their own outlet jurisdiction, may be acting contrary to the laws of a cardholder's legal jurisdiction. Likewise, some cardholders may attempt to complete transactions that are illegal in their jurisdiction but legal in the merchant's outlet jurisdiction. Such transactions may have legal or regulatory impact on card associations and banks, which may adversely affect their reputation.

- A merchant must comply with applicable laws and a transaction must be legal in both the cardholder's jurisdiction and the merchant outlet's jurisdiction. For enforcement purposes, the cardholder's jurisdiction is defined as the jurisdiction of the issuing bank.
- A card issuer (bank) may systemically send a decline response to an authorisation request for a transaction that has been determined to be illegal.
- A merchant must not knowingly submit any transaction that is illegal or that the merchant should have known was illegal, for submission into the payment system.

Failure to comply with the above may result in penalties up to US$50 000 and/or termination of the merchant's agreement.

Processing a range of payments

Guests can make payments in a variety of ways: cash (local or foreign currency), cheque, credit card, debit card, travellers' cheques or vouchers.

Cash

When a guest makes a cash payment, proceed as follows:

- On check out verify that all service dockets have been charged for and posted to the relevant room number.
- Print the invoice, present it to the guest and allow guest to verify amounts charged.
- When cash is handed over, count the total in front of the guest to prevent any dispute.
- Validate notes under an ultraviolet lamp if possible. (This will not work with foreign currency as all notes do not have this security feature.)
- On the cash payment system enter the amount of cash tendered in the correct currency.
- Place the money in the cash drawer and take out the correct change from the cash drawer.
- Check that the correct change has been handed to the guest by counting it before the guest.
- Place the counted change, the bill and the receipt in the bill folder and hand the folder to the guest.
- Retain the other copies for record purposes and file correctly according to procedures.

Credit/ debit cards (see Annexure E)

Here are a few handy rules as issued by banks to companies for completing an electronic transation:

Keep the card throughout the transaction:

If you hand the card back to the customer after you have swiped it through the Paypoint terminal, you will not be able to carry out all the necessary checks to ensure that the transaction is legitimate

Check the front of the card:

Each specific brand of card account numbers begin with the same number.
> *Visa* accounts all begin with a "4"
> *Mastercard* account numbers all begin with "5"
> *American Express* account numbers all begin with "37"
> *Diners Club* account numbers begin with "36" or with "38"

A four-digit number on Visa and Mastercard cards, known as the pre-printed Bank Identification Number or BIN, must be printed above or below the embossed account number on the front of the card. This number must match the first four digits of the embossed (raised) account number. (Refer also to the section on Credit Card Security features.) If the numbers do not match make a Code 10 call. (Refer to the section on fraudulent tansactions.)

Swipe the card through the paypoint terminal:

Swipe the customer's card through the magnetic strip reader in the direction as indicated on the specific machine.

Request authorization: (See Annexure F)

If the amount to be paid by the customer is above the floor limit, the paypoint terminal will automatically dial the Authorisation Centre for authorisation.

Possible responses from the paypoint terminal:

Approval	Decline	Hot Card
- The transaction slip will print automatically	- If you do not receive approval, return the card to the customer.	- If you get this reponse from the Authorisation Centre, keep the card, phone the Authorisation Centre and follow their instructions.
- The account number printed on the transaction slip must match the embossed (raised) account number on the front of the card.	- Discreetly and politely inform him/ her that the bank has declined the transaction.	
- If the numbers match, ask the customer to sign the transaction slip and compare the signatures. The signature on the back of the card should match the signature on the transaction slip.		

- If the signatures do not match, make Code 10 call (Refer to the section on fraudulent transactions.)		-

Get authorisation and REMEMBER CODE 10

Code 10 is a universal code which provides merchants with away to alert the authorisation centre that a suspicious transaction is taking place.

- Call for "CODE 10" authorisation if
  - you believe you have a counterfeit or altered card,
  - the presenter / transaction looks suspicious,
  - the signatures don't match,
  - account number of the printed sales voucher differs from that on the card, or
  - the customer does not have his card with him and insists on purchasing goods with a credit card number only.
- Dial the ABSA authorisation centre on 086 010 0017.
  - The Code 10 operator asks a series of questions that can be answered with yes or no responses
  - Follow the operator's instructions – NEVER ENDANGER YOURSELF!

Check the signature panel on the back of the card:

The card must be signed. If not signed ask the customer for positive identification and ask him/her to sign it in front of you. Compare the name on the ID with the signature and name on the front of the card.

Obtain and compare signatures:

The customer must sign the transaction slip. The signature on the transaction slip should match the signature on the back of the card. If it does match, return the card to the customer with a duplicate of the transaction slip (you must always keep the copy with the original signature.) If not, keep the card and make a Code 10 call. (Refer to section on fraudulent transactions.)

BEWARE OF THE BOGUS LETTER OF AUTHORITY

One of the newer tricks used by credit card fraudsters is to present a falsified letter of authority which authorises the presenter to use someone else's credit card. Always insist that the credit card and its true owner be present when payment is made, or ask for an authorisation code. Remember "CODE 10 authorisations". "Card not present" practices that you should be wary of: It often happens these days that companies and business leaders address a handwritten or typed letter to businesses authorizing the use of their credit cards for hotel bills, telephone calls, meals etc. The following may indicate a forgery:

- Letterhead appears unprofessional.
- Spelling and grammatical errors.
- Handwritten letters.
- Only a cellphone number given as contact.

Keep the original transaction slip:

Keep the original transaction slip for at least 180 days for your records and for protection against possible disputes, which may result in chargebacks if the copy of the transaction slip is not retained.

How to do a manual credit card transaction
(see Annexure G)

In the event of a power failure, you may have to resort to processing a mnual transaction.

Faulty magnetic strips on cards may also result in transactions having to be done manually.

Here are a few handy rules to keep in mind when performing a manual transaction:

(a) Keep the card throughout the transaction
   If you hand the card back to the customer after you have processed it through the manual machine, you will not be able to carry out all the necessary checks to ensure that the transaction is legitimate.

(b) Make an imprint of the card:
   Use the zip-zap machine to make an imprint of the customer's card. (Check that all card details are clear on the voucher.)
   This will prove that the card and the cardholder were present at the time of the transaction. Make sure the security character (for example the stylized "MC " for Mastercard cards and the "Flying V" for Visa cards) appears next to the expiry date. (Refer to section on Credit Card security features.)

(c) Check the front of the card:
   Each specific brand of card account numbers begin with the same number.
   Visa accounts all begin with a "4"
   Mastercard account numbers all begin with "5"
   American Express account numbers all begin with "37"
   Diners Club account numbers begin with "36" or with "38"
   A four-digit number on Visa and Mastercard cards, known as the pre-printed Bank Identification Number or BIN, must be printed above or below the embossed account number on the front of the card. This number must match the first four digits of the embossed (raised) account number. (Refer also to the section on Credit Card Security features.) If the numbers do not match make a Code 10 call. (Refer to the section on fraudulent transactions.)

(d) Capture the transaction:

   In the case of a Point of Sale (POS) terminal:
   – Key-enter the transaction (card details) on the POS terminal.
   – The terminal will automatically dail the Authorisation Centre for authorization.
   – If the transaction is approved, a transaction slip with the authorization code will be printed. If it isn't approved, return the card to the cardholder. Discretely inform him/her that the transaction has been declined.

In the case of a zip-zap machine:
- If the electronic POS terminal is out of order, use the zip-zap machine to make an imprint of the card.
- Phone the Authorisation Centre and ask for an authorization code.
- Have the the card in front of you so that you can provide the following information:
  o Your merchant/company number
  o The cardholder's name
  o The card number and expiry date
  o The CVV/CVC2 number (see Annexure I on Credit Card security features)
  o The transaction amount
  o Any other information required by the Authorisation Centre.
- Complete the zip-zap voucher by ensuring that details are clear and legible and that the following information is included on the voucher:
  o The merchant/company name and location
  o A brief description of the merchandise or service provided
  o The transaction date
  o The transaction amount
  o In the case of a restaurant, the tip amount

If the transaction has not been approved, return the card to the customer. Discretely inform him or her that the transaction has been declined.

Important: *Do not process the transaction or phone the cardholder's bank for authorization when the Authorisation Centre (covering all banks) declines the transaction.*

(e) Check the signature panel on the back of the card:
The card must be signed. If not signed ask the customer for positive identification and ask him/her to sign it in front of you. Compare the name on the ID with the signature and name on the front of the card.

Important: *Do not accept an unsigned card*

(f) Obtain and compare signatures:
The customer must sign the transaction slip or zip-zap voucher. The signature on the transaction slip should match the signature on the back of the card. If it does match, return the card to the customer with a duplicate of the zip-zap transaction voucher (you must always keep the copy with the original signature.) If not, keep the card and make a Code 10 call. (Refer to section on fraudulent transactions.)

(g) Keep the original transaction slip:
Keep the original zip-zap transaction voucher for at least 180 days for your records and for protection against possible disputes, which may result in chargebacks if the copy of the transaction slip is not retained.

Also see Annexures H & I

Credit card rules for your specific industry

The banks have specific industry rules for restaurants, casino's and forecourt (garage, petrol cards & fleet cards)

Restaurants, food service establishments:
The tip amount must be added to conclude the transaction. In the case of electronic transactions, swipe the supervisor's card or use your supervisor's PIN to access this option. In the case of manual transactions, include the tip amount on the zip-zap voucher as separate line before the total. If the tip amount is zero, the zero must be added as the tip amount to conclude the transaction.

Cheques

Cheques are generally not accepted unless prior arrangement has been made with management.

If a guest pays by cheque, do the following:

- Ask if the cheque is guaranteed to cover the full amount of the bill.
- If so, ask to see the cheque guarantee card to confirm this. The card number must be written on the back of the cheque in the space provided.
- Print the invoice, present it to the guest and allow the guest to verify the amounts charged.
- On the payment system, enter the amount of the cheque tendered in the correct currency.
- Place the cheque in the cash drawer.
- Place the bill and the receipt in the bill folder and hand the folder to the guest.
- Retain the other copies for record purposes and file correctly according to procedures

If the guest pays by travellers cheque the same process is followed, except that the passport number of the guest must be entered on the travellers cheques to validate them. Proceed as for cheques described above to complete the transaction.

Tokens and vouchers

If a guest has a token or voucher, this may be taken off the guest's account without management authorisation, provided that the voucher/token numbers and expiry dates are checked and verified

Keep the voucher and attach to relevant documentation for filing. The guest receives the bill with the discounted amount printed on it. In the case of a voucher card, update the amount on the card using company procedures to include the latest transaction and return the voucher card to the guest.

Voucher cards are typically issued to staff of companies/organisations that provide frequent business to the hotel and have a contractual agreement to that effect, for example, flight staff of a particular airline may be entitled to accommodation (pre-paid by their company) and discounts on their meals on presentation of their voucher cards.

Storage and filing

Procedures for filing and storing guest accounts correctly

- Bar, restaurant and telephone charges are generally automatically charged to guest accounts. The supporting dockets signed by the guest must be filed with the relevant room number.
- Deal with one thing at a time and ensure that documentation is filed correctly to ensure that nothing is lost or misfiled.
- All cash, cheques and credit card vouchers must be placed in the cash drawer when received.
- Make sure that the cash drawer is securely locked when not in use.
- Always sign out of the computerised system to safeguard computer data files from being tampered with when leaving the front office desk.

End of shift

Procedures for closing the payment point and handing-over correctly at the end of the shift

- Remove the cash, credit cards, cheques and disbursement vouchers from the cash drawer and complete the required company printout.
- Verify that the float amount is the same as at the beginning of the shift and sign the float count sheet. In larger hotels the entire cash drawer is removed and handed in. The next shift brings its own cash drawer.
- Place the cash drawer printout and content (cash, cheques, credit card slips) in a banking envelope, hand it to the manager on duty to check. Obtain the signature of the manager on duty and then counter sign it yourself.
- In view of rising crime the normal practice is to place the sealed banking envelope in the drop safe in the presence of the same manager on duty – or hand over the banking envelope as per company cash-handling procedures and security measures.

Did you know?

Vouchers and tokens can be exchanged for goods or services to the value stated on the voucher or token. The difference between a voucher and token is that tokens are usually promotional gifts that are valid for a limited period of time, while vouchers may be obtainable/issued as required or by special arrangement.

Did you know?

All documentation relating to daily recording of services and purchases, relevant computer printouts (normally two readings), financial reports etc. and supporting documents must be kept for at least five years

- When reconciling the cash drawer and there is a cash shortage or extra cash
  - recheck cash counted
  - recheck float
  - recheck pay outs/refunds/Forex
  - recheck that none of the pre-listed dockets/credit card vouchers have been recorded in the wrong column.
- If there is still a discrepancy, this will be investigated the next day. Company policy normally states that the responsible cashier may have to pay in any shortfalls. If the cash drawer reconciliation shows extra cash, check everything! There may have been a mistake, which will mean that there will be a shortage on the next shift.

In the workplace

THETA

At the point of sale in your shop - usually a cash register - you need a system that will capture the price, and preferably also the product code. (As mentioned above, bar coding makes this a quick and easy process.) Whether or not you use an automated system, you need to be able to do the following:

- Manage a cash float at the point of sale to give customers change for their purchases.
- Generate a customer receipt for the purchase, and keep a record of it yourself.
- Accept other forms of payment from customers (more customers today are using credit cards and debit cards for safety reasons), and keep records of these transactions.
- Clear the till regularly and safely for security reasons; and
- When clearing the till, reconcile the amount of cash in the till with the receipts issued. (Discrepancies need to be recorded on a cash discrepancies report form, signed by the cashier, and investigated by a supervisor or you, the business owner).

In the workplace

THETA

Below are guidelines for improving work efficiency:

- Keep work areas tidy so that it is easy to find things when they are needed.
- Never leave till drawers open or leave cash lying unattended on counters or desks. Dealing with losses is time-consuming and may cost an employee his or her job.
- Place cash, cheques, credit card vouchers in the till drawer immediately after processing them.
- Work efficiently, and keep paper work up-to-date – but not if it means keeping a guest waiting. Guest service comes before paper work!
- If cash revenue is particularly high, it is advisable to bank it at intervals during the shift. Make sure that the cash to be banked is counted with the duty manager and signed that the amount is correct.

THETA

Efficient service

Prompt service is important as it creates the impression that the employee

- is familiar with company procedures and knows what s/he is doing
- is able to identify and address customer needs efficiently
- cares about customer satisfaction

Customers love efficiency and customer satisfaction impacts on company profits. Remember that 'time is money!'

Unit 2:

Security

Unauthorised access

Impact on organisation

It is of crucial importance that payment points are protected from unauthorised access to prevent theft and tampering.

The consequences of unauthorised access to especially cash in pay point will have negative implications for both the staff member and the company as described by THETA in the following guidelines:

- *Inaccurate transactions*: The presence of unauthorised persons in one's work area increases the risk of inaccurate transactions. Not only will the company suffer from account imbalances and profit losses, but the customer may be upset by being charged incorrectly etc. This impacts on guest satisfaction, which in turn affects repeat business.
- *Personal accountability*: Staff who handle and process payments are personally responsible and accountable for computer transactions and for any outstanding payments while on duty.
- *Profit losses*: If payment points are not secured properly, even small amounts of cash/cheques etc. that are misplaced/stolen can lead to account imbalances and eventually have a huge impact on company profits. This invariably affects the employee who may be paid less to overcome losses.

Securing pay points

Cash and card pay points

There are two different types of pay points:

- tills or billing equipment with cash drawers
- speed points or manual card machines

Recommended ways of securing tills or billing equipment with cash drawers:

- Keep the till drawer closed at all times and do not leave any cash outside the till drawer.
- Do not allow any unauthorised person into your work area.
- Make it a habit to double-check all transactions.
- Never allow a manager or cash-up officer to remove any cash from your till drawer without counting it in front of you and signing a receipt for it.
- The same principle applies when receiving cash from a manager or cash-up officer. Always check it in front of him/her and sign a receipt for it.

Recommended ways of securing speed points or manual card machines:

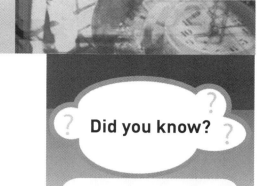

- The service counter should be high enough to keep equipment out of reach.
- No unauthorised person should be allowed into the pay point area, including fellow staff members.
- Most systems require an authorisation code to gain access to the system which needs to be entered before any transaction is carried out. KEEP YOUR PASSWORD/CODE SECRET. If another person gains access to the system with your password/code you will be held responsible for any losses.

Unauthorised payments (See Annexures H & I)

Unauthorised use of a credit card constitutes fraud and is an serious criminal offence. All the major banks and credit card companies have extensive anti-fraud campaigns to protect cardholders as well as merchants against the fraudulent use of cards as means of payment.

See Annexure I "Combat card fraud" for more details in this regard. This annexure also gives a detailed overview of the security features of credit cards to look out for and be able to identify false and tampered cards.

Types

Unauthorised payments can originate from a variety of sources, such as the following:

- cheques that are not bank guaranteed
- the amount on the cheque exceeds the value that the cheque is guaranteed for
- the value of the bill exceeds the credit card limit
- the credit card company declines authorisation of the amount requested
- the credit card in no longer valid. See the expiry date on the card
- the signature on the credit card does not match the guest's/customer's signature on the credit card slip

Discretion

It is important for staff to be discreet. Unauthorised payment may be offered for the following reasons:

- The customer/guest may be offended by unfounded suspicions of him/her.
- Perpetrators and fraudsters may sense that they have been compromised and may try to get away without being caught.

Did you know?

Limited cash at payment points
The SA Police Services recommend that only a limited amount of cash be kept at payment points for security purposes. If the amount of cash at a payment point is limited, losses will be limited in the event of theft or robbery. During busy periods, especially at month end or during peak check out time, limited amounts of cash are easier to tally up and process.

Assessment activity 1:

Simulation

If the college has a restaurant or cafeteria, you may do practical work by actually working at and operating the payment point. If not, divide into groups of three.

Fifteen scenarios are listed, covering setup, operation and cashing up of the payment point:

1. Activate the machine
2. Replace a till roll
3. Complete a cash/cheque/credit card payment
4. Request more change
5. Print bills, etc.
6. Wrong price entered
7. Cash shortage at end of the shift
8. Too many items of one sort entered
9. Paper jams while printing customer receipt
10. No till rolls available and there is a long queue of waiting customers
11. Customer do not have enough money to pay for the goods
12. Bank refuses credit card authorisation
13. General power failure occurs
14. Change received is not correct
15. Fraudulent /stolen credit card used to pay for goods

Each student is allocated five scenarios. Where necessary, another student may role play as a customer. You must each demonstrate these five scenarios using the payment point machine.

It is important to develop responses to the scenarios, highlighting security issues that you may encounter. You may use your notes and learning materials to assist you. You should also highlight customer service issues as they arise.

Unit 3:

Dealing with customers in a polite and friendly way

It is important that all staff understand how operational issues impact on customer service, from the porters, laundry staff, cooks, cleaners, front office, housekeeping staff, etc. up to the general managers.

Politeness and friendliness

The manner in which employees communicate with customers is a reflection of what the company is about, what it stands for and what makes it unique. Does the customer sense a sincere warm and friendly welcome or just a cordial greeting?

Whenever staff members speak to guests, they must be polite, friendly and courteous.

Consider & apply the PLEASING principle when dealing with customers.

P – always be Polite

L – Listen to customers

E – Empathise, Ensure feedback

A – Ask questions, display a good Attitude

S – Smile

I – show Interest

N – Never say NO upfront - always try to make an effort

G – Go the extra mile

Greeting customers

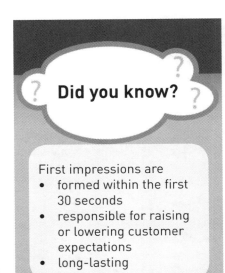

All staff should be trained (not simply instructed) to greet guests in a friendly and courteous manner that conveys the warmth of the organisation. It is important that guests and visitors feel welcome and comfortable in the hotel. Guests should also leave with a farewell in a warm and friendly manner.

Guests/customers often make a decision about staff or the organisation in the *first few minutes* – these are the crucial minutes for creating a positive first impression. Customer satisfaction has a direct effect on a company's popularity and profitability as it influences the guest's future decisions of either returning or finding another venue and it has been proven by research that satisfied guests return and recommend the organisation to their friends, family, colleagues and business associates.

Unit 4:

Dealing with unexpected operational situations while maintaining standards of customer service

Unexpected situations

Discrepancies with cash

When reconciling the cash drawer and there is a cash shortage or extra cash

- recheck cash counted
- recheck float
- recheck pay outs/refunds/Forex
- recheck that none of the pre-listed dockets/credit card vouchers have been recorded in the wrong column.

If there is still a discrepancy, this will be investigated the next day. Company policy normally states that the responsible cashier may have to pay in any shortfalls. If the cash drawer reconciliation shows extra cash, check everything! There may have been a mistake, which will mean that there will be a shortage on the next shift

Shortage of supplies /change

It must be standard practice to check that there are sufficient supplies and change at the beginning of each shift.

It may happen during busy periods that supplies/change run low. When this happens

- notify the duty manager so that s/he may bring the supplies/change to you
- try not to keep the customer/guest waiting
- ask customers/guests to use an alternative pay point, if available
- check and sign for change as swiftly as possible

Customer disputes

The following are typical situations where customer disputes arise:

- The customer/guest queries the amount of change given. Firstly check how much the guest has handed over as payment and then check the change again. If a mistake was made by a staff member, s/he should apologise immediately to the guest and correct the mistake. If the guest made the mistake, staff should accept that it was a mistake and not see it as a personal attack of any kind on the staff member.

- In the case where the guest disputes the amount of the bill, identify the relevant items that the guest is querying. Quite often it is a misunderstanding on the part of the guest. Then simply explain in a very friendly manner what the charge is for. If the pay-point operator made a mistake, s/he must apologise immediately to the guest and correct the mistake. All voids must normally be authorised by the duty manager or other supervisor.

Float shortages

The following is standard procedure in the event of a float shortage:

- All float shortages must be reported to the duty manager *before processing payments in the system*.
- Count the float in front of the supervisor or manager and sign the relevant documentation recording the shortage as well as the count.
- The manager must be aware of any shortages so that s/he may follow-up and check these with the previous shift's tally-up and double check the total from which the float was allocated.

Problems with customer payments

Customers are people and the following situations call for friendly discretion in handling your response to the customer/guest:

- If the guest hands over too little cash, politely point this out. Thank the guest when s/he gives the correct amount.
- Above certain amounts authorisation has to be obtained from the bank to process the transaction. If the speed point machine advises to call the bank, obtain authorisation as described in the company procedures manual since certain codes identifying the company may be required by the bank.
- If a staff member suspects that s/he has been handed counterfeit cash, a stolen credit card or a stolen cheque, call the duty manager immediately. It is important that the suspicion not be obvious to the guest. Simply pick up the telephone and ask the duty manager to come to the payment point immediately.

Equipment malfunctions

Even in our age of electronic machines, equipment malfunctions now and then.

- When the payment point equipment malfunctions, advise the manager responsible for the computer systems immediately.
- In the event of manual transactions, make sure that all relevant details of the transaction are recorded/written down accurately so that this information can be entered into the computer later when it is functioning properly again.
- In the event of a problem with the speed-point machine, inform the duty manager or supervisor immediately. If it is a manual machine, process the transaction as described above.

Counterfeit money/suspected card/cheque fraud

If there is reason to suspect that counterfeit cash, a stolen credit card or a stolen cheque is involved in any transaction, simply pick up the telephone and ask the duty manager to come to the payment point immediately. Be discreet when requesting the assistance of the manager because the suspect guest must not be alerted to any possible suspicions.

If the guest realises that s/he is suspected of fraudulent behaviour, one of two things could happen:

- If the suspect is guilty, s/he may try to make an escape.
- If the guest is innocent, s/he will be offended by such suspicions, which could result in lost future business.

The motto is still – better safe that sorry.

Errors or voids

When an incorrect transaction is processed accidentally, the transaction must be voided and repeated. All voids must be authorised by the manager.

Retain all documentation relevant to the mistake, write the reason for the mistake on the slip, place the slip in the till drawer and contact the duty manager to sign the slip, which will be handed over to the payment point operator as a 'void'.

Some company procedures allow that all voids be kept until cashing-up time and then only are they signed by the manager. Ensure that you are familiar with the correct procedures as you are accountable for any shortages or losses.

Assessment activity 2:

You are required to develop and complete a training manual for the set-up, operating and cashing-up of a payment point. The pay-point has an electronic credit/debit card machine, cash drawer as well as manual credit card device.

Include the following aspects:

- All operational procedures: wrong item/price entered, voids, refunds, etc.
- Behaviour guidelines for customer interactions
- Security precautions

You should use diagrams, pictures and flow charts to illustrate your manual.

Topic 4:
Handling and recording refunds

Module 1

Dealing with customers and processing refunds where necessary thus understanding the importance of maintaining good customer relations and continuing business with the customer

Overview

The student should be able to ...

- describe the procedure for handling refunds and why the need for refunds may arise
- understand the implications of not giving a customer a refund on request
- know how to deal with a customer dispute appropriately including the reporting procedure

Unit 1:

Refunds

Customers often feel that they are entitled to a refund for some reason. Staff at the pay point are usually the first to hear about the customer's problem. When you deal with such customers, keep the following points in mind:

- Customers requiring a refund need sympathetic handling, because they usually unhappy or upset about something.
- All establishments need to make refunds, either in cash or credit, from time to time.
- Most refunds are the result of some error or bad service rendered to the customer.
- All refunds must be appropriately authorised as applications for refunds can potentially be of a fraudulent nature.
- The processing of a refund must be appropriately recorded according to company procedures, including the authorisation. Not following the prescribed procedures may put the staff member at risk. For example, if cash is refunded without being correctly recorded, the staff member may risk being accused of cash discrepancies or even of theft.
- All refund applications must be properly recorded to enable management to take corrective action to prevent the same problem re-occurring.

Reasons for refunds

There are three basic reasons why a customer may ask for a refund. Customers are generally upset, or appear to be very angry because of bad service, a delivery error, etc. and therefore need to be treated very politely and diplomatically. The reasons are as follows:

- *Institutional errors*: The staff may have made an error in processing a meal. For example, a customer asked for roast chicken breast and was served a drumstick. Another error could be that a customer requested a birthday cake in advance for a special occasion and it was not delivered/presented as requested at the end of the meal. These are valid reasons for customers to be really upset as they were caused great inconvenience and even embarrassment before their friends. The person dealing with these customers needs to be very tactful and diplomatic.
- *Opportunistic customers*: Sometimes customers may 'try it on' - take a chance to see if they can get a refund of some sort, even though they are not really entitled to it. These opportunistic customers usually appear very angry and upset in order to intimidate the establishment's staff. This is why a senior member of staff should deal with the problem and authorise the refund after investigating the incident.
- *Problem customers*: A customer may be the cause of the problem him-/herself. For example, when ordering a meal, s/he did not mention an allergy to bacon. Hock was used in the preparation of the lentil soup and so the soup made him/her ill. In this case it is also

preferable that a senior member of staff investigate the incident, and make a decision as to whether or not the guest is entitled to some form of compensation.

Typically in all these cases the pay-point staff are often first in the firing line and get the first blast of anger. Organisations usually have a prescribed procedure for staff, guiding them how to deal with this type of problem. If this procedure is followed and the staff members remain calm, the incident can be defused and remedies offered. The problem usually becomes complicated and more difficult to resolve if staff members take the customer's anger personally and respond angrily. A shouting match easily destroys the whole atmosphere and creates a bad image of the institution as well.

Procedures for validating and issuing refunds

All organisations have a standard procedure for validating and issuing refunds. Staff members should never deviate from the prescribed procedures; these procedures are designed to protect you as staff members as well as the establishment.

In the workplace

Points to remember when refunding:

- Issuing a refund means money is leaving the business – it is an expense for the business.
- A refund can only be processed if a senior member of staff has authorised it.
- Refunding means that money is taken out of your cash drawer resulting in a shortage. There must then be some prescribed documentation to justify the shortage (refund payout).
- A refund claim is open to fraud just as any other payment transaction; the refund claim must, therefore, be validated before the refund is issued for your own protection.

General principles

If the establishment owes the guest a refund, the following procedures should be followed on checkout because the advance deposit exceeds the final account:

- A pre-checkout folio must be printed and signed by the guest as proof of acceptance of the balance received. It is essential that the guest sign the folio personally and not the cashier on behalf of the guest.
- The duty manager must authorise all refunds and sign the pre-checkout folios as evidence thereof.
- The cashier disbursing the funds must do the transaction on the computer system .
- Attach a copy of the registration card to the folio to check the guest's signature.
- Management must review the listing of refunds after close of shift to ensure that pre-checkout folios are printed and authorised for all items.

- Management must confirm the validity of exceptions.
- If the guest's deposit was paid by cheque the balance should not be refunded at checkout.
- Confirm the guest's details and the accounts department will make out a cheque and send it to the guest.

Credit balances

Quite often guests cancel bookings they have made and the deposit paid must then be refunded as they will no longer make use of the services of the establishment.

Refunding a deposit to a guest must be done as follows:

- Print a copy of the full account for the guest to check.
- The refund must be done on the computerised system once the guest has confirmed that the account is correct and the refund has been authorised by a senior staff member.
- Hand the guest the folio to sign to acknowledge receipt of the refund.
- The original copy (normally the top one) must be returned to the guest; the other copies must be filed correctly for banking purposes and internal back up.
- Attach the registration card to the folio to verify signatures.
- If the deposit was paid by cheque the following procedure will apply:
  - Confirm the guest's details.
  - Inform the guest that a cheque will be drawn from the accounts department and sent to him/her.

Unit 2:

Implications of not giving a customer a refund on request

There can be quite a number of consequences when a refund is not made to a customer when s/he is actually entitled to one. The most common implications are

- the customer being dissatisfied
- the customer retaining a negative experience of the service
- the customer not using your service again and telling others about his/her 'bad' experience.
- the company losing potential guests and income

It has been proven by research that customers tell more people about bad service they have experienced than about good service.

Guest expectations

Every person making use of the services of a hotel, restaurant, guesthouse, etc. has some expectations of the service, food and general experience s/he is about to have.

In the workplace

Each guest is important and has the following expectations when making use of the services and facilities of your organisation:

- Make me feel important.
- Don't lie to me.
- Keep your promises.
- Give me understandable information.
- Be sensitive to my needs.
- Listen to my advice on improving your service or product.
- Be fair; if you expect me to pay for something, I expect value for my money.
- Treat me in such a way that I will come back again.
- Don't underestimate my intelligence; that would be insulting.

Methods to deal with customer-related issues

Customers are the most important people in a business. If they do not buy the food, sleep in the rooms, etc. there will be no income and after a short while no longer any business. Customers are the very reason for the existence of the business – to satisfy some special need. Dealing with customer- related issues is, therefore, a very important part of conducting a good business. Not everything you do in your business will always please all customers and some difficulties may arise.

Be aware of the following when you are required to explain unpopular policies:

- Know the proper language, terminology or 'scripting' while explaining difficult policies.
- Always let the **positives imply negatives** when explaining policies.
- Always emphasise the benefits for the customer.
- Accept complaints graciously and relay them to management.
- Offer different options.

When the guest is really wrong, try the following:

- Always put yourself in the guest's shoes.
- Share the problem with him/her by saying, "I understand your perspective".
- Ask open-ended questions.
- Give reasons; try to negotiate a comfortable solution.

When the guest is still upset after your best efforts

- understand and accept that there may be a personality clash
- do not take the customer's complaint as directed at you personally
- find someone else who may relate better to the customer
- send a follow-up note or make a follow-up call

In the workplace

Case 1: I had a really horrible experience at the stated restaurant. I will get straight to the point, my friend and I were having a light lunch, when with disgust she noticed mould on the crust of the wholewheat sandwich which we were eating. The sad thing about our experience was that we had eaten most of the sandwich. I complained to the manager, got an apology and a refund which actually didn't make any difference to me. Two days later I phoned the restaurant to speak to the manager in question, and let him know that my friend and I were both ill, he suggested that we send him the bill from the doctor and he would be happy to refund it.
Michelle: August 29, 2007

Case 2: I would like to share my experience at a Fordsburg fast food outlet with you. Last week I ordered two pizzas. My boyfriend discovered a small piece of metal wire in the piece of pizza he was eating. I called the outlet to advise them of my finding. The manager of the outlet promised to send over a replacement pizza which did not arrive. She also gave me two excuses for why the pizza has a piece of metal wire in it: 1. This could have happened when they were cleaning the "screens". 2. The meat supplier could have been the problem. The manager had tried to brush me off with these excuses and did not intend sending a replacement! I then looked at the fast food chain pamphlet and called the company that handles complaints etc for the chain. I lodged a complaint with them. They advised me that the area manager would be in contact with me in a matter of a few days. On Friday the area manager, Andrew, did call me apologising for the unfortunate incident and asked me whether I would like a replacement meal or a refund. I accepted a refund and asked for it to be delivered to my residence. I am still waiting for my refund.... The money does not concern me that much. The justice and fairness to all is foremost in my mind. My appeal is that more of us should stand up for our rights and not be defeated by those that want to give us excuses for not delivering the service we pay for. Something for you to think about: What if it had been your little son or daughter eating this piece of pizza?
Dylan: 21 February, 2005

Unit 3:

Dealing appropriately with customer disputes

Most hospitality establishments follow the same basic rules and only the finer details vary from one organisation to the next.

The basic procedure is as follows:

1. There are two ways an organisation can become aware of a problem:

- *Staff*: For instance a customer has arranged a party, ordered flowers for the tables and paid for them. The flowers have not arrived (they were sent elsewhere in error) and the florist has closed for the day. Staff and management know that this is a genuine problem before the customer becomes aware of it. The organisation then needs to take remedial action; for example, arrange for champagne to be available and debit the cost of the flowers from the total bill. In a case like this, staff firstly become aware of the problem and alert a senior member of staff to resolve it before the customer even becomes aware of the problem.
- *Customer*: Often the customers become aware of the problem first. For instance, they may have ordered one bottle of wine with their meal but were billed for two bottles. The first action after apologising for the error would be to contact the appropriate senior member of staff. The senior member of staff will investigate the incident and take remedial action, like correcting the account or authorising a refund.

2. *Refund book*: Once the senior member of staff is sure of the facts, s/he will authorise the refund. This is done by describing the incident in a refund book, which will be similar to the example given below.

Date	Details	Cash refund	Credit refund	Authorised by	Cashier

3. *Cash refunds*: If the refund is to be done in cash, the cash is removed from the cash drawer and given to the customer. There is usually a duplicate book for the customer to sign acknowledgement that s/he has received the cash. The bottom copy goes into the cash drawer to justify the reduction in cash. If the refund is a credit refund, an adjustment is made on the customer's bill. No cash changes hands but when the customer pays the bill, there will be a reduction on the bill for the agreed amount.

4. *Credit card refunds*: If the refund is a credit or charge card refund a voucher which is very similar to a credit or charge card voucher

must be completed. However, it will state: 'refund'. An imprint of the customer's card must either be taken, or the card must be run through an authorisation machine, according to the establishment's procedures. The customer must sign the voucher and retain his/her copy. However, when the customer eventually receives a statement from the credit or charge card company, s/he will find that the original full account has been debited (deducted) from the card and the refund credited (returned) to the card account.

If the establishment uses a mechanised method of accepting credit and charge card payments and an error has been made which is noticed *before the voucher is signed* there will be a prescribed procedure to void the error voucher created. Always follow the establishment's

---

TONY'S RESTAURANT

CREDIT NOTE

Name _____   Date _____
Address _____   Issued by _____
                               Authorised by _____

Credit to the value of _____

---

procedure for doing this.

5. *Refund refused*: If the senior member of staff is not satisfied that the refund can be justified, s/he will not authorise it. The senior staff member will deal with the customer in private away from the public access areas. If there is no authorisation for a refund, even if it is only for a tiny sum like R0, 50, no refund should be made, because the whole story may not be known.

In different organisations the basic procedures will be as described above. However, there may be variations in the documentation to be completed and in the specific members of staff who are authorised to

Case studies

Scenarios:

1. A tourist from Australia visited your hotel. On check-in he made a payment of R5 000.00 by credit card. His final account amounted R4 398.00. The hotel has to refund him.
2. A guest enjoying a meal at your restaurant called the waiter halfway through his plate of food and complained that the meat was off. The guest demanded a refund.

- You must describe in both cases, step-by-step, the process you would follow to deal with the question of a refund; how you would assess the validity or not of the refund and how you would process or reject the refund. Clearly indicate all persons involved in the process as well as the documentation that should be completed. Develop sample documentation and complete it.
- Visit a restaurant and find out the most common reasons for refunds in the specific restaurant as well as how the staff deal with customers in this regard. Suggest ways of reducing the need for such refunds. A written report must be completed for this exercise.

Role play

Form groups of three:

- a customer
- a staff member, and
- an observer

Every group must develop a minimum of three different situations where refunds are requested by customers. In at least one of the scenarios the refund should not be warranted.

Each student must complete at least one role play as the staff member. The observer must take notes on the behaviour and responses of the staff member in each case.

issue refunds. Follow the procedures for the specific institution and make sure you know them well.

Summary

Deal with customers and process refunds where necessary thereby understanding the importance of maintaining good customer relations and thus continuing business with the customer

Customers often feel that they are entitled to a refund for some reason. The staff at the pay point will normally be the first to hear about the customer's problem. When you deal with such customers, bear in mind specific points to resolve the situation in a win-win way.

There are three basic reasons why a customer may ask for a refund:

institutional errors, opportunistic customers and problematic customers. Customers are generally upset, or appear to be very angry because of the bad service, delivery error, etc. and therefore need to be treated very politely and diplomatically. All organisations will have a standard procedure for validating and issuing refunds. Staff members should never deviate from the prescribed procedures; these procedures are designed to protect you as a staff member as well as the establishment.

There may be quite a number of consequences when a refund is not made to a customer when s/he is actually entitled to one. The possible negative consequences for the establishment must be taken into consideration before a final decision is made in this regard.

Customers are the most important people in the business. If they do not buy the food, sleep in the rooms, etc. there will be no income and after a short while no business. The customer is the very reason for the existence of the business. Dealing with customer-related issues is, therefore, a very important part of conducting a good business. Not everything you do in your business will always please all customers and some difficulties may arise.

Every person making use of the services of a hotel, restaurant, guesthouse, etc. has some expectations of the services, food and general experience s/he is about to have. When these expectations are not met, a customer becomes unhappy. When dealing appropriately with customer disputes, most hospitality establishments follow the same basic rules and only the finer details vary from one organisation to the next. It is important to train staff well in dealing with unhappy customers.

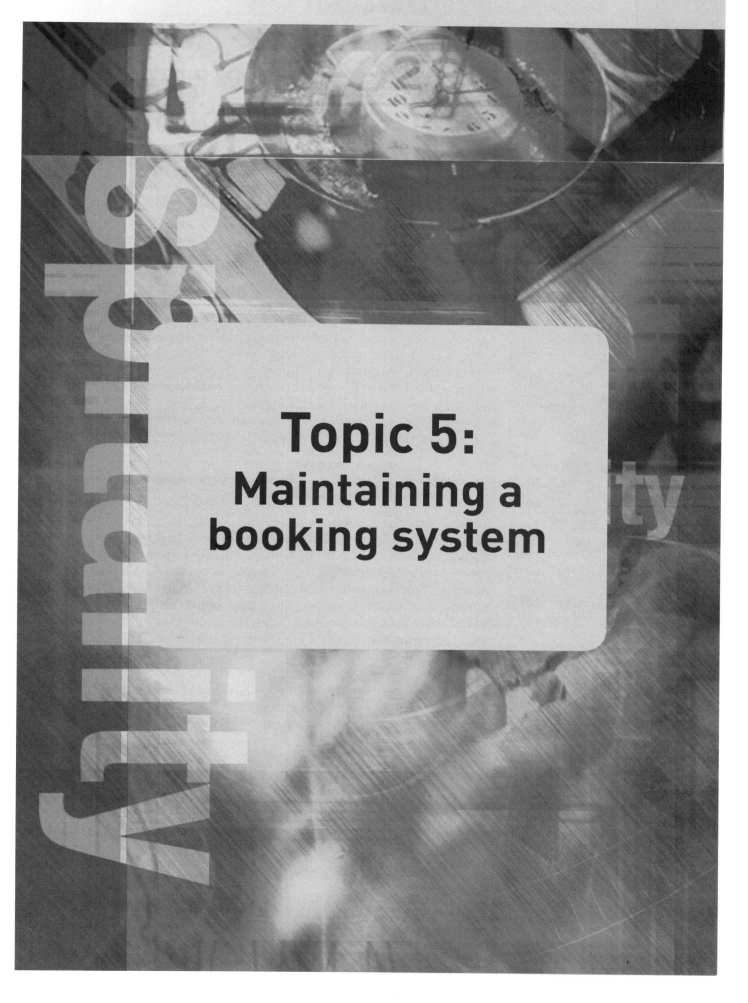

Topic 5:
Maintaining a booking system

Module 1

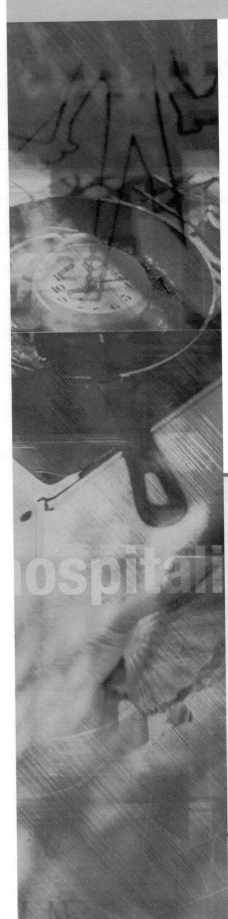

Maintaining, determining, recording and confirming bookings on manual and computer systems

Overview

The student should be able to ...

- explain the importance of giving accurate, knowledgeable and timely information to customers
- explain the importance of providing an efficient booking service
- explain the importance of taking deposits for bookings and demonstrate the appropriate procedures
- understand the importance of keeping bookings up-to-date and following up when they are unconfirmed
- explain the importance of keeping other departments informed of bookings status

In the workplace

South Africa rides tourism wave

Almost 8.4-million tourists visited South Africa in 2006 – over a million more than in 2005, representing a 13.6% increase – as the country broke its annual tourist arrivals record for the second year running. "We had an increase of more than 73 000 visitors from Europe, almost 30 000 more visitors from North America, and over 30 000 more visitors from Asia, Australasia and the Middle East," the Minister of Tourism and Environmental Affairs said. While the country's growth rate for overseas arrivals kept pace with international industry growth, a 16.9% growth in arrivals from Africa far exceeded the international benchmark. One key market that did not show growth, van Schalkwyk said, was China. He said he was confident, however, that SA Tourism could turn this around.

Jobs and business opportunities created in tourism have special significance for economies such as ours. They help to spread opportunities beyond our major metropolitan areas to rural areas. They create incentives, not only to remain in rural areas, but also to develop, take pride in and showcase local hospitality and culture.

29 October 2007 Ministry Tourism & Environmental Affairs

Unit 1:

The importance of giving accurate, knowledgeable and timely information to customers

Making a reservation is often the first contact between a potential guest and a hotel. The mental picture the potential guest forms of the hotel, its staff, service, etc. is formed through this first contact. It is, therefore, essential, even critical, for the reservations clerk to provide prompt and accurate service in order to present a good first impression to the guest. There is strong competition within the hospitality and specifically the hotel industry in accommodation sales. Any potential guest experiencing problems or slow service from the reservation section will soon try another institution before confirming a reservation or returning to that hotel. An effective and efficient reservations system is the artery for the lifeblood of hotel.

The reservations department does not only sell accommodation. Through room bookings the reservations staff help generate income for all the other departments of a hotel, for example, the food and beverage department, internal shops and other specialist service offerings. Every empty room in a hotel does not generate income but incurs expenses. Hotel rooms are a saleable commodity and are strictly limited by factors of time and number. If a room is not sold on a particular night, the revenue from that room is lost forever. The reservation section contributes to the hotel's profits by maximising room sales in terms of beds/sleepers and an improved average room rate.

Any guests phoning a hotel to reserve a room would like to

- receive a quick reply to their request or enquiry
- receive a firm 'yes' or 'no' reply
- have reservation details recorded accurately in a manner that inspires their trust
- be treated politely.

The same applies when a guest makes a booking over the Internet where s/he is not dealing with a person but a system which represents the hotel and its levels of service. Internet/websites should not be a frustration to a customer but assist in a clear and logical way with the reservation being made. Personal follow-up on Internet booking creates a very positive image of the personal care attitude of the institution.

For a reservation system to function effectively, set procedures should be established for the handling of requests, the updating and amending of information and the generation of confirmations. These procedures help to ensure that any request from a guest will be dealt with quickly and accurately, both when calling in person and for Internet bookings.

Unit 2:

The importance of providing an efficient booking service

It is reasonable for a guest to expect that when a reservation or room booking is made at a hotel, the hotel will honour its commitment in accepting that reservation and guarantee that the room will be available when the guest arrives.

Sources of reservations

Requests for reservations may come from a number of sources. The following are the most common:

A direct reservation

Direct reservations are reservations that are handled directly by a hotel. These requests may come to the hotel in a number of ways:

- Face-to-face

An individual walks into the hotel and makes a direct reservation

- Telephone

An independent traveller makes a reservation by telephone, directly to the hotel.

- Letters or fax

Individuals or groups make reservations in writing, usually directly to the reservations department.

- E-mail and Internet bookings

These are often used for reservation requests. It is the quickest method of making reservations and generally involves no personal contact with any hotel staff up to the point of arrival at the hotel.

Reservation network systems

A growing number of hotel reservations are from guests who have been referred to the hotel by another hotel in the same chain or marketing group, via affiliate or non-affiliate reservation network systems or a central reservation system.

An affiliate reservation system is a hotel reservation system used by all hotels within the same hotel chain/group, like Holiday Inn, Formula One, Protea Hotels, etc. This means that guests can make reservations for future or onward accommodation at any hotel within the same group.

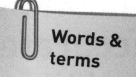

Words & terms

A reservation in the context of the front office of a hotel means the booking or reserving of a bedroom by a guest, and involves a particular type of guest-room being reserved for a particular person or persons, for a certain period.

A non-affiliate reservation network is a subscriptions system that is designed to connect independently operated hotels. The system allows guests to make future reservations at any hotel within the network.

Central reservation systems can deal either directly with the customer or with the hotel. Most of the major hotel groups operate a central reservations system whereby the agent in the central reservation office checks the room availability of the nearest hotel where the customer wishes to be. If accommodation is available, all relevant details will be recorded directly into the computer terminal at the central reservation office. This system saves potential customers costs as they generally have the option to make use of a toll free number.

Agencies

Guests may also make reservations through a travel agent. The guest usually makes a payment to the travel agent and not the hotel. The travel agent then sends the confirmation to the hotel, and issues an accommodation voucher on its behalf for the guest as proof of payment and booking. Travel agents receive a commission fee from the hotel for their services and for recommending the hotel to guests.

Importance of an efficient booking service

An efficient booking process ensures the availability of the room as specified, upon the arrival of the guest. This is of vital importance to a hotel because it:

- provides guests with the first impression of the hotel
- sells the main product of the hotel (accommodation rooms)
- generates customers for other departments and
- provides important service delivery management information to other departments

See Annexure M

Sample Training Manual: How to make a booking

Unit 3:

The importance and appropriate procedures of taking deposits for bookings

Reason for taking a deposit

Hotels usually require group booking or long-stay guests to pay a deposit in advance (it can vary from one night's accommodation to the full amount) to secure a booking. If the guests fail to show up or cancel their booking on the actual day of arrival, the hotel may retain the deposit as compensation. Some hotels may return the deposit to the guest or company, depending on the hotel policy. See *In the workplace* notes in this regard.

In the workplace

Cheetah B-Safari

This safari takes you 'behind the scenes' and gives you the opportunity to interact with the researchers, ecologists, vets and guides while discovering the fantastic world of wildlife in southern Africa. You will come face to face with the magnificent cheetah, the Cape hunting dog, the African elephant, vultures and much more. Not only will you have a fantastic time but your participation will also help to save the endangered cheetah.

Costing

This eight-day safari is available at a cost of ZAR 22, 00.00 per person sharing. This is based on a minimum of four persons participating in total, and allows for a maximum of seven participants. Larger groups may be accommodated on special request. This cost **includes** board and accommodation as laid out above, all land transfers in a comfortable air-conditioned mini-bus, guides, all tours, presentations and activities as laid out above, entrance fees, VAT and government tourism levies. **Not included** are drinks, dinner on day one, lunch on the last day, items of a personal nature, gratuities, travel insurance and flights. **Please note** that owing to the nature of this experience, times and plans may need to be adjusted slightly as we proceed. Please bear with us should this become necessary.

Terms and conditions for booking

- A 30% non-refundable deposit is payable at confirmation of booking.
- A balance of 70% is payable 56 days before commencement.
- A 60% refund for cancellation is payable 42 - 56 days prior to commencement.
- A 50% refund for cancellation is payable 28 - 42 days prior to commencement.
- Cancellation within 28 days is subject to full forfeiture.
- Payment of deposit implies acceptance of terms and conditions.
- Cancellation must be made in writing.
- An administration fee of ZAR 500.00 per person will be charged for amendments made after confirmation.
- B-Safaris reserves the right to use a similar lodge/hotel if the intended lodge/hotel is not available. This may affect pricing.
- The itinerary costing is subject to availability and currency fluctuations.
- Terms and conditions are subject to change without notice.

Procedures for taking bookings

See Annexure M for training
manual on how to make an
electronic booking

When the advance deposit has been paid, the amount is recorded and the details of the deposit transferred from the reservation file onto the registration form. The front office confirms the receipt of the deposit with the guest on arrival. The deposit received is then transferred from the advance deposit account to the guest folio.

Information of advance deposits received by the reservations department and payments received by the front office cashier must be recorded and passed on to the accounts department. This is mostly done within an integrated electronic reservations accounts system. The accounts department is responsible for the monitoring of guest accounts, monitoring credit limits and seeking prompt settlement of ledger accounts through the front office. Advanced computer software systems designed specifically for hotels to deal with all these aspects in a user-friendly way are available.

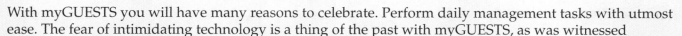

In the workplace

Hospitality Suppliers
Accommodation Booking & Management Systems   **SAP-RAPIDE**

myGUESTS International
mySQUIRREL Professional Hospitality Management Solutions

myGUESTS International – the champagne-class professional hospitality management system that is affordable on a beer budget.

With myGUESTS you will have many reasons to celebrate. Perform daily management tasks with utmost ease. The fear of intimidating technology is a thing of the past with myGUESTS, as was witnessed by many visitors at the INDABA 2006. With over 25 years of unshakeable experience in developing business solutions SAP-RAPIDE understands users' fears. With the aid of this intuitive system with a short learning curve you will soon be up to speed, even if you have limited computer knowledge. No hype, no frills and glossy packing, just value added functionality, contributing to help you increase revenue, avoid cost and improve service. Whether your establishment is a bed & breakfast, SC, guest house, lodge etc., with myGUESTS you receive a robust and modern system and a secure investment in technology. Let the following tasks become sheer business pleasure:

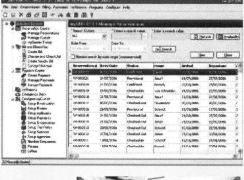

- **Availability tracking**
- **Reservation management**
- **Payment management**
- **Guest billing**
- **Information reporting.**

Toast management efficiency and effectiveness and bid farewell to

- **sub-standard service to guests**
- **outdated, costly and inaccurate manual record-keeping**

- **loss of potential business**
- **inconsistent operational procedures**
- **loss of valuable business information**
- **creeping administration costs.**

Manage your business now from a single point of control. Extract strategic information that is consistent, accurate, on time, complete, relevant and traceable. Thus enhance decision-making, competitiveness and improve productivity. There is no need for a large capital investment or additional hardware costs and maintenance. Simply install on your computer and run. Annual licence fees - uuh - not with myGUESTS!!

Amongst the numerous fine features you also benefit from the following:

- **On-demand management**
- **Be informed and react faster**
- **Enjoy a professional edge even as a small business**
- **Automated day-to-day control**
- **Operational transparency**
- **Improved utilisation of your time.**

mySQUIRREL Inventory Management Solution
A significant cost to most Small and Medium-sized Enterprises (SME) is the inventory it carries for its customers. An effective management and minimised inventory investment can provide a competitive advantage. mySQUIRREL is a pragmatic add-on to myGUESTS and can also be used as a stand-alone application. This flexibility makes it an economical solution for SMEs. mySQUIRREL is simple and provides up-to-date inventory status on demand. Maintain continuous service for your customers by eliminating shortages and 'out-of-stock' situations.

Visit some of the following websites to see what computerised booking systems look like and can do:

AlpTech IT Services, Inc.

Hotel/motel reservation and management system targeted at small to medium lodging businesses.
http://www.alptechcorp.com/

Applied Technologies

Reservation software for bed and breakfasts or inns. Reporting functionality and interface to accounting system.
http://www.guestall.com/

BookingCenter.com

Management and marketing system for small and middle-sized hotels; includes free Internet bookings module.
http://www.bookingcenter.com

DSC Hotel Systems

Providers of integrated reservation, front/back office, accounting and marketing software solutions for accommodation establishments.
http://www.dschotel.com/

FrontSuite

Front and back office automation system and Web-based multi-property central reservation system.

http://www.frontsuite.

Guesthouse

Reservation, room management and billing software for guesthouses, small hotels, motels, hostels, and bed and breakfasts.
http://www.guesthouse-software.com

Innes Systems

Hotel management software. Features include reservations, accounting and guest history. Touchscreen Point-of-sales available for restaurant, barbershop or bars. Conference room scheduling. Tracks catering and equipment.
http://www.InnesSystems.com

Unit 4:

The importance of keeping bookings up-to-date and following up when they are unconfirmed

A non-guaranteed reservation is a reservation in which the guests have simply agreed and confirmed that they will arrive, without paying any deposit in advance. The hotel then holds the non-guaranteed room until a specific cancellation time, normally to 18h00 on the day of arrival. If the guest has not booked in by the cancellation time, booking is cancelled and the room released. The hotel then has no further obligation towards the guest and can sell the room to another guest or even to the original guest if s/he arrives late and the room is still available. This cancellation time is sometimes called the *release time*. A release time is stated in order to avoid loss of income for the hotel because of guests who fail to arrive and because there is no deposit that can be retained by the hotel. If a room is not sold on a particular night, the income from that room is lost forever.

In the workplace

Hotel occupancy up
South Africa's tourism boom has had a predictable knock-on effect on the performance of the country's hotels.

In its latest tourist accommodation survey, Statistics South Africa (Stats SA) reported a 6.4% increase in occupancy rates at hotels, guest houses and other forms of accommodation in 2006 as compared to 2005 – from 17,227,200 to 18,330,900 individual stays at hospitality establishments.

These 18,3 million stays indicate how many bookings for accommodation had to be made at hospitality establishments, as well as changes that might have been necessary before the guests finally arrived!

Unit 5:

The importance of keeping other departments informed of the bookings status

Any hotel operates as an integrated system although there are many departments. All departments benefit from the reservation details collected by the reservations department. Such details may include an accurate estimate of the number of guests staying in the hotel, meal bookings, special services required, or an indication of when the hotel is expected to be full.

Reservation information can be used by the hotel and by individual departments to

- prepare sales forecasts
- prepare weekly or monthly staff schedules, menus and purchase requirements
- relate sales forecasts to expenditure budgets (for example, money available for staff wages and purchases)
- control costs, including materials, labour and overheads
- carry out long-term planning (for example, renovation of rooms and expansion programmes)

In the workplace

City Lodge

Single image inventory: Quicker handling of reservations in all City Lodge hotels. The benefit of Amadeus Hotel Multiproperty electronic booking system is that it provides all guest data on a single central database. "Since all City Lodge hotels access the same central guest file information, all customer-relevant data is transparent at all customer touch points," explains Warren Loots, Managing Director of HISA, the Amadeus Hospitality certified distribution partner for South Africa.

City Lodge has a high percentage of return guests and can now improve guest satisfaction even if the guest's favourite hotel is fully booked. The front office manager suggests a different hotel matching the guest's special wishes straight away – be it a sea view or a Table Mountain view. Stuart Mattinson says: "The shared guest information among all City Lodge hotels enables a real caring business relationship that matches the City Lodge credo: 'People caring for people'. With the transparency gained through the Amadeus Multiproperty solution, we make sure that a return guest is treated as a special guest in every single City Lodge hotel – even if it is his first stay in that respective property." All employees have access to the central guest information on each individual guest at any time and in any City Lodge hotel. So from the classic feather pillow to the New York Times every morning for breakfast or the allergy to nuts or apples – everybody in the City Lodge team is familiar with individual guest preferences. City Lodge can keep track of everything a guest has ever requested in order to anticipate every wish during future stays. And the Amadeus Multiproperty system also makes sure that very special guests – for instance at their 15th stay at a City Lodge hotel – will be recognised and treated accordingly. Of course the application also provides the necessary tools for specially designed one-to-one marketing initiatives, responding to specific guests' wants and needs.

Module 2

Recording and confirming bookings on both manual and computer systems

Overview

The student should be able to ...

- determine the availability of services and communicate this clearly to customers; offer alternatives if appropriate
- record and confirm a range of bookings
- be able to promote the establishment's facilities appropriately
- deal with a range of customers politely and efficiently

Unit 1:

Communication of the availability of services to customers

After checking if a room is available, the reservations clerk either accepts or denies the booking. If a room is available, the request is normally accepted. The reservations clerk then records the guest's details onto a reservation form or a computer terminal.

The reservations department may choose not to accept a booking (this is called denying the booking). Denying the booking happens when

- a hotel may not have the specified accommodation available on the requested date(s).
- a hotel is fully booked.
- a guest is known to be on the blacklist. (A blacklist is a record authorised by the hotel management of the names of persons not welcome in the hotel for various reasons.)

When denying a specific reservation request, the reservations clerk should always be polite and helpful and should follow these procedures:

Do the following, if the specific accommodation requested is not available:

- Firstly apologise and then explain to the customer that the particular accommodation requested is not available. Offer to help with alternative accommodation or dates at the hotel. Accommodation may also be offered at another hotel in the group or network.

Do the following, if the hotel is fully booked:

- Apologise and explain that the hotel is fully booked. Offer alternative dates or accommodation at the hotel or in another hotel in the group or network. (It is important to keep a record of denied bookings for cumulative historical data for management analysis and rooms maximisation over the long term.)

Do the following, if the guest is blacklisted:

- The information communicated to the guest in this instance depends on the reasons for the guest being blacklisted, for example, the guest has previously been a nuisance. You may also accept the request but on a cash-only basis if the guest is known to have a bad payment record. Complicated cases should be referred to reception.

Never lie to a guest about the reason for denying a booking; it will damage your personal and the hotel's reputation in the long run.

Unit 2:

Recording and confirming bookings

Standard reservation form (See Annexure J)

Telephone and personal bookings are normally noted on a standard reservation form.

Benefit of a standard reservation form:

- It acts as a check list to ensure that all the relevant information is obtained.
- It is a reminder to tell the guest certain things (price, etc.)
- It can easily be processed.
- It is less likely to be lost.

If the request for a reservation is accepted, the reservation clerk then completes a reservation form (either manually or online on the computer), recording all the necessary details concerning the guest and his/her stay.

- Date of receipt of reservation
- Name, address and nationality of the client
- Arrival date
- The length of stay
- The departure date
- Type of room required
- Method of payment
- Any special requests
- Advance deposit
- Signature of clerk processing reservation

It must be remembered that in many cases the enquiry may not come from the potential guest personally, but from a third party, acting on behalf of the guest.

The reservation form is the only document that contains all the relevant information about the prospective guests and their accommodation requests. It is, therefore, important that all the details be recorded accurately. The reservation details capture important information that is essential to other sections and departments within the hotel.

If a computer system is being used, the details are normally typed directly into the system. Whether the system is manual or computerised, the principles of recording the information are similar. When obtaining the reservation details from the guest, the reservation clerk should also explain the differences between a guaranteed and a non-guaranteed booking. Should a guest decide to guarantee his/her booking, the reservations clerk must then obtain additional information concerning the method of guarantee (for example, credit card, prepayment or deposit).

Advanced reservation chart (conventional chart) (see Annexure K)

The type of charts used by the reservations office can vary from hotel to hotel. The reservation office and front desk must have an up-to-the-minute visual picture of the room status of the hotel whatever system is used.

This booking chart covers one calendar month with dates clearly marked at the top and the room numbers and their descriptions on the side. The chart is used in smaller hotels, where room types may differ substantially. It is particularly common in older resort hotels that have the following characteristics:

• A great variety of rooms
• A long average guest stay (three or more nights)
• A long lead time of reservations
• Some repeat business

In hotels where bookings are made several months ahead, charts for each month are prepared. The chart is normally located with the receptionist who allocates a room at the time of booking and notes this in the diary. Entries on the chart are made in pencil, with the name of the guest or a reference number next to the booking to facilitate changes that may occur through cancellations, etc.

Guidelines for use

• Entries must be made in pencil to allow for alterations.
• Arrows should run from the centre of each day as this corresponds with the hotel 'day' of midday to midday.
• If it is a short-stay booking, the folio number from the diary should be used rather than the guest's name.
• Chance bookings, extensions of stay, **rooms off** and early departures must be noted so that the chart is always accurate.
• When a room reservation has been confirmed, it is then marked as confirmed on the chart and great care must be taken that all entries are correctly checked and charted.

Often booking may be taken by 'juggling' the existing bookings. This means that an entry may be changed two or three times before guests arrive at the hotel and consequently they are not informed of their room number until they actually register. A conventional chart can be very time-consuming to keep up-to-date and lower occupancy often results from errors. Modern computerised systems are much easier to use and record changes.

Density chart or accommodation availability chart

Large hotels use a density chart to record their bookings. Rooms are classified into groups of similar type and no allocation of a specific room is made until the guest arrives.

The density chart is used in the following circumstances:

- By modern hotels where all rooms are similar
- When guest stay is short
- When chance bookings, extensions, early departures, etc, need to be continually noted on the chart
- Management uses the chart to compare the number of rooms let on the chart, with the actual number of guests in the hotel on a given day.

Hotel diary

Immediately after updating the accommodation availability chart, the reservations clerk must enter all of the booking details into a hotel diary. However, if the hotel operates a computerised reservations system, this will be done automatically.

The details recorded in the diary are placed in order under date of arrival; this helps in the preparation of an arrival list.

The hotel diary should include the following:

- Guest's name
- Type of accommodation requested
- Length of stay
- Rate and terms quoted
- How and when booked
- Contact telephone number
- Reservations clerk's signature
- Remarks

If confirmation is given or received, this too may be entered into the hotel diary. A major advantage of the diary is that it acts as a back-up for the information on guests who are due to arrive, especially if the original reservation form is misplaced. On a computerised reservation system this information is hyperlinked from the initial reservations details.

Stop-go charts

In large hotels there would be a bottleneck if every reservation clerk had to refer to the booking chart every time s/he handled a reservation request. This is overcome by a visual 'stop-go' chart which is prominently displayed in the reservation office. It summarises the information on the main chart. It shows at a glance whether or not a booking can be accepted. There is space for each day of the year.

Other methods of recording reservations

Advance reservation – power scan

The advance reservation chart is a manually operated scan. All the rooms of the hotel are charted on a flat board. A clear white transparency on a roll with all the days and dates of the year at the top,

revolves from right to left at the touch of a button. Special coloured marking pens are used to block in room allocations. With this type of scan the room reservation for every room for any given day can be brought into view

The rack system (Whitney)

A rack system can operate both status and advance reservations, each of which can be installed independently. A hotel operating a reservation rack does not necessarily have to complement it with a room status system.

A Whitney system is an example of a rack system. Advance reservations filed in a rack system operate in basically the same way as the reservation diary, but instead of bookings being entered into a diary, they are entered on a 'rack slip' or Shannon and this rack slip is filed visibly under the date of arrival. The big advantage over the diary is that reservations can be filed alphabetically. Checks can be made very quickly to see if a guest has a reservation.

The reservation slip is filled out for every booking and put into a metal carrier. This is stored in the reservation rack under the arrival date. Strict alphabetical order must be maintained right up to the day of arrival. Tour entries are entered into individual rack slips in the same way as other bookings. If a booking is cancelled, it is not removed, simply crossed through. These reservation racks are stored on the walls of the reservation office in full view of all reservation clerks. They extend as long as the period of time over which bookings extend. Only the top line with the most important information is visible, when the slips are filed.

Some hotels colour code reservation slips so that easy visual checks may be made of a day's reservation profile.

Central reservation system

Large groups of hotels that are area-linked by computer usually operate their own central reservation system. Information on the availability of accommodation within the chain of hotels is fed into the computer and by telephoning the central reservation number the customer can be directed to the location and type of hotel which is able to meet his/her requirements.

Other centralised reservation systems that are not attached to any particular group are also in operation. These work on a commission basis. Hotels that wish to join the scheme provide details of their location, accommodation and facilities. The information is fed into a computer so that when an enquiry is made to the centralised reservation service number, the customer can be directed to the hotels with the available type of accommodation.

In order for the scheme to function efficiently, it is essential that the reception offices of the hotels within the scheme inform central reservations of the up-to-the-minute availability of rooms to let at all times. Failure to do this could result in double-bookings, loss of goodwill and unnecessary charges being levied against the hotel for the service.

Confirming reservations

Confirmation of a reservation is a written acknowledgement sent either by the hotel to the guest or vice versa, depending on the hotel's policy regarding room reservation details. It confirms that a request for a room or rooms has been made with the hotel and is written evidence that a contract has been entered into between the hotel and a prospective guest.

As a part of the confirmation process, the reservation clerk, or the central reservations office, may assign a reservation confirmation number to each booking, generated from either a manual or a computerised system. The reservation number assures the guest that a booking has been made and this reference number should subsequently be quoted in the case of cancellation of or amendment to the original booking.

Large hotels very often have a large number of transient guests whose bookings are on short lead times. They do not attempt to confirm any bookings, except in the cases of a guaranteed reservation from a local company or agent.

Maintaining reservation records

The maintenance of reservation records consists of two main types of activity:

- the filing/recording of the original booking, and
- the modification of bookings because of changes to reservation details

Filing paper-based bookings

In older paper-based manual reservation systems all details of bookings and cancellations are stored in filing cabinets under the date of arrival of the guest. Letters are usually stapled together with the most recent letter or telex from the guest at the top of the file.

In computerised booking systems, the information is stored electronically and printouts are made on the arrival of the guest and again on departure.

Compiling reservation reports

The final step in the reservation process is the compilation of reservations reports. Information from these reports can assist management of the hotel to maximise room sales by controlling room availability and forecasting potential room sales.

Other departments can also make use of this information for their own forecasting and planning.

Management reports available through a reservation system can vary depending on the needs of the hotel and capability of the reservation system. The most common reports prepared by the front office are as follows:

Daily reports	Weekly or Monthly reports
Expected arrivals and expected departure lists (see Annexure L) Lists of guests who are due to arrive or depart on a particular day	Turn-away report A report on the number of reservations denied
Group status report A list of groups due to arrive or depart, with information on the group size and whether their bookings are guaranteed or non-guaranteed	Revenue forecast report A report on the projected revenue from future room sales
Special arrivals list A list of special guests, VIPs or guests with special requests	Geographic statistics report Gives an indication of where guests come from that use the hotel e.g. local vs international guests
Room availability report A list showing the number of rooms sold or available	Financial reports Indicate the overall performance of the hotel
Night audit report Report of all the financial transactions of the day.	

Based on the purpose of the information required, reports are prepared and compiled on a daily basis (for example, the arrivals & departure list - essential for the smooth operation of the front desk and the housekeeping department), while others are prepared on a weekly or monthly basis (for example, reports on the number of guests, number of rooms occupied, number of reservations from different sources, no-shows, or walk-ins).

Reports presenting information over longer periods of time give management not only data and information enabling more accurate forecasting of occupancy, future revenue potential and market mix of the hotel, but also information on how to focus marketing strategies and promotions.

(For reports see Annexure K & L)

Unit 3:

Promoting the establishment's facilities appropriately

Facilities and services:

Accommodation

The sale of rooms is one of the main products to be provided by a hotel. It is also very often the principal source of hotel revenue. The accommodation product does not just consist of a guest-room – single or double – but also the additional facilities and services which are applicable to that room e.g. does the room have a sea view?, is there a mini-bar? Are there in-house movies?, etc.

Conference facilities

The corporate market is also the source of group business. Many companies will have hotel conferences, sales training classes, business seminars and annual conventions. It is essential that the hotel sales team keep a careful check on these activities in order that they can offer the company the appropriate hotel facilities and services.

Exhibition

Exhibitions are often presented as part of a conference.

Functions

Hotel facilities can be used for function such Business lunches, corporate annual dinner dances, departmental farewell parties, weddings, birthday and Christmas parties.

Restaurants

The hotel may operate and manage an in-house restaurant. Another option is franchising or out sourced basis. For example, Spur restaurants at Holiday-Inn Hotels

Very few guests arriving at a hotel for the first time are aware of the various services and facilities available offered by the hotel. Reception staff need especially to explain to guests the various types of accommodation and other hotel facilities available, and encourage them to use such services and facilities during their stay. The objective of this *up-selling* is to significantly increase the income/revenue of the hotel from sales of additional services.

Reception staff may help to promote sales by

- encouraging guests to use the full range of the hotel services (for example, business centres, coffee shops, bars, restaurants, gyms, spas, etc.)
- suggesting an upgrade in accommodation

Photographs courtesy of Gautengpics

Useful techniques in selling facilities

Reception staff may promote sales of hotel services by employing certain useful selling techniques. These may include the following strategies:

Offering alternatives

Guests are not always aware of the range of services available in a hotel. Reception staff can promote the sales of the services by suggesting the most appropriate service to the guest, or offering alternatives for the guest to choose from.

Two strategies that can be used when offering alternatives of accommodation to customers are the *top-down* and *bottom-up* approaches:

- **The top-down technique** requires the reception staff to start from the most expensive option and then offer progressively cheaper ones if the guest does not intend to take the more expensive offer. This method is most appropriate with guests whose prime concern is comfort and service rather then cost.
- **The bottom-up technique,** on the other hand, requires the receptionist to begin with the cheapest option, and then persuade the guest to take progressively more expensive packages. This method is most appropriate with guests whose prime consideration is the cost of the service. If the most expensive option is offered first, the guest will most probably not be interested further.

Suggestive selling

This is an important sales technique for front office staff. It involves describing a specific service and offering to book it immediately for the guest. It is important to remember that when suggestive selling is used, too much pressure on the guests must be avoided.

In the workplace

Suggestive selling

A receptionist may recommend to a couple travelling with their baby the full range of the hotel services by offering to hire a baby-sitter on that evening, reserving a table in the hotel's à la carte restaurant, or describing the laundry facilities and baby meals available from room service.

How to choose a selling strategy

Reception staff need to anticipate what will motivate a guest to use a service. This skill is acquired only by years of service and dealing with customers and guests.

In general the following may be said:

- Well-dressed affluent guests are less likely to be on a tight budget and may be more concerned with the quality of service than costs.

- Guests whose full accounts are settled by their companies tend to spend more than guests paying for themselves.
- Guests who want to impress business clients or colleagues tend to spend more on high-quality services.
- Guests who desire comfort are more likely to treat themselves to expensive services.

In the workplace

When deciding on a selling strategy, the receptionist needs to determine whether the guest will be attracted by being offered a special promotional price or be more interested in the exclusivity of expensive service.

Photograph courtesy of Gautengpics

Unit 4:

Dealing with customers politely and efficiently

It is crucial to remember that every interaction with a guest is an opportunity to sell. This may be accomplished by giving guests information and opportunities to make choices. When a receptionist speaks to guests, it is important to speak clearly and to make eye contact periodically. Guests like to be given attention and treated like important people, valued by the hotel. For many people going on holiday this is a once-a-year or perhaps a once-in-a-lifetime opportunity. Correct interaction is important for repeat business; when guests feel they have been treated very well they want to return. This is especially true of business people. Next time they are in town they will not look for alternatives, but will call and book at the same hotel straight away, because they feel that they are valued and receive good service there.

Booking agencies

Booking agencies fulfil a very important role in the hospitality industry. They have extensive networks, especially on the Internet to advertise accommodation, conferences and other related services. The primary service of booking agencies is accommodation and not travel. Travel agencies specialise in packaged tours and rarely deal with individual customers seeking accommodation, mostly in foreign countries.

The customer deals with the agency all the way up to the point of arrival at the destination. The agency communicates with the hotel or accommodation establishment, makes all the reservations, bookings, pays deposits and even full accounts.

This is a positive service to the hotel as booking agencies facilitate effective and efficient bookings, normally on-line and interactive, providing all the required details for bookings.

Hotels pay a commission to the booking agency for referring guests to the hotel, saving on extensive marketing costs and campaigns.

A good booking agency also renders a better customer service to potential guests as it can offer the client a variety of destinations and accommodation options, saving the customer the time and effort in searching for these him or herself.

Customers with communication difficulties

The hospitality industry needs to cater for all types of people, including those with communication difficulties. Communication difficulties can stem from a variety of sources such as culture, language and physical impairments. These people are customers just like others and should be treated with special care.

Culture differences

Culture may be defined as the attitudes, values, language, dress, customs and behaviour of a group of people. In South Africa, with its very heterogeneous population, inter-cultural communication is a very relevant issue in the hospitality industry. Hotel front office staff inevitably have to deal with intercultural situations.

The disruption of a smooth communication process can have more serious effects than hurt feelings or indignation; the hotel or guest house could lose a valuable client or company contract.

Cultural role expectations and prescriptions vary greatly among different cultures, for example, the role of woman in westernised society differs greatly from that in some African and eastern societies.

Although intercultural communication has possible stumbling blocks, there are methods that can be employed to help produce more effective communication among cultures.

- Try not to judge people of other cultures and take time to make intercultural communication more effective and meaningful; learn from other cultures.
- Base decisions in the workplace on skills, qualifications and abilities rather than gender, race, socio-economic status or creed.
- Treating others with respect, sensitivity and consideration is vital in conveying the message that they are accepted for who they are and what they believe in. This improves the trust factor and results in better communication.

Key points to remember

- Eye contact

Make a little less eye contact than usual if necessary – but do not avoid it completely

- Gestures

Gestures vary from one culture to another. 'Latin' nations (Spanish, Greek, Italian, and Portuguese) tend to use very big gestures, whereas eastern cultures appear to be very submissive. Do not be intimidated by loud voices and excessive gestures. Cultures using smaller gestures to complain should be taken just as seriously as those who are animated.

- Personal space

This may vary according to culture. Be sensitive to the indications that people give regarding their need for space. If a person moves back slightly, realise that he or she needs more space. Most African people tend to require a smaller personal space, and tend to touch more than others. Oriental (Japanese, Chinese, etc.) people require a large personal space and do not like to be touched.

Foreign or regional language

In cases of language difficulties, consider the following:

- Speak slowly and clearly and use your hands to explain what needs to be said.
- If necessary, draw pictures.
- If one knows a staff member who speaks the guest's language, ask that colleague to assist.

Using alternative methods to communicate shows guests or foreigners that one is sensitive to their needs and is trying to accommodate them as best as one can. This makes the person feel important and promotes repeat business.

Different level of language

In a different situation, when a customer appears aloof and uses complicated words, it is important to swallow one's pride; don't hesitate to stop and ask for the meaning of a word that is not understood if it affects the perception of what the customer needs.

A speech impediment is not necessarily an indication of a lesser intellect. Neither is the use of high, complex language a sign of superiority of a guest over the service provider.

Customers, guest and clients are vital to any business and should always be treated with importance.

Serving customers with speech impairments

Deal with guests with speech impediments in exactly the same manner as you would any other guest.

A common mistake staff tend to make when dealing with someone who has a speech impediment is that they look down, or past the guest whilst the guest is speaking to them, that they correct the guest's attempt to communicate, or finish the guest's sentences. This should never be done.

In general be aware of the following:

- If you do not understand something do not pretend that you do; ask the customer to repeat what s/he said and then repeat it back.
- Be patient; take as much time as necessary.
- Try to ask questions that require only short answers, or a nod of the head.

Did you know?

South Africa The Foreign Tourist Picture:
Number of tourists: 7,369,000
Spend – per person per day: ±R1 536
Average length of stay: 8 nights
Main overseas source markets: UK, Germany, USA

South Africa's Top 5 Overseas Markets (2005):
1. UK: 469 599
2. Germany: 249 504
3. USA: 233 417
4. Netherlands: 116 244
5. France: 101 139

South Africa's Top 5 Average Spending Markets 2005
1. Mozambique: R18 237
2. India: R11 392
3. Angola: R11 336
4. Brazil: R10 589
5. Canada: R9 235

Purpose of Visit to South Africa, All Tourists:
Holiday 30.9%
Visiting Friends and Relatives 21.8%
Shopping 24.9%
Business - Travel 8.6%
Business - Tourism 5.4%
Other 8.4%

Foreign Tourist Activities in South Africa:
Shopping 87%
Nightlife 63%
Social 44%
Visiting Natural Attractions 27%
Beach 26%
Cultural, Historical, Heritage 26%
Wildlife 24%
Business 14%
Theme Parks 12%
Casino 10%
Sport 7%
Trading 8
Adventure 6%
Medical 5%
Health 2%
Source: SATourism 2006

- Concentrate on what the customer is saying; concentrate on listening and communicating.
- Avoid barriers like glass partitions and distractions such as noisy, public places. Do not speak for the customer or attempt to finish her or his sentences.
- If you are having difficulty understanding the customer, consider writing as an alternative means of communicating, but first ask the customer if this is acceptable.
- If no solution to the communication problem can be worked out between you and the customer, ask if there is someone who can interpret on the customer's behalf.
- Discuss matters that are personal (for example, financial matters) in a private room to avoid staring or eavesdropping by other customers.

Customers with special needs

Serving customers who are blind or visually impaired

- Speak to the customer when you approach her or him.
- State clearly who you are; speak in a normal tone of voice.
- Never touch or distract a service dog without first asking the owner.
- Tell the customer when you are leaving; never leave a person who is blind talking to an empty space.
- Do not attempt to lead the customer without first asking; allow the customer to hold your arm and control her or his own movements.
- Be descriptive when giving directions; give the customer verbal information that is visually obvious to persons who can see. For example, if you are approaching steps mention how many and the direction.
- If you are offering a seat, gently place the customer's hand on the back or arm of the chair and let her or him sit down by her or himself.
- When dealing with money transactions, tell the customer the denominations when you count the money s/he is receiving from you.
- Ensure that the customer has picked up all of her or his possessions before leaving.
- Ask if the customer needs assistance in signing forms. Offer to guide her or his hand to the appropriate space for signature.
- Offer assistance if the customer appears to be having difficulty locating a specific service area.

Serving customers who are deaf or hard of hearing

- Gain her or his attention before starting a conversation (tap the person gently on the shoulder or arm).
- Identify who you are (show them your name badge).
- Look directly at the customer, face the light, speak clearly in a normal tone of voice, and keep your hands away from your face; use short, simple sentences.
- Ask the customer if it would be helpful to communicate by writing or by using a computer terminal.
- If the customer uses a sign-language interpreter, speak directly to the customer, not the interpreter.

- If you telephone a customer who is hard of hearing, let the phone ring longer than usual; speak clearly and be prepared to repeat the reason for the call and who you are.
- Discuss matters that are personal (for example, financial matters) in a private room to avoid staring or eavesdropping by other customers.

Serving customers with mobility impairments

- Put yourself at the wheelchair user's eye level. If possible, sit next to the customer when having a conversation.
- Do not lean on a wheelchair or any other assistive device.
- Do not assume the customer wants to be pushed. Ask first.
- Provide a clipboard as a writing surface if counters or reception desks are too high; come around to the customer side of the desk/counter during your interaction.
- Offer assistance if the customer appears to be having difficulty opening the doors.
- Make sure there is a clear path of travel.
- If a person uses crutches, a walker, or some other assistive equipment, offer assistance with coats, bags, or other belongings. Offer a chair if the customer will be standing for a long period of time.
- If you telephone the customer, allow the phone to ring longer than usual to allow extra time for her or him to reach the telephone.

Serving customers with cognitive disabilities

- Be prepared to provide an explanation more than once.
- Offer assistance with and/or extra time for completion of forms, understanding written instructions, writing cheques, and/or decision-making; wait for the customer to accept the offer of assistance; do not 'over-assist' or be patronising.
- If a customer has difficulty reading or writing, she or he may prefer to take forms home to complete.
- Be patient, flexible, and supportive; take time to understand the customer and make sure the customer understands you.
- Consider moving to a quiet or private location, if in a public area with many distractions.

In the workplace

Remember:

- Provide access to facilities and services.
- Relax.
- Listen to the customer.
- Maintain eye contact without staring.
- Make the customer feel comfortable.
- Treat the customer with dignity, respect, and courtesy.
- Offer assistance but do not insist.
- Ask the customer to tell you the best way to help.
- Deal with unfamiliar situations in a calm, professional manner.

Important guests

Many hotels pay special attention to important guests. Important guests may include the following people:

Photograph courtesy of Gautengpics

- VIPs (**v**ery **i**mportant **p**ersons) for example, frequent-stay guests, celebrities, guests in expensive rooms, guests with security risks, executives from the hotel's head office, and so on
- CIPs (**c**ommercially **i**mportant **p**ersons) may be guests and executives of large corporate account-holders, important journalists and media staff, travel agents and tour company staff and guests whose companies could bring a lot of business to the hotel in the future
- SPATTs (**sp**ecial **att**ention guests) are guests who may need extra care and attention, such as handicapped guests, elderly or ill guests, and long-stay guests

These important guests tend to be given special services or amenities during their stay. Such services may include the assignment of the guest's room before they arrive; the complimentary use of hotel transport; registration in their room; and being greeted and escorted by special staff when they arrive.

In order to alert staff to the arrival of important guests, a list of important guests is produced and sent to other sections of the front office and to all other operating departments.

Customers requiring bookings for groups

When a customer requires a booking for a group there is a significant amount of additional information that is required to make the booking. If the customer is experienced in this type of booking, like booking agencies or travel agents, this will generally not be a problem.

Information that is required is typically: size of the group, number of single and double rooms needed, special dietary requirements of group members, physical needs or any special treatment, daily itinerary and mealtimes, etc.

The logistics to accommodate groups, places additional requirements on, for example, the porter services (large numbers of suitcases to be moved in short space of time, offloading from the bus and loading the bus again at the end of their stay), parking for the bus, etc.

Group bookings can easily become a nightmare as each group member wants to have preference in the allocation of rooms, people not wanting to share rooms with specific individuals, etc. The staff member must firmly but politely inform group members that they deal only on instructions from the group leader to make changes to allocated rooms, meals, etc.

Did you know?

Travel groups trends and patterns in the Western Cape during the peak summer period.
Travel group sizes varied from 1 to 60 (organised tours), whereas the average travel group was 3.8 persons. The biggest proportion of travel group, however, was the medium sized group of 3-6 persons (40%), followed by those travelling in pairs (36%). Six per cent of visitors travelled in groups of 7 to 12, whereas 3% travelled in groups of 12 and more. The domestic visitors mainly travelled in groups of 3-6 (typical family size) as compared to the international travellers, who mainly travelled in pairs.
http://www.ctru.co.za/files/research2006Festive seasonvisitortracking report.pdf

Assessment activity 1:

Assignment

- Describe step-by-step the complete booking process for at least three different scenarios, each in a different type of establishment. (You may make use of flow charts.) Include typical correspondence, confirmations, special requests, deposits, etc.
- Specifically describe how the process may differ for different guest types and establishments and the different information that will be required in each case.

This exercise must include a complete set of mock documentation for each of the three scenarios.

Examples of different scenarios:
- Travel agency group booking for an old age home holiday at seaside hotel
- a VIP guest – famous music star wishing to stay incognito
- a disabled guest in a wheel chair
- a female business woman
- Managing director of new airline investigating accommodation options for air crews at your hotel which is close to the airport
- Family of four staying one night en route to holiday destination
- Japanese tour group of 25 people (a) for overnight stay, (b) week-long stay
- Family with baby twins aged 2 years
- Cabinet minister and officials' overnight stay
- Honeymoon couple, etc.

Assessment activity 2:

Field trip

1. Visit a hotel that has minimum accommodation and a restaurant-based food service. Your lecturer must make the necessary arrangements well in advance to ensure that the hotel manager is willing to give students the required information.
2. Ask as many questions as possible and collect brochures, etc. to use in the assignment.
3. During the tour of the hotel, obtain information on
- the types of customers generally served
- each department's purpose, function and services rendered
- the staff details of at least two departments and their specific roles and responsibilities, as well as other departments/areas that they work closely with (their internal customers).

4. Ask your lecturer to pre-arrange with management to allow you to observe someone taking a reservation by telephone or face-to-face.
5. Complete the assignment according to the following outline:
- Describe the hotel visited and its services.
- List the departments involved in provision of, for example, breakfast and the booking of a room.
- Describe the role and responsibilities of reservations staff in informing other departments of the booking status and how they actually do it. Why is this important? Which members of staff are involved in these activities?
- Give three examples of how a receptionist can sell more services to customers through having knowledge of all the hotel services available.
- The importance of meeting customer expectations in terms of knowledge of services and facilities.
- Any other information, not directly connected with the hotel that a guest may require.

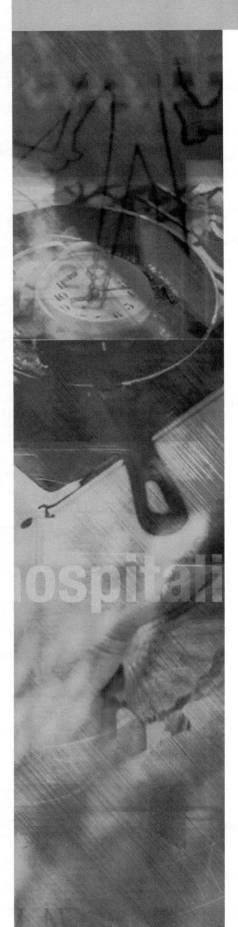

Module 3

Maintaining both manual and computer booking systems

Overview

The student should be able to ...

- amend bookings in accordance with procedure
- describe what action to take, given a system failure or manual error
- work in an organised and efficient manner
- adapt procedures for a range of situations

Unit 1:

Amend bookings

In our modern age of communication and information, the schedules of people change by the hour and this has an effect on hotel bookings; a change to or cancellation of a booking is quite frequently requested. Remember that a booking constitutes a legally binding contract between both parties, regardless of whether it is made in writing or verbally. If either a hotel or a guest wishes to alter or cancel the reservation, they can do so only by mutual agreement.

Change in services / facilities, date or time, customer's personal details or number of people

In these cases an amendment or cancellation form is completed by the reservation clerk and attached to the original reservation form and correspondence (in a computerised system this is recorded digitally in the system). At the same time, the room availability chart should be amended accordingly (done automatically in computerised systems).

Cancellation of bookings:

In the case of a booking cancellation, various details are recorded to ensure that the correct booking is cancelled. It is also necessary to show who is responsible for cancelling the booking, that is, who in the hotel received the cancellation and who on behalf of the guest made the cancellation. If any discrepancies should occur, the reservation clerk will be able to spot the error right away.

The cancellation details should include the following information:

- Date of original booking
- Guest's name
- Date when the booking is cancelled
- Name of person who cancelled the booking
- Cancellation number
- Name of reservation clerk who received the cancellation. As with denied bookings, all the details of cancelled bookings must be kept for historical data.

Unit 2:

Actions to take in case of a system failure or manual error

In the event of a computer problem or breakdown, inform the supervisor immediately and then proceed as follows:

- If guests wish to check out when the computer system is still not operational, manually prepare the guest folio, ensuring that all dockets and costs are added. Process the payment manually as well.
- Once the computer system is back on line, all these charges and payment transactions must be posted to the software system and the handwritten documentation stored for reference.
- If the speed point machine goes off-line from the bank while an authorisation is being processed, write the credit card number, the three control digits at the back of the card and the expiry date on the guest's registration card. Process the card manually, and hand this to the supervisor who will process it once the speed point is back on line.

As a contingency plan, most establishments do random printouts of guest accounts and keep them on file so that they may refer to them in the event of equipment/system failure.

Some establishments have a direct telephone link from the speed point to the bank with a backup power supply so that in the event of a power failure or telephone line problem, credit card payments can be carried out uninterrupted.

Unit 3:

Working in an organised and efficient manner

Working in an effective and efficient manner can also be referred to as total quality management (TQM). It is a philosophy of management that is driven by the constant attainment of customer satisfaction through the continuous improvement of all organisational processes.

- This includes ensuring that all staff work in an organised and efficient manner – from front office staff, porters, cleaners, kitchen staff, waiters, up to the general manager.

In service-type organisations the problem is often to reconcile the conflict between professional service to customers and administrative procedures.

Photograph courtesy of Gautengpics

There must be a continuous focus on the following aspects:

- Intense focus on the customer (internal and external)
- Concern for continual improvement (Very good is not good enough)
- Improvement in the quality of everything the organisation does (food, services, rooms, facilities, etc.)
- Accurate measurement of critical performance areas (bookings, finances, meals, etc.)
- Empowerment of employees – involving the people rendering the actual service in the improvement process, teamwork, etc.

Remember the following aspects in the service industry:

- The customer is participant in the service process.
- Services cannot be stored; they are time-perishable and if they are not used they are likely to be wasted.
- Unlike physical products, services are less tangible and more difficult to explain or communicate.
- Benefits derived from services tend to be associated with feelings and emotions.
- In service organisations, work activities are people-orientated and the characteristics of the staff are particularly important in determining organisational effectiveness.
- Measurement of output is difficult and there is unlikely to be a single, important criterion by which to measure performance.

Unit 4:

Adapting procedures for a range of situations

Complaints, comments and suggestions

At the end of every shift all specific guest comments, complaints and suggestions should be written in the hand-over book and passed on to the relevant head of department as soon as possible.

Complaints, suggestions and comments must be recorded and passed on to the appropriate person/department for the following reasons:

- The responsible departmental managers must have the opportunity to resolve a complaint as quickly as possible, and must be given the opportunity to apologise to the guest on behalf of the company - even if the complaint is already resolved to the satisfaction of the guest.
- Complaints can give insight into how work performance can be improved: making services better, faster, cheaper and more service-oriented. If one has learnt something as a result of handling a complaint, it must be shared with managers and colleagues so that they can take the same action in future.
- A lost guest is lost revenue. The longer one takes to resolve a problem, the more likely it is that the guest will be lost to a competitive establishment.

Guests need to know that members of staff are able to deal with problems that may arise. There is nothing as frustrating as being sent/transferred from pillar to post to resolve a complaint or problem. A staff member taking responsibility for resolving the matter gives the guest confidence in the company, and strengthens the trust relationship between the guest and the company.

Errors in accounts

If an error is picked up in a guest's account, proceed as follows:

- Check supporting documentation for verification.
- Make an adjustment as described in section 3.2 (Account adjustments).
- Print out the documentation and hand to the guest for checking.

In the event that a guest has already paid:

- Inform the supervisor
- Notify the guest and apologise for any inconvenience.
- If the guest was undercharged, politely ask the guest to pay the balance. If the amount is miniscule (for example, under R20) it may be better to write off the expense than to lose a good customer.

If the guest was over-charged, offer to refund the amount in a suitable method of payment particular to the organisation and guest's needs.

Accounts not pre-prepared

When there are too many departures and insufficient staff, it may happen that some accounts are not ready by the time a guest wishes to depart. In such an event, proceed as follows:

- Call the manager/supervisor to assist/speak to the guest.
- Alternative terminals may be used in urgent cases, for example, the porter's terminal.
- Work swiftly and accurately and process one payment at a time. Be pleasant, polite and calm; do not panic.
- Offer waiting guests a seat and refreshments and assure them that they will be attended to as soon as possible.

Always check departures the day before so that backup/assistance may be organised in advance if there are too many departures. A little preparation goes a long way. If the establishment caters for business people a typical crunch time is early morning as the businessmen depart; it may be wise to ask guests at what time they expect to depart the next morning so accounts can be prepared in time for the early morning rush.

Guest disputes regarding accounts

If a guest queries a charge on his/her account, proceed as follows:

- Check the supporting documentation and guest signatures on dockets from other departments, for example, bar, restaurant, etc.
- If the dispute is legitimate (it should have been charged to another room number or it is not the guest's signature; etc.) make the adjustment on the account as per company procedures.
- If the charge appears to have been correctly posted but the guest still disputes it, request the assistance of the supervisor.
- There are occasions when it is preferable to make an adjustment for a small amount that is in dispute (for example, a telephone call for R25.00 that the guest claims not to have made) than to risk losing a loyal guest, so a certain amount of flexibility is necessary.

There may be occasions when Housekeeping informs Reception that items of linen and other hotel property are missing from the room. If the guest has not yet checked out, the front office duty manager must be called to handle the check out of this guest. An attempt must be made either to recover the property or to obtain payment for it from the guest.

Case study scenarios

If possible, this assessment should take place in the workplace. Alternatively a simulated environment may be used.

- A real or simulated reservations environment or front desk must be used. Practise receiving enquiries and bookings by telephone, fax and face-to-face.
- Handle a *busy front desk* for at least 30 minutes under observation (or a detailed role play).
- Deal with eight to ten scenarios, some to happen simultaneously (for example, a simple request for room rates over the telephone, receipt of a faxed booking confirmation, arrival of a guest with no reservation, etc.)
- Follow the bookings procedure, including making a booking, confirming, taking a deposit, giving information, informing other departments, etc.

Summary

Maintaining, determining, recording and confirming bookings on both manual and computer systems

Making a reservation is often the first contact between a potential guest and a hotel. The mental picture the potential guest forms of the hotel, its staff, service, etc. is formed by these first impressions. It is, therefore, essential, even critical, for the reservations clerk to provide prompt and accurate service in order to present a good first impression to the guest. The reservations department does not only sell accommodation; through room bookings it helps generate income for all the other departments of a hotel, for example, the food and beverage department, internal shops and other specialist service offerings. If a room is not sold on a particular night, the revenue from that room is lost forever.

There are various sources of reservations: direct guest reservations, network systems and agencies.

Two types of reservations are made: guaranteed reservations and non-guaranteed reservations.

It is important to follow appropriate procedures when taking deposits for bookings.

Other departments in the hotel must be kept up-to-date on the status of reservations as they have to plan for their services, i.e. meals, laundry, the bar, etc.

Bookings may be recorded either manually in a paper-based system or in an electronic computerised booking system. The system must indicate availability of services and rooms. A standard reservation form requiring certain details is used in both systems. Various chart systems are in use in the industry for obtaining an overview of room availability: conventional advance reservations chart, density charts,

hotel diaries, stop-go charts, Whitney rack system or a computerised central reservations system.

Once reservations have been made, written confirmations are required by either the hotel or the guest. The reservation information is maintained as an original booking or as subsequent changes made to the reservation. Reservations are stored on paper under date of arrival of guests or electronically in computer booking systems. This information is also used to compile various reports: reservation reports, expected arrivals, departures, room availability, group status reports, special guests or VIPs, turn-away report and management forecast reports.

Once the guest has arrived the establishment's facilities and services must be promoted to generate additional income for the business. This can be done in a variety of ways: offering alternatives by using the top-down or bottom-up techniques, as well as suggestive selling. The choice of which selling technique to use depends on the type of guest and his/her needs.

Some customers may experience communication difficulties owing to cultural and/or language difficulties. These must be treated with understanding and respect.

There are also customers with special needs: speech impairments, visual impairments, deafness, mobility impairments and cognitive disabilities.

Group bookings require special attention as these generate substantial income for hotels from a single source with normally limited risk.

Bookings or reservations need to be amended as customer travel plans change and these must be recorded accurately.

At times when computerised booking systems are out of order owing to network or other technical problems, data must be recorded according to system failure company procedures to ensure customers are still served and taken care of in an efficient way.

Guests may have complaints, compliments and or suggestions to improve the hotel's services; these must be promptly brought to the attention of management. Any errors in customer accounts must be rectified as soon as possible, even to the extent of writing off small outstanding amounts in the interests of customer care.

Topic 6:
Maintaining effective working relationships

Module 1

Contributing towards the smooth running of the department and working effectively with fellow workers

Overview

The student should be able to

- understand and implement the organisation's procedures for resolving conflict
- understand the importance of internal communication systems and demonstrate written and verbal procedures
- suggest ways to improve internal communication
- describe own area of responsibility and be able to prioritise work appropriately
- describe the organisation's reporting levels and lines of authority
- understand why good relations influence levels of productivity

In the workplace

South African brand King Pie gets international service excellence award
King Pie was awarded the coveted international BID 2007 Quality Award on 28 May 2007 at the Times Square Marriott Marquis Hotel in New York. The award is aimed at companies that "are symbols of commitment to leadership, technology and innovation which make them models for other companies of their sectors". The award to King Pie was based on the innovation and technology used to implement its business strategy (King Pie Model) as well as its focus on leadership. The King Pie Model elements referred to are: A well managed cold chain including freezers in store as well as frozen trucks; centralised production plants that comply with their "Good Manufacturing Procedure" guidelines; effective marketing campaigns and training programmes; a rationally designed outlet blueprint including their unique chip machine, display trolleys and new decor elements to improve outlet aesthetics. These elements resulted in spectacular growth as well as re-establishing, the King Pie Brand as one of the leading Quick Service Brands. King Pie's motto says it all:
"What gets measured will be done...
What gets done can be rewarded...
What you reward will be repeated...
And what gets repeated will become a habit!"

Unit 1:

Conflict

There are four main types of conflict

Intra personal	Interpersonal
Conflict within an individual (conflict of interests, moral values).	Refers to conflict between two different individuals.
Intra group	Inter group
Conflict that takes place within a specified group.	Conflict that exists among groups of people.

Words & terms

Conflict may be defined as a disagreement of ideas and opinions between at least two people. Although conflict most often occurs among people, we can also experience internal conflict when we have to make decisions and don't know which choice to make.

Causes of conflict

The reasons and causes of conflict may be broadly categorised into three groups. Very often conflict situations result through a combination of two or more of these groups.

- Conflicts over resources

These are normally the easiest to identify and resolve. They occur when two people want the same thing and there is not enough to satisfy both needs at the same time. The resource is probably the first point of contention to be identified in a conflict situation and the heat of the dispute will most often be focused there. The use of the resource may represent the entire problem but that is seldom the case.

- Conflicts over psychological needs

Each person has many psychological needs such as power, friendship, belonging and accomplishment. The desire to fulfil these needs is commonly manifested in the need for material things – a person who, for example, appears to be upset about the use of a material resource, may also be upset about not having the authority or power to decide on who gets to use the resource. These types of internal motivations are not easy to pinpoint clearly and therefore conflicts of this nature are more difficult to resolve. If a person is unwilling or unable to express a psychological need, the conflict is unlikely to be resolved

- Conflicts involving values

Values are the basis of a person's belief system and this makes conflict over such matters very difficult to resolve. A challenge or conflict concerning a person's values is often perceived as a challenge to the person's very being. People tend to respond to such conflict from within their deepest-seated defensiveness and tenacity. Conflicts that involve value-system differences are, therefore, very difficult to solve as they involve abandoning old patterns and choosing to make new responses.

Conflict management styles

There are different methods and strategies for managing conflict and each individual has a personal conflict-management style. It is possible for individuals to change their conflict-management styles by learning new and more effective ways of managing conflicts. An individual person's response when confronted with a conflict situation depends on the individual's personal goals as well as the importance of his/her relationship with the other person or group.

Listed below are five basic strategies for conflict management

Style	Useful when	Consequences	Characteristics
Competition (forceful or aggressive, winner takes all approach)	there is physical threat, or when the goal to achieve is more important than the relationship	Power play; loss of relationship; resentment	Dominating, abusive, arrogant, bossy, yelling
Avoidance (withdrawal)	there is a danger to your safety	Feeling hurt, misunderstood	Indecisive, apologetic, submissive, timid
Accommodation (smoothing)	the relationship is more important than your goal	No solution, possible later resentment	Submissive, agreeable, quiet
Compromising (each party gives something up, in the interest of resolving conflict *now*)	time is limited and there are things you don't mind giving up. Only a temporary solution	Possible that conflict will resume again later; can maintain relationship on the short term. Expect something back later for what you gave up now	Direct, good listening, everyone gives a little
Joint problem- solving (cooperation, win–win solution)	there is time to negotiate and develop a mutually satisfactory solution and the relationship is important	Satisfactory long-term solution; improved relationship; everyone feels they have won, are better off	Good listening, creative, accepting, honest & open

Conflict management tools

These tools are described in more detail below; study them as they can be used not only in the workplace but also in all other spheres of your life.

Effective communication

Consider the following in effective communication:

- Be clear in your own mind about what you wish to communicate.
- Explain your ideas as well as feelings completely and concisely.
- Ensure that the receiver hears your intended message and check that you really hear what the other person is trying to say.
- Make a serious effort to understand other people's ideas and feelings.
- Learn to listen openly and carefully to the other party; pay specific attention to their responses to your messages. Do they understand what you are communicating?

- Avoid emotional responses as far as possible, as these complicate the situation.

Positive assertiveness

Non-assertive behaviour includes not expressing your own feelings, needs, ideas and ignoring your own rights to express yourself. This type of response to conflict normally results in a steady build-up of resentment within you for not being able to resolve the conflict. At some stage this may reach a breaking point where you 'explode' and cannot control yourself in a situation.

Aggressive behaviour is exactly the opposite of what is described above: it results in trying to dominate, even humiliate others and bully them into your way of thinking.

Positive assertive behaviour is being able to express your feelings, needs and ideas and standing up for your rights in a non-emotional way that does not violate the rights of others.

Group problem-solving

Considerations:

- All group members should try to work together – jointly decide who else should or should not be present, for example; an independent person should chair the meeting/session if possible.
- Each member should have a chance to share all relevant information; carefully try to separate facts from personal opinions.
- From information shared and the facts jointly define the real problems in an orderly fashion. From these problems, develop solutions and set objectives for the group.
- Brainstorm as many different solutions to the problem as possible. Just doing this jointly is a conflict-resolving exercise in itself.
- Jointly agree on solutions for the problems identified and decide who should take the relevant/appropriate action.
- Schedule a follow-up meeting to monitor progress jointly. If the selected solution is not producing the desired results, review the action plan and adjust adopt other methods, strategies and implementation steps.

Did you know?

To be able to manage conflict effectively people need special 'tools'. These tools include good communication skills, ability to use group problem-solving processes, behaving assertively in an appropriate manner and being able to work cooperatively with others.

Possible outcomes of conflict

- Lose-lose

Both parties in the conflict feel that they have lost out; generally animosity follows and the conflict is not resolved. The chance of conflict recurring is exceptionally high.

- Lose-win

One party is unassertive and allows the other party to win, despite the cost to him-/herself. The loser experiences internal conflict which could at some stage in the future result in conflict with the other party once again.

- Win-lose

One party forces a solution on another leaving him/her feeling dejected and defeated. The loser experiences internal conflict which could at some stage in the future result in more conflict with the other party.

- Win-win

Both parties feel that they have won; this can be achieved through compromise and collaboration. The solution is of such a nature that a good working as well as personal relationship is maintained for a long time. The chance of the conflict recurring is very limited.

In the workplace

Guidelines for dealing with conflict

1. Know your personal goals, wants and needs.
2. Build on areas of common agreement.
3. Be assertive not aggressive.
4. Empathise with the other person's views and feelings.
5. Be honest about making mistakes or feeling uncertain.

Conflict resolution

Methods for resolving conflict

The collaborative problem-solving outline

1. Admit a conflict exists.
2. Confront the problem.
3. Brainstorm possible options.
4. Select the best possible option.
5. Put a plan in motion.
6. Feedback and review.

The three-step conflict resolution procedure

Step 1: Complete a conflict analysis map.

- Define the issue by describing it in a short statement.
- List the parties involved.
- List the needs and fears of each person.

Step 2: Design solution options.

Step 3: Negotiate with an independent third-party, if necessary.

Unit 2:

Importance of internal communication

The following are the most common forms of communication in the hospitality industry:

- Verbal
  - face-to face
  - telephonic; Skype
- Written (for example, letters, memos, reports)
- Email; written Skype
- Faxes
- Representative or third party (for example, leaving messages with answering service or machine, pager, receptionist, secretary, etc.)

Communication channels

Every job function within any organisation is interdependent on other departments in the organisation to function successfully. These interdependent relationships are based upon communication - the life blood of every organisation. The channels of communication vary from one organisation to the other; however, they all fall into two basic types:

- Formal

Formal communication refers to: standard operating procedures, organisational policy, legislative information, team briefings, memos, appraisal discussions, training sessions, coaching, telephone calls and letters.

- Informal

Informal communication usually occurs as face-to-face, one-to-one conversations, but may also be small group discussions. In informal conversations the atmosphere is normally very relaxed and normal protocols are not followed. This type of communication usually also involves the expression of more personal feelings and opinions on matters under discussion. It is very often used to 'sound out ideas/opinions' before communication and formal discussions begin.

Photograph courtesy of Gautengpics

Importance of constructive communication

In both informal and formal communication the importance of a constructive exchange of ideas and/or views cannot be over emphasised.

The following benefits flow from effective communication:
- Helps you to improve the service.
- Strengthens the team effort.
- Informs both internal and external customers of the latest situations.

Good communication internally as well as externally is the key to any successful business. Everyone needs to be kept informed. Well-informed staff at all levels know what to expect, what is expected of them and understand what they can contribute to the business. Wherever or whatever your work, good communication skills are necessary to achieve results. Every employee needs to know about appropriate communication channels, company structures, his/her role within the job function and the different situations that require contact with management positions.

Photograph courtesy of Gautengpics

In the workplace

Customer Service
Foodies have been known to travel hours for a taste of the grilled black figs with tangy lime sauce, a medallion of veal tenderloin with woody mushrooms, or a slice of Valrhona chocolate cake with roasted banana ice cream.

But perhaps the tastiest thing served at the world-famous Inn at Little Washington is the service itself. Few restaurants – indeed, few businesses of any kind – seem so adept at fulfilling their customers' every need. Founded in 1978 by chef Patrick O'Connell, and Reinhardt Lynch, who oversees the business, the Washington, Va., hotel and restaurant has won nearly every hotle & food service award in the USA. Recently, Zagat's ranked the inn's 100-seat dining room as America's best.

Regardless of what business you're in, there's a lot to learn from the Inn at Little Washington's approach to keeping its customers happy. And while most chefs would sooner bite into a Big Mac than reveal a cherished recipe, O'Connell agreed to share one – the Inn's five-course system for, as he puts it, "delivering the perfect experience."

"It's not enough for staffers to be courteous. They must also convey an extraordinary degree of competence."

Measure the customer's mood: People, O'Connell believes, aren't impressed by what you know or what you can offer until they see that you care. And you can't possibly care in any meaningful way unless you

have some insight into what people are feeling and why. Enter the "mood rating". When a new party arrives in the dining room, the captain assigns it a number that assesses the guests' apparent state of mind (from 1 to 10, with 7 or below indicating displeasure or unhappiness). The mood rating is typed into a computer, written on the dinner order, and placed on a spool in the kitchen where the entire staff can see and react accordingly. Whatever the circumstances, O'Connell's goal is crystal clear: "No one should leave here below a 9." To that end, restaurant staffers spare nothing in their attempt to raise the number -- be it complimentary champagne, extra desserts, a tableside visit from one of the owners, even a kitchen tour. "Consciousness to the extreme is great customer service," O'Connell says. "If guests ran into terrible traffic on the way over here, or are in the midst of a marital dispute, we need to consider it our problem. How else are we going to ensure that they have a sublime experience?"

Cultivate staff expertise: It's not enough for staffers to be courteous, O'Connell believes. They must also convey an extraordinary degree of competence. Employees are encouraged never to stop learning about their job, the Inn, and anything else that might take the team closer to perfection. In line with that philosophy, all staffers – from managers to waiters to hosts – are assigned research projects and expected to become the resident experts on their subject, which can range from wild mushrooms to French merlots and vintage port wines. And staffers are called upon to demonstrate their expertise by giving presentations to their co-workers. It doesn't end there. Dining-room staff are each assigned a notable restaurant critic and asked to memorize everything from the reviewer's culinary hot buttons to his or her favorite words. The goal here is less to please any particular critic than to cultivate a deeper understanding of the opinion makers who can make or break a restaurant's fortunes. Indeed, staffers even are assigned to eat at a local restaurant, write a review in the style of their assigned critic, and present it to their fellow employees. "You have to know what controls the marketplace and what controls the perceptions of your customers – and ultimately your bottom line," says O'Connell. "Rather than maintaining a passive adaptation to these critical players, we study them."

Unit 3:

Improve internal communication

The most common breakdown, distortion and misunderstandings within communication occur in the vertical communication lines - communication which moves up and down the hierarchical network from subordinates to managers, as well as from managers to subordinates.

The increasing size of organisations has the effect that the lines of communication are constantly extended. It is common sense that the more people a message has to pass through up or down an organisational structure, the greater the chance of distortion or breakdown. The experience in business has been that generally as the size of the organisation increases, communication decreases and morale declines.

There are two solutions to resolve this problem in larger organisations:

1. Improve the communicative ability of all employees.
2. Open communication channels should be established, especially for feedback. Management should encourage the use of suggestion boxes and letters and the establishment of informal communication opportunities such as social and sporting events to bridge so called social 'distances'. Policy and procedures for communication should be laid down. Top management should communicate directly with all staff using effective and efficient communication tools.

Principles of communication within organisations

In the workplace

Guidelines for improving internal communication

- Communication should follow the lines of authority.
- Policies and procedures should control bypassing of the command structure.
- The content of messages should be stored in recoverable format.
- Messages should be structured and restructured to meet audience requirements.
- An awareness of potential barriers to effective communication is a first step towards avoiding misunderstanding.
- By building feedback into communication situations, members of organisations can help to avoid communication breakdowns

Unit 4:

Own area of responsibility and Prioritising work

Own area of responsibility

Good working relations are created when employees and employers know both their responsibilities and their rights and use this knowledge to their mutual benefit and to the advantage of those they serve in the industry.

The organisational chart defines the areas of responsibility and co-operation with co-workers and managers. The job description elaborates on specific duties and responsibilities. This should be clarified when starting in a new job to ensure that each person has a clear understanding of his/her own area of responsibility.

In the workplace

What consequences may there be for the operation of a hotel should a reservations clerk fail to adjust the room availability after dealing with a cancellation of booking? This illustrates the consequences when a person does not complete all tasks within their personal area of responsibility – it will negatively affect the operations of the establishment as well as a negative impact on other staff areas of responsibility as they will have to compensate for this error in the execution of their duties.

In every job function and working environment there are some tasks that are more important than others. There are also tasks for which you will be dependent on others before you can perform them, as well as tasks that others are dependent on you to perform for them to be able to fulfil their job requirements. There is a mutual inter-dependency among staff within departments as well as among departments for the organisation to be able to function effectively and efficiently.

It is, therefore, important for employees to have skills to make informed decisions on how to prioritise their work within this inter-dependent working environment – what needs to be done first and what the priority sequence is leading to the final task.

Impact of prioritising work

Prioritising work means allocating time to tasks and ensuring all are done within a specified time limit. Efficient time management is, therefore, essential for the supervisor to ensure that deadlines are met, individual as well as team goals are achieved, resulting in achieving business goals and profit margins.

As a supervisor you must manage not only your own time, but realise that you are responsible for managing the time of your subordinates as well. You as a supervisor are accountable for how your team manages time. Supervisors must ensure productivity of staff by setting task, production and time targets and monitoring and following up to check that tasks are on schedule according to the planned timeframe. It is your responsibility as an employee to inform your supervisor immediately that you are unable to meet your timelines as this will impact on the team as a whole, other departments and the organisation as a whole. When problems are encountered in time, alternative plans can be put in place to ensure that targets are still achieved.

Priorities and consistency of effort among all your group members really count and depend on good communication channels and good internal communication among team members.

In the workplace

How to control your time

- Make a daily TO DO list with respect to goals (preferably at the same time every day).
- Set priorities according to the ABC system (see below).
- Beware of the time rut (inflexibility and doing only what is scheduled).
- See what can be delegated.
- Don't fill up with low priorities.
- Spend time on As and not Cs.

Six steps for using time efficiently

1. **Set objectives** - Surveys done on successful people show that what they have in common is written goals. Write your goals down, keep them handy and remind yourself of them often. Also, list your long-term goals and goals for the next six months.
2. **Know how you spend your time** – Complete a time log for a week (daily at 15-minute intervals write up what you did) to see what you do and how much time you spend on each activity/task. This will help you plan for the future.
3. **Set priorities** - Use the 80/20 rule. This is called the Pareto Principle, named after an Italian economist-sociologist. It states that the significant/important items/tasks in a group usually constitute a relatively small portion of the total items/tasks in the group. In practice it means that 80% of what you produce/have to achieve in your job comes from 20% of the tasks – the challenge is to identify the critical 20% tasks and do them effectively & efficiently first and the rest will be easy.

Set priorities- in terms of urgency and importance:

ABC METHOD:

A = high value   B = medium value   C = low value

The secret is to do the As first. Don't do Cs at the expense of As and Bs.

How to differentiate between important and urgent activities (categories of time use):

- Important and urgent

These are tasks that must be done immediately or in the immediate future.

- Important but not urgent

These are things that can be done now or later. They can be rescheduled to a later date.

- Urgent but not important

These are things that appear to be important and need immediate action, but which we could assign a low priority if we examined them objectively; they look urgent but are not really part of the 20% of critical tasks.

- Busy work

These are those activities that are marginally worth doing.

- Wasted time

Anything you feel morally guilty about having done – extended lunch/ tea breaks, not urgent private matters attended to in work time, etc.

4. **Do one major thing at a time** – focus your time, effort and resources on completing the task at hand, then the next one, etc.
5. **Schedule your work** – first things first for others that depend on completed tasks.
6. **Delegate** – not everything can or needs to be done by you.

Unit 5:

The organisation's reporting levels and lines of authority

Channels of communication

Importance of channels of communication

Since authority and responsibility are delegated through a chain of command and associated channels of communication, it is very important to follow procedure to ensure that all relevant personnel are informed.

It is important that people in a chain of command are not left out. This may result in conflict as a particular person may expect to be included in the channel of communication because of his/her position. Ignoring channels of communication often results in people at a more junior level being singled out as a 'scapegoat' since management was not aware of decisions and actions carried out by the individual.

Channels of communication are, therefore, also a means of protection and accountability for lower levels of staff. If you can prove that you informed your supervisor of a problem and s/he did not do anything to solve the problem, you are protected if it becomes a crisis since you followed the correct channels of communication and have records to prove it. The same applies if you as a supervisor cannot resolve a problem and follow the correct channels to inform the next level of management.

Communicate with your supervisor

Generally your immediate superior is your entry point in your organisation/department's channels of communication. It is, therefore, very important that communication with this individual be effective.

Guidelines for communicating effectively with your superior

Receiving instructions

Effective listening skills are vital when you receive instructions from any person in a supervisory position. You should pay careful attention, be objective in your observations, not make immediate judgments and think about what is being said. You should ask questions to ensure that you understand what is expected and ask questions to clarify uncertainties. Receiving instructions is not a passive process; it is a two-way exchange. Often the supervisor has difficulty in communicating clearly what s/he means and wants. This is the root of many conflict situations: "I meant you must have

Words & terms

The term *chain of command* is often associated with and implies channels of communication. The channel of communication follows the chain of command. Instructions and information in an organisation originate at the top, and then proceed toward the bottom from one management level to another **without skipping out any levels or crossing over into different channels of communication.** The same procedure is followed by information, requests, complaints and suggestions originating at the bottom of the chain of command and following the channels of communication to the top.

..." "I thought that you meant that I should ..." Statements like this form the beginning of many conflicts that could be avoided by asking questions when the instruction is given.

It involves the following:

- **Listening:** paying attention and showing interest through body language, eye contact and encouraging gestures such as a smile or a nod.
- **Questioning:** asking questions to ensure you understand what is being said and to clarify details, methods, standards, timelines, priorities, etc.
- **Summarising:** stating comments and instructions in your own words to ensure that you understand. Similarly, the person giving the instructions is sure that you clearly understand what s/he means. This will also help you remember what you are being asked to do.

Carrying out instructions

Begin immediately to act upon the instructions/tasks you have been given by your supervisor. Do not postpone or waste time in taking action; you are expected to complete the task within the agreed timeframe. If you experience any problems with the execution of the task, immediately ask your supervisor for information or advice.

When you have completed the task

- report back to your supervisor about the outcome of your work
- ask for feedback about your performance in order to help you evaluate your own performance and improve your skills

Reporting back

Regularly report your progress on activities to your supervisor. The intervals of reporting progress will depend on what has been agreed on between you and your supervisor. You need to use your judgment because at times it may be necessary to communicate with your supervisor outside of the agreed times, for example:

- You may encounter problems that prevent you from completing the required task.
- If you have made an error, it is good practice to be honest about it and present a solution for correcting the mistake and possible problems that may arise.

It is important that you report back to your supervisor to show that you have initiative and are capable of making decisions within your scope of responsibility by

- giving your supervisor appropriate detail without overloading him/her with unnecessary information
- taking responsibility for decisions rather than constantly seeking confirmation and approval from your supervisor for each step. When new in a job this may be necessary but as you become more confident, make decisions yourself.

The procedure for keeping your supervisor informed will be as agreed or as organisational procedures require. It may be verbal or written. When problems are communicated to your supervisor, it may be good practice to keep a written record of such communication.

Organisational charts

Importance of an organisational chart

An organisational chart allows personnel to see their role in the organisation in the context of their fellow workers as well as where they fit into the whole organisation. This visual presentation of the organisation is very valuable in demonstrating the support systems and services available to personnel as well as indicating the different channels of communication within the organisation. It serves to highlight visually each individual's correct channel of communication, up as well as down.

Example of the typical hierarchical structure of an organisation

A simple example of a hierarchical structure for a department or an establishment may look like the following example:

- General manager
- Departmental manager
- Supervisors
- General staff

The example could be completed by including other departments and the staff who work in them as follows:

- General manager
- Food and beverage manager; restaurant manager; front house manager, personnel/trainee manager
- Head chef; head receptionist; housekeeper; secretary
- Sous chefs; supervisors; receptionists
- Chefs; food service staff; room attendants
- Kitchen staff; cleaning staff; porters

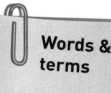

Words & terms

An organisational chart maps the hierarchical structure of the organisation.

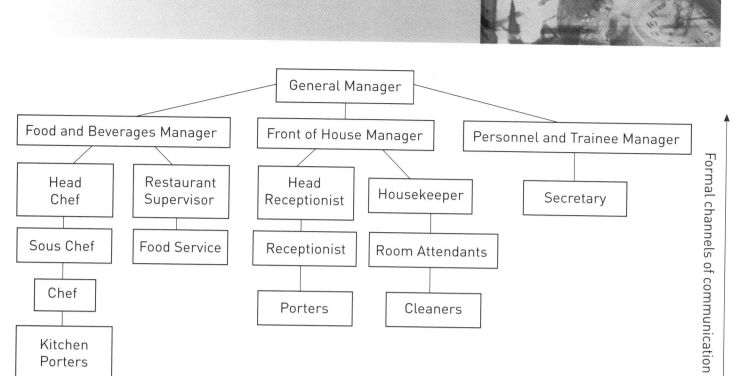

Normal informal channels of communication

Formal channels of communication

Unit 6:

Good working relations influence levels of productivity

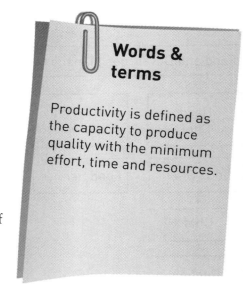

Effective working relationships and good teamwork improve the service delivery of the hospitality organisation. Cooperation among individuals as well as between one department and the next is critical in delivering a better service to the customer, resulting also in less wastage of both time and resources, the key concepts of productivity. Good working relations enhance co-operation between individual staff members and departments.

The most recent research provides support for the satisfaction – performance relationship. When satisfaction and productivity data is gathered for the organisation as a whole we find that organisations with more satisfied employees tended to be more affective than organisations with less satisfied employees. This conclusion may well be the reason for the fact that work satisfaction causes productivity.

Technological innovations especially in the telecommunications industry, such as International Central Reservation Systems and many more have improved productivity significantly. Productivity is a critical success factor in any private organisation and has a significant impact on the overall performance and profitability of a business. Productivity has become a major issue in the service industry. In order for productivity to be achieved and improved, standards should be set and employee performance measured accordingly.

Managing quality

Quality is central in the hospitality industry management model. It is the interface among all three primary areas and the shared goal of the organisation, employees and customers. There is no doubt that quality in the hotel industry is an important issue. Organisations should use this word in their advertising and promotion directed at their customers and in their standards of performance manuals directed at their staff.

What is meant by quality?

The British Standards Institute defines quality as *the totality of features and characteristics of a product or service that bears on its ability to satisfy a given need*. Today hoteliers and the hospitality industry as a whole are more consumer-orientated; therefore the modern concept of quality is 'fitness for purpose'. The industry must provide the best that the customer's money can buy and should be aware of the customer's attitudes and perspectives in order to be able to provide quality.

Measurement of guest satisfaction

Quality control and quality audits should be conducted to check the institution's quality performance. By implementing quality control and quality audits, the manager can influence customer satisfaction, which should be measured on a regular basis

A good quality management system doesn't guarantee that there will be no complaints. Complaints should, however, not be seen as negative. It is important to monitor complaints for feedback purposes and take action to resolve the complaint as soon as possible. The organisation, employees, customers, productivity, service and income should be managed in such a way that real quality is achieved.

Conclusion

Good strategic and hospitality management is very important for an organisation to be successful. Successful strategic management involves the formulation, implementation and evaluation of strategies that should not only be planned very carefully, but also be implemented through action plans. Monitoring and control are also very important as they provide valuable information for the future. The organisation, employees, customers, productivity, service, income and quality all form key areas of the hospitality institution. The strategies that are formulated and implemented by focusing on the key areas determine the success of the hospitality establishment now and in the future.

In the workplace

Why do customers leave and what drives customer loyalty?
When it comes to customer loyalty, it is vital for organisations to understand why customers stay and why they leave. This way companies can increase customer loyalty and reduce customer defections (remember, it is ten times more expensive to get a new customer than it is to keep the existing one). Adopting a customer-centric stance will inform management about what motivates customers' behaviour, thereby enabling the organisation to proactively develop a profit-generating loyalty strategy.

Happy customers are loyal customers
Emotions play a greater role than price in the decision to defect, and poor customer service is the most likely cause of generating the negative feelings that motivate a customer to leave. In today's free market, customers can generally acquire similar products at similar prices, from a range of local and global suppliers, so why stay with a supplier who provides poor service? One survey found that in 83 per cent of cases of defection, a 'triggering event' caused customers to end the business relationship and emotion was a critical factor.
In his article, The Customer Loyalty Solution, Arthur Hughes explains that most people leave a company because they feel they have been mistreated or ignored. While management usually thinks price is the reason for defection (which may be true in some cases) customers usually leave because they have been neglected or abused somehow. When they write a letter, send an email or make a phone call – often no one replies.

Module 2

Understanding the importance of treating internal customers with respect and regarding confidentiality as a professional conduct issue

Overview

The student should be able to ...

- treat colleagues in a polite and helpful manner and understand why this is important
- understand why confidentiality is important in the work environment
- show respect through professional conduct
- obtain assistance when difficulties in performing responsibilities arise and implement corrective action
- adapt performance appropriately, given a number of different situations

Unit 1:

Treating colleagues in a polite and helpful manner

All staff members are responsible to their employers and to themselves for making an effort to establish and maintain effective relationships with their immediate work colleagues as well as with staff working in other departments. It is in your personal interests if you relate and work well with your colleagues; you will be happier at work and gain greater job satisfaction. The company will also benefit directly from good staff working relationships because staff working cooperatively in a team provide a higher standard of customer service.

In the workplace

Guidelines to be kept in mind when dealing with other staff

- See all other members of staff as *internal customers*. This means that a service-orientated relationship exists between you and them.
- In order for you to perform your job effectively you need your colleagues' assistance and vice versa; they are dependent on you to work with them.
- If you and your colleagues do not give one another the very best service as *internal customers*, none of you will be able to perform your jobs effectively and efficiently which will result in poor customer service.
- You should be polite and helpful to others. Greet colleagues with warmth and friendliness every day. Rather greet someone too often than not often enough, even when you feel depressed or not well.

Techniques for working effectively in a team

A team as whole can only be successful if every member of the team is a team player and does his/her part.

Adopting the following practices and attitudes towards your fellow workers will help you establish and maintain effective inter personal working relationships at work.

Having a positive attitude and behaviour

Your attitude and the way in which you conduct yourself and behave at work, will determine how other team members respond to you. Are you the one that others always have to beg to get something done? Are you often late? Do you care about standards of work? Are you trustworthy about meeting deadlines, etc? If you behave irresponsibly, do not expect a positive attitude from others.

A good team player displays the following attitudes and behaviour:

- Smiles often.
- Maintains eye-contact when speaking to others.

- Asks open questions to extend the conversation, i.e. questions that require more than a 'yes' or 'no' answer.
- Is friendly.
- Maintains a positive attitude to work and other team members.
- Has a sense of duty and willingness to serve; is trustworthy about doing what s/he says s/he will do, within the agreed timeframes.
- Accepts responsibility and admits to mistakes, but rectifies them as well. Does not just blame everyone and everything else for his/her own failure to perform up-to-standard.
- Finds solutions, and does not just list and create problems.

Value others

It is an easy way out just to judge others. Do not judge others; rather focus on listening and making sure you understand your fellow workers. Make sure that you

- receive all questions in a respectful manner (remain calm even if you are presented with a negative attitude)
- receive all questions with equal value (value each team member's input; do not see questions as an attack on you personally)
- respond to questions in a clear and concise/short manner (you will break the flow of your discussion/ presentation and decrease understanding of your message if you give lengthy answers).

Treat everybody equally

Every team member is an individual with his/her own personality. Team members will be different from one another in a number of ways, for example, some may be argumentative or dominant, and others may be quiet. How you handle your interactions with each member of your team will determine your success as a team member. Do not abuse your strong personality traits to dominate others and create a team environment where only the strong can survive. Team success means every one feels valued as an important team member.

Photograph courtesy of Gautengpics

Unit 2:

Importance of confidentiality

Some information that may be available to the staff of an institution can cause a great deal of harm if the general public becomes aware of it.

Examples of confidential information in a business:

- Telling people about the findings of the health inspector. This could lead to fewer people visiting your restaurant, resulting in fewer sales, leading to possible retrenchments in staff.
- Favoured client status of some customers which allows them a discount. It is the privilege of management to make decisions in this regard.
- Revealing the identity of a celebrity who would like to stay or use the service/facilities incognito.
- Revealing where the money safe is situated and how access to it is controlled.
- Revealing what time money is taken to or collected from the bank, who takes the money, along what route, etc.
- Any information as far as the security set-up and procedures are concerned.

In the workplace

Guidelines that should be followed regarding confidential information

- Never gossip about or criticise your guests or colleagues.
- Don't divulge personal or sensitive details regarding your guests or colleagues. You could be held legally liable by doing so.
- Guests and members of the public are never to be told the room number of any guest; it could embarrass or even endanger a guest. First get their express permission.
- Never give out information regarding hotel occupancy rates; this is confidential business information.
- Treat the hotel's internal operations and future plans with confidentiality.
- Never give out any information you may have regarding salaries – yours or anyone else's.
- Protect confidential documents and confidential work on your computer. Use passwords where possible.
- If you are busy with a guest and the phone starts ringing, excuse yourself and attend to the call. It is rude to lift the handset and still be talking to the guest with you. The caller doesn't know what is happening and confidential information could be overheard.
- Never give any information to members of the media; always refer them to the general manager. Remember that all guests are entitled to their privacy
- If your manager is unavailable, do not give out information about where and with whom your manager is, should a person wish to speak to him/her. Rather try to assist the guest yourself or refer him/her to someone who will be able to assist him/her
- Be wary of the chatty caller who asks a lot of inappropriate questions; s/he may be from the media looking for a story and fishing for juicy bits of confidential information.
- Never give information regarding contact details of guests, for example, home address, telephone numbers, room number assigned to a guest for the duration of their stay.
- Never divulge any information regarding financial details of your guests.

Unit 3:

Showing respect through professional conduct

A professional working relationship exists solely for the purpose of getting work accomplished. The purpose of personal relationships is to develop a form of personal connection that facilitates good communication among people. It is important to remember that the primary purpose of the relationships with other people at work *is to get a job done*. We may work with or for someone we come to regard as a friend. We need to keep reminding ourselves that the topic of most of our conversations is not personal. it should be professional. This is especially true in times of conflict and disagreement on work issues; the working relationship between us then has nothing to do with how we feel about each other. It is about getting the job done.

Professionalism at work

Professionalism refers to behaviour that will enhance your performance and image at work. It is about doing your best and going the extra mile. Professionalism can turn a good employee into a great employee. It is about character and attitude. It is professional to:

- Be on time for appointments
- Smile at clients
- Help even though it may not be in your job description
- Return people's calls
- Complete tasks on time

Respect must be earned. This requires a level of admiration and esteem for the person who is respected. Intimidating, abusive or personally remote leaders do not deserve respect. They haven't earned it.

People generally respond according to the way they are treated. If you give a little you will invariably get a lot back. Make people feel important and give them a sense of personal worth. Most people will respond constructively if treated with consideration and respect and as responsible individuals who wish to serve the organisation well. There are, however, always some members of staff that abuse consideration. This has to be dealt with very firmly the first time it happens; if not, it just becomes more difficult to deal with over time.

Did you know?

The characteristics of professionalism
- Take pride in their work
- Show personal commitment
- Show initiative
- Do whatever it takes to get the job done
- Are always looking for ways to make things easier for others
- Are eager to learn and take on new challenges
- Listen to the needs of others
- Are team players
- Can be trusted with confidential issues
- Are honest, trustworthy and loyal
- Are open to constructive critique on how to improve
- Are accurate

Unit 4:

Dealing with job performance difficulties

There are many factors that play a role in the life of an individual making it difficult for him/her to fulfil job functions and areas of responsibility.

These factors can generally be divided into two categories:

- factors resulting from skills and competency deficiencies owing to lack of training, and
- non-training issues, normally inter and intra-personal issues

In all cases the staff member needs positive support in order to overcome such difficulties and obstacles.

Strategies for overcoming obstacles

Inadequate training

Skills, competency and knowledge of a person can be improved through staff development and training. This training and development can take many forms: hands-on training, coaching, mentoring, attending training courses or seminars, retraining, etc. The staff member's mentor or manager should provide guidance in this regard to the staff member.

Inappropriate inter-personal style or manner

This is normally the result of personal style and habits formed over years. Behaviour modification needs to take place. External training and coaching can be given in this regard but an in-house expert should preferably monitor this to ensure that the behaviour changes on a permanent basis.

Lack of commitment

Commitment cannot be given to a person; it is an internal personal decision that needs to be taken by an individual. Incentives can, however, assist in some way. An improvement in relationships among members working with the individual in conjunction with goal setting and the establishment of incentives should take place. This process must be carefully monitored by the department manager.

Underdeveloped personality

Personal skills training should be provided by a counsellor. Team-building activities conducted by team members should be organised to encourage integration.

Unclear job description

The staff member needs to gain clarity from management. All staff members should have a detailed job description in writing. This should annually be reviewed during the performance assessment to adjust the job description as a result of changed working conditions, personal development and growth and experience gained by the individual.

Poor work methods

This is once again a retraining issue. This training could take place in one of the manners discussed earlier:

- demonstration
- mentoring by senior worker or manager
- attending courses and seminars
- re-training at in-house facility, external training institution like an TVET college, a university etc.

Appropriate advice in this regard needs to be given by the staff member's mentor or manager.

Work environment

Fears, insecurities, conflict, resentment etc. in the work place are best solved by frank and open discussion among the parties concerned and a mediator, if necessary.

In the workplace

Managing Employee Performance

Managing employee performance is the process of creating a work environment in which people are enabled to perform to the best of their abilities and provided with the support they require to do so. Managing an employee's performance begins once they assume their role and ends when they leave the company. Performance management is about the importance of measuring and recognising accomplishments rather than activities. To overcome performance obstacles, you need to develop elements and standards that centre on what your employees achieve, not what they complete. Rather than employee appraisal or review, today's organisation is more about maintaining and improving performance while managing expected results and accomplishments. The traditional method of evaluating employee performance is reactive, with evaluative methods conducted after the event takes place. It rewards the activities an employee performs, rather than that employee's ability to do the right things to reach specific objectives.

Identifying Poor Performers

Just about every organisation has its fair share of poor performers. But even though the employee may be partially responsible for the poor performance, there are other contributing factors. Some issues that directly affect the performance of employees and eventually the organisation include:

- Lack of knowledge: lack of knowledge is a common problem among managers, who commonly believe that employees will figure it out for themselves. All employees deserve to receive the proper knowledge and training to effectively function in their roles. Without the functional and cultural knowledge of the company, an employee cannot be expected to attain any type of performance objective.

- Not clearly defining performance objectives: employees may understand what is required for them to do their job, but may not have been given any performance expectations. It is your responsibility to define the critical elements and set specific performance standards to achieve.
- Lack of support: most employees state that support from their company and their superiors is essential for them to have confidence in their jobs. When employees receive support, it builds confidence, gets them more involved and allows them to strive to do their jobs better. Discuss with them what they require from you to become better performers.
- Inconsistency from superiors: another annoyance for employees is management inconsistency. Mixed messages, unclear directives and the lack of defined measures are just some of the issues that are at the root of poor performance.
- Inadequate tools: think back to a recent time when you had to work on something and did not have the right tool at your disposal. How did you feel? Frustrated? Now, think of your staff when they are asked to do something or have to meet a specific performance objective set forth by you or the company. Ask them what they need to do a better job. Provide the right tools, infrastructure and environment so that they can reach their goals.
- Not having a clear direction: effective performance management begins with a clear strategic direction. From this, employees derive the critical elements, specific performance measures and attainable standards.

Unit 5:

Adapting performance appropriately according to different situations

Dealing with individual characters

The following guidelines should help you work effectively with some of the different types of characters who may present you with problem behaviours in the working environment. Unfortunately, we cannot always pick our work colleagues and have to learn to work with them, especially in times of high unemployment.

Argumentative staff members

Team members may from time to time appear argumentative. When you deal with argumentative team members, remember the following:

- Control your own temper – two inflated ego balloons just need a prick to make a big bang. Try to deflate ego balloons as they are not easily pricked when deflated and do so with much less noise.
- Respond to the content of the member's comments not the attack; rephrase arguments in a calm and responsive way.
- Try to find merit in the member's comment; express your agreement and move on.
- Try to find out in a non-threatening way what is irritating the team member, in private at another time in a relaxed setting.

Dominant staff members

Dominant team members usually take over. They are often the first person to talk and rarely give other people a chance to express their opinions. When dealing with dominant team members try the following techniques:

- Interrupt with statements like, "That's an interesting point. What do the rest of you think about that?"
- Give other team members a chance to influence the discussion with statements like "Great point. What can you add to that Gail?"
- Seek the team's opinion of the comments by asking questions like, "Does anyone else have a different opinion?" or "I can see your point. Can anyone else think of another possibility?" or "Great idea. Victor, given your experience with this matter, can you add anything to what Chris has just raised?"

Quiet staff members

Quiet team members are team members who rarely contribute and often appear apart from the group. When you deal with quiet team members, remember the following advice:

- Ask for, but do not force, the team member to give his/her opinion in a friendly manner.
- Maintain eye contact with those who appear shy when you ask a question.
- Try to find out in a non-threatening way the reason why the team member is not contributing, in private at another time (Do they feel that they have nothing to contribute, feel insecure in the group, have less education, experience, etc?)
- Give the team member an opportunity to succeed (utilise his/her knowledge, skills and experiences in some way).

Assessment activity 1:

Conflict role play

Divide into groups of four. Each group must choose at least two conflict situations and prepare a role play on how to handle the conflict situation. Each group member must be involved in at least two role plays. Roles include

- supervisor running the meeting
- argumentative staff member
- quiet staff member and
- other staff members

Those of you not role playing should complete observation forms for each scenario.

Assessment activity 2:

Case study

Imagine you are a housekeeping supervisor in a busy business hotel. Four housekeeping assistants report to you and are responsible for cleaning one floor of 40 bedrooms in an eight-hour working day. Do the following:

- List all the tasks that need to be completed during a typical day.
- Prioritise the tasks using the ABC method.
- Allocate duties to each member of staff (including yourself).
- Prepare a work schedule to ensure that all tasks are completed within the timeframe. Do not forget break times for staff.

Indicate how you will handle the following situations and reschedule the work according to each scenario:

- One member of staff has to go home at lunch time because he is ill.
- There is a blocked toilet in a bedroom.
- The linen supply is late.

Summary

Maintaining effective working relationships contributes towards the smooth running of the department and working effectively with fellow workers.

In the working environment there will be conflict at some stage among people. Conflict may be interpersonal, intra-personal, inter-group or intra-group. Conflict originates from three main areas: resources, values and psychological needs.

There are various styles with which to manage conflict: competition, avoidance, accommodation, compromise and joint problem-solving.

The following are useful tools for dealing with conflict: effective communication, positive assertiveness and group problem-solving. Good use can be made of the three-step conflict resolution procedure. The outcomes may be lose-lose, lose-win, win-lose and win-win, the latter being the best outcome often resulting in long-term solutions.

Internal communication within any organisation is very important and takes place along communication channels in a formal or informal way. There are various ways to improve internal communication within the framework of principles of communication within especially larger organisations.

To ensure service delivery is of a high standard in the hospitality industry, work needs to be prioritised by each worker. There are six steps that can be implemented in order to use time effectively.

Within any organisation specified reporting levels and lines of authority exist. Everybody in the organisation needs to be able to communicate correctly and effectively with his/her supervisor – receive instructions, carry them out and then report back on what has been done. The organisational chart is a visual representation of the hierarchical management levels and lines of reporting and communication within the organisation.

Productivity is the capacity to deliver quality service with the minimum of effort, time and resources. Quality service delivery is the life blood of the hospitality industry.

The organisation and its different sections/departments/divisions need to see one another as internal customers. Staff must follow certain guidelines in order to deal effectively with one another and develop techniques to promote good team work. Professional conduct in the working environment is of the utmost importance. Staff need to be trained to deal with different situations and individual characters in their working and public service environments.

Information within any organisation is confidential and all employees must treat information as such – especially in the hospitality industry where staff also have access to certain types of guest information.

Sometimes staff experience difficulties in achieving the required levels

of performance. This can be owing to factors resulting from skills and competency deficiencies or because of non-training issues. A variety of strategies and methods exist to deal with these situations and include re-training, better job descriptions, personal development, improving working conditions and/or work procedures.

Topic 7:
Application for a job or work experience placement

Module 1

Preparing a curriculum vitae, comparing skills for available positions and submitting applications with appropriate correspondence

Overview

The student should be able to ...

- identify job opportunities/vacancies that are appropriate to his/her skill level and personal attributes
- determine appropriate contact strategies and activities to progress opportunities that may be available
- prepare appropriate correspondence in accordance with the contact approach
- understand the importance of a CV or resume and compile one appropriate to the opportunity

In the workplace

"While unemployment statistics may be dispiriting for young people entering the job market, opportunities exist for those who know where to look. "South Africa's workplace is rapidly evolving, creating new and exciting jobs. The trend for a flexible worker has created significant job opportunities." says Tracey Czakan, MD Kelly Personnel. While qualifications are important, not everyone can study. Many need to become economically active when they leave school. There are opportunities for working while learning and gaining skills. It is essential to gain the necessary skills to make you employable, says Czakan. Basic skills can be obtained at little or no cost. Become resourceful; it is not as difficult as you think, says Czakan, offering tips for school leavers seeking work:

- Look for learnership opportunities. A great way to earn while you learn and receive a qualification.
- Keep your eye on job trends and find out where the opportunities are and which skills are needed.
- Read books, magazines and newspapers, particularly about the industry you want to work in.
- Job-shadow or volunteer for a short while to gain experience.
- Communication skills are essential. You must be able to communicate in English, the accepted business language.
- Basic computer skills are essential in any job.
- All businesses demand that you have customer service skills.
- Find a mentor. The quickest way to learn is by looking at what others did before you.
- Teach yourself.
- Be an entrepreneur - don't wait for someone to give you a job.
- Networking is a good way to find out where jobs are.
- Be reliable and responsible.
- Be passionate. Show you are committed to your own success.

Cape Times, July 03, 2005 Tracey Czakan, MD of recruitment agency Kelly

Unit 1:

Job opportunities/ vacancies appropriate for your skill level and personal attributes

Self-assessment (getting to know yourself)

The most important aspect of finding a job is realising that you are actually selling your personal skills to a prospective employer. Knowing your skills, capabilities and competencies is, therefore, necessary. A good hard look at yourself and what is important to you is one of the first steps in preparing for a job search. Self-assessment means determining who and what you are. Getting to know yourself better will enable you to have a reasonable idea of what kind of jobs you are interested in and qualify for.

You will need to find answers for the following questions:

- What job will suit me and my temperament, skills, knowledge and life style?
- What am I capable of?
- What can I do?
- What do I want to do?
- What are my interests?

The time spent on a detailed self-assessment will definitely be to your personal advantage. The information gathered about yourself can be used to compile your Curriculum Vitae (CV), covering letter and your preparation for interviews.

A thorough self-assessment should cover the following areas:

- Personal values
- Educational qualifications
- Work experience
- Personal accomplishments
- Favourite subjects
- Physical capabilities
- Specific skills and abilities you have
- People you admire in the working world
- Hobbies/outside interests

Career information

To be able to compare and find more information on different jobs you need to know what sort of information to collect. Step one is to make a list of as many questions as possible for each career you are interested in, for example:

- What are typical salaries and other benefits (financial potential) at the different job levels, both immediately and in the future, in this field?
- What employment possibilities exist in this field? Is the job field saturated or are opportunities opening up? (Certain tourism sectors have more potential now before 2010 than, for example, South African Airways which has just announced plans to retrench 30% of its staff during the second half of 2007)
- What is the nature of the work available at certain companies?
- What are the career paths in this field of work?
- What are the prospects for career advancement in this field?
- Is there any possibility that this job may become obsolete in future?
- Procedures and sources of information to contact organisations and employers?

Use the information collected in your answers to help you make a career choice that closely fits your skills, education, interests, aptitude and temperament.

Search broadly

It is important to do proper research on careers to have enough quality information about the different options available. Be systematic and read as much as possible about each job you investigate. A broad search for career opportunities will provide you with more choices and will help you find a career that best suits your skills and personality.

Use formal (magazines, newspapers, Internet, etc.) and informal (friends, family, etc.) channels in your search. Use your networking skills - compile a list of all possible contacts in your church, family, friends, sports club, youth association, etc. Also think of professional or other institutions (business associations, Chamber of Commerce, personnel agencies, etc.) in your area where you could speak to a person of authority and discuss career options. Read about the different careers – your local library will have a section on career guidance.

Newspapers or magazines as a source of information

Most large newspapers have special employment pages and special inserts on specific weekdays and on Sundays. Articles about the jobs people do can also be found in magazines and trade-specific newspapers such as engineering news, small business news, etc.

Department of Labour as a source of information

The Department of Labour offers free professional guidance and host placement centres in 22 major towns and cities. The department is linked to many companies and firms and can provide part-time positions until a permanent position comes your way. It also provides training courses in different career aspects at a minimal charge.

Organisation as a source of information

Make a list of all the possible private companies and organisations that offer the career you are interested in. Add information obtained from advertisements in newspapers, the Yellow Pages, an address list from your local Chamber of Commerce and names from family or friends.

You can then send your curriculum vitae (CV) with a covering letter to each company. Some companies may decide to keep your CV and use it for further reference, should a suitable vacancy occur while others do not do this and may or may not inform you; remember then to keep a lookout for jobs they advertise.

Employment agencies

Employment agencies specialise in finding suitable candidates for various positions within organisations. These agencies are listed in telephone directories, in the Yellow Pages, as well as in newspapers under the Classified Advertisement section. They are not supposed to charge for their services. Visit them personally and register your interest with them or contact them on a regular basis. Some personnel agencies will ask you to complete a database form so they have your details on record and can search their database of applicants for specific skills when a vacancy is registered with them. When doing this, ensure that you complete all details as clearly as possible otherwise the database search may not include your profile.

Friends and relatives as a source of information

Inform friends and family that you are looking for a job. They may know of vacant positions or may even offer you employment themselves or know about specific skills their employer is looking for. When receiving such a job offer to work for family or friends, discuss and think about it seriously because working for or with family & friends can often cause interpersonal conflict and interference.

Vacancy boards as a source of information

Vacancy boards are found in shopping centres, employment offices, at student advisory centres, or outside factories and warehouses. Unfortunately they are not always kept up-to-date, so it is possible that the job advertised has already been taken.

Unit 2:

Appropriate contact strategies and activities for processing opportunities that may be available

Make a list of the companies, names, titles, positions and telephone numbers of people to contact at prospective organisations. It is important to find out as much as possible about the company and to ensure that the contact information is accurate and current. This is crucial when you contact the organisation for information or go for an interview.

Using the telephone

The telephone interview is an important tool in searching. Information about possible openings can be gathered. You can also market yourself by using the telephone and save the time and cost it would take to visit the company in person.

Employers often use a preliminary telephonic interview as a pre-selection method, to cut down on the number of people to interview. When you are called by a company it creates an opportunity that must be used to present yourself as a confident, well-organised and skilled person for the job. Keep in mind that first impressions are lasting. From the moment you make contact with the employer, they are judging you and forming an opinion. Although the telephone conversation may last only one or two minutes it could give you the edge over the other competitors if it is handled correctly.

Written and electronic contact

A letter can be sent to potential employers when you are looking for possible job openings. Fax or e-mail your enquiry. Attach a covering 'business letter' as this will make a good impression and is accepted business practice.

To make the best impression the letter should

- preferably be typed or handwritten clearly and neatly on plain white paper
- have no spelling mistakes or corrections
- consist of only one page

Some companies explicitly require handwritten application letters and use these as part of their evaluation process to screen potential candidates.

Personal contact

You may make personal contact with potential employers, personnel agencies, families and friends, contacts, library, etc. You may visit places of work to enquire about actual opportunities available.

Determining actual opportunities

When contacting organisations determine the following:

- What qualifications are generally needed to qualify?
- What specific qualifications are required?
- What skills/experience/qualities are required?
- What is the potential for personal growth and development?
- What is the working environment - indoors or outdoors?
- What is the dress code in this field?
- Is it possible to study further while working?
- What are the working hours? Is flexitime allowed or are shifts required?
- Are specific physical qualities needed, for example, strong hands, good eyesight?
- What are the conditions of employment?
- Average pay?
- Is on-the-job training offered?

You also need to consider travelling to and from work: How will you commute to and from the company? How far is the workplace from your present home? How long will travel-time take? What type of transport is available and how suitable is it? How much will this cost you per week/month? This may make some companies not a viable option for you unless you are prepared to relocate.

> ### In the workplace
>
> A new generation of graduates from tertiary education institutions, together with the latest crop of matriculants, has joined the masses who will be hitting the road this week looking for a job.
> The only thing that is certain about what they are facing is that it is definitely not going to be easy and, if one is to believe the statistics that are put about, very few of them stand a chance of gaining permanent employment in the weeks and months to come. That doesn't mean, however, that they should give up without a fight. What they need to do is get the basics right and to do everything they can to improve their chances of being included in the diminishing percentage that will be successful.
> There are a number of publications that offer advice on how to make the job-search process more effective and the latest – published – is called Jobinfo: Your Complete Employment Guide.
> There are many exciting opportunities available to young people, both in South Africa and abroad. The secret to taking advantage of these is to follow a methodical approach to searching for the right one. The process to follow is to choose the right area of work via research and self-awareness; to develop an effective job-search strategy by acquiring the necessary skills and techniques; and to access the job market, local and abroad, through advertisements, recruitment agencies and new technologies, including the Internet. There is also a "bonus section" consisting of a summary of labour-law aspects that are relevant to job seekers and employers in South Africa. The fact is that there are people being appointed to positions all the time. The issue is how to become one of those.

Jobinfo begins by looking at what it is about those who are successful. Among the characteristics they have are the following:

- They have recognised the changes in the ways companies go about hiring and what they expect from candidates.
- They don't rely on other people – they know finding a good job is their own responsibility.
- They have a positive attitude – they know their own strengths and can describe them clearly.
- They are motivated – they spend time planning their job-search strategy and establish specific goals for themselves.
- They focus their efforts – they find fields of work that are relevant to their experience, they identify the best companies to approach in these fields, and contact them.
- They communicate well – they listen carefully, try to understand what they hear, don't talk too much, and ask good questions.
- They learn from previous experience, rather than continuing to use the same ineffective tactics.

Unit 3:

Appropriate correspondence in accordance with the contact approach

Seeking and applying for a job requires specific paperwork called correspondence. This may include initial letters, application forms, etc. The way in which you conduct this correspondence and complete the paperwork is very important as this is often the first contact you have with the company. Sloppy paperwork, inaccurate and incomplete forms create a bad impression from the very beginning and the company may quickly decide that you will not be able to deliver the required standard of work if your application is messy.

Application forms

It is common practice for employers to require applicants to complete printed application forms. This ensures that they acquire the same basic information from all candidates. The company uses the information on the form to see if the person applying is suitable for the vacancy s/he wants to fill, for instance, whether the person has the necessary educational qualifications for the position. It allows for comparison among applicants and may be used as a pre-selection or sifting tool by the employer.

The company also looks at how the person has filled out the form. Is it clean, neat, accurate and not scribbled over, etc? It is, therefore, evident that the job application forms must be completed correctly.

Tips for completing an application form

- Read the entire form carefully before starting to write any information.
- If possible make a photocopy and fill the copy out in pencil first and then the original form in pen once you are satisfied that you have all the relevant information correct in the photocopy.
- Use block letters when asked to do so.
- Write clearly. Use legible handwriting or type if possible.
- Make sure it is neat and tidy.
- Make sure your facts, e.g. dates, are correct. A common mistake is to give your birth date as the date when you fill in the form.
- Fill in all details asked for.
- Write N/A (not applicable) if the section doesn't apply to you as this shows you haven't left it out by mistake. Don't just leave it blank.
- Avoid crossing out or smudges.

- Carry your CV with you as it should contain most of the information needed to fill out an application form.
- Keep the form clean and unstained (dirty fingers!)

Curriculum vitae (CV)

Drafting your CV is the end result of all the searching and information-gathering done in the preparation stage. The information gathered during the job-sector search and the self-assessment must now be utilised to draft a suitable CV. The CV brings together all the information collected about you, the career you want to follow, your skills, abilities, etc. in one document.

Why is a CV important?

A CV is **an essential document for obtaining a job**. The first impression any company has of an applicant is often from his/her CV.

Seize the opportunity to make this first impression a good one. Often the CV alone is the deciding factor as to whether you are invited to continue with the selection process or not. The CVs received along with educational criteria are often the basis on which employers decide to short-list candidates for positions. The CV usually acts on behalf of the applicant. The employer reads it, forms an opinion of the applicant and then makes a decision whether it's worth his/her while to see the applicant in person for an interview.

The purpose of the résumé is to make an impression on the person evaluating the CV so that you will be considered for an interview. The easier the CV is to read, the better. A dog-eared, messy-looking CV with incorrect data creates a bad impression from the start and you will not be there to alter the perception. It pays dividends to ensure that every detail is correct. Having a CV ready means no time will be wasted if an opportunity arises – you can apply immediately.

The layout of the CV

There is nothing more frustrating for an employer or interviewer than having to search for information required in a muddled CV. This immediately places the candidate at a disadvantage.

Be aware of the following aspects when you prepare a CV:

- Take care with the layout. The information must be arranged in a clear logical format.
- Divide the information into sections under separate headings.
- The main headings should be as follows:
  - Personal details
  - Educational qualifications
  - Employment history
  - Career objectives
  - Achievements
  - Leisure interests
  - Support documentation (certificates, references)

Words & terms

Curriculum vitae (CV)

A CV is a personal history that gives a prospective employer the following information about a specific person:

- What that person has done up to that time in his/her life (specifically educational and work experience).
- What the person is capable of doing (skills, strengths, achievements).
- It provides a brief account or personal record of the person's life, that is, school, work experience and personal details.
- It is basically an advertisement of the person presented on paper.

Did you know?

Curriculum Vitae (CV) is a Latin phrase meaning 'schedule of your life'. You will also hear it referred to as a résumé.

- Set out the CV with the heading on the left-hand side and information opposite on the right-hand side.
- Keep underlining and sub-headings to a minimum.
- Space the contents to facilitate easy reference.
- List facts in natural and logical sequence.
- Previous job history should be in reverse chronological order, that is, your last job should appear first.
- Clearly indicate start and end dates of study or previous jobs (they must be correct and easy to find).

The Format of the CV

Personal details on your CV

NAME:	State full name: forenames and surname.
ADDRESS:	Include postal code.
IDENTITY NUMBER:	This information can be used to check your age, citizenship, or for a security check.
TELEPHONE NUMBER:	Include business and work telephone with area code if applicable.
DATE OF BIRTH:	Age is an important consideration for some positions and for some companies.
MARITAL STATUS:	This can affect ability to travel and benefits such as medical aid.
SEX:	It is not always obvious from a name whether a person is male or female, e.g. Ashley
RELIGION:	If you are not religious this aspect may be omitted.
NATIONALITY:	Companies sometimes have restrictions in terms of employing people from other countries.
DRIVER'S LICENCE:	Some jobs require a driver's licence. State which code you have.
HEALTH:	Write 'excellent' only if this is a certainty. Otherwise rather state 'good'. Honesty is always the best policy, as the company will probably expect you to undergo a medical examination.
LANGUAGE ABILITY:	Indicate all official languages you can read, speak and write, plus any others if applicable.
CRIMINAL OFFENCES:	It is always better to be honest than to commit a falsehood and have the company establish this only later. Providing false information in a job application is a valid reason for immediate termination of service in terms of labour law - beware. There is no need to disclose parking offences.

Educational qualifications on your CV

SECONDARY EDUCATION:	List last school attended, dates, highest standard passed, subjects passed, and extramural activities.
HIGHER EDUCATION:	List institution attended, dates, type of certificate obtained, major subjects, distinctions obtained, extramural activities.

Employment history

LIST JOBS:	Begin with most recent, i.e. reverse chronological order.
DATES:	Give start and end dates of employment as month and year. Do not

leave time gaps in your CV as this will lead employers to wonder why you omitted the information. If you have been unemployed for a period of time, list it.

NAME AND ADDRESS OF EMPLOYER:

State name and address of employer.

TYPE OF INDUSTRY:

State field of work, e.g. communications.

PRESENT POST OR PREVIOUS POSTS:

State title of post. State responsibilities of each post. Note skills required to exercise responsibilities, and achievements. Also list promotions whilst with an employer. Give number and type of employees under your control and the tasks for which you were accountable.

SALARY:

Provide salary of only the most recent job.

REASONS FOR LEAVING:

State as concisely as possible. Don't criticise past or present employers. State lack of advancement opportunity or personal reasons if applicable.

Leisure and personal interests on your CV

List leisure activities participated in, that is, sports (specify which sport/s you enjoy playing or watching), hobbies, community work.

The employer can deduce what kind of person the applicant is from this information, whether a group-orientated or more self-orientated person.

Outline career objectives on your CV

Give a brief account of what you intend to achieve in the short, medium and long term in terms of your career. State what actions you are taking to realise your objectives.

Outline achievements on your CV

This includes additional training, volunteer work, related accomplishments, and awards. You could give a brief description of each achievement.

Supporting documentation

The following documentation may be required when you submit a CV:

Certificates: Don't attach every certificate ever received. These can be produced when you go for an interview. State in the CV that they are available on request and keep to the most important ones, i.e. school, college, university certificates.

References: Quote references or indicate that references will be provided on request. Let the referees know of their nomination so that they are prepared to provide information concerning your work performance.

Customising the CV

Carefully read every advertisement. Underline the job requirements (criteria) asked for. Go over your skills and find those you already have that fit the new job. Highlight these requirements in your application letter and CV. You should not use the same CV for all job applications. Communicate the message that *you* have the skills, experience and qualifications that match very closely those required for the particular job.

Identify portable skills, that is, those skills that can be transferred from one occupation to another. Typical examples include being able to communicate with people, plan and organise, and handle responsibility.

Presentation of the CV

Besides the factual information contained in the CV, the prospective employer makes other deductions from the way the CV is presented. If it is clean, neat, concise, easy- to-read, and relevant; the applicant appears to be a careful, thorough, well-prepared, systematic person. If, however, it is dog-eared, sketchy, incomplete and disorganised; the applicant gives the impression of a careless, disorganised candidate - hardly the sort of employee the company will want to hire.

The CV must be perfect. Check it and then **double and triple check** it. The end result is important – it may make the difference between success and failure! Spelling should be correct and the CV readable. Ask someone proficient in the language you are presenting your CV to proofread your draft copy for syntax or spelling errors. They can often see errors and omissions not immediately evident to you.

• Paper

Use a good quality A4 size white bond paper for the CV – minimum 80g. White paper is preferable to colour as most organisations are conservative and it is better to play safe and keep to standard white or off-white paper. Sometimes copies are made of CVs to distribute to interested parties and coloured paper doesn't always copy well. Do not print in colour as this makes bad photocopies – keep to black ink on white paper.

• Language

Most companies use English as their business language. Use straightforward language. Don't try to impress the interviewer by using long words. Keep technical expressions, abbreviations and long words to a minimum. Choose your words carefully in order to give your CV maximum impact. Do not be too shy but be modest. Never undersell yourself - sound dynamic and enthusiastic to secure the job.

- Legibility

It is recommended that you have the CV typed even if you have a very neat handwriting. Employers are busy people and lose interest if they have to struggle to read the handwriting. The end result is worth the trouble. Use only one side of the paper so that the typing does not shine through to the front page and disturb the reader.

Writing up the CV

- Length

A CV should ideally be as short as possible, not more than 3-4 pages maximum. The effect should be restrained and business-like. Excite the interviewer's interest so that s/he can ask you to expand at the interview. Put yourself in the best light possible in the most concise way without leaving obvious gaps.

It is advisable to draw a dividing line between providing a comprehensive summary that has all the necessary details without overdoing it and boring the interviewer or swamping the important information in irrelevant data.

If the CV is too long the employer will lose interest. Keep it to only a couple of pages if possible. Include only essential information. The interviewer should be able to scan your CV in 2-3 minutes. Revise and delete unnecessary words. Keep educational information to a minimum. Summarise your previous job duties and responsibilities in three to four good sentences, if possible reflecting some of the job requirements of the position you are now applying for. This shows your experience is suitable for this new job.

- Duplication

When duplicating the CV, photocopy it on a good photocopier – copies must be of basically the same standard as the originals; no grey, smudged or black photocopy lines must be visible on the photocopies. Make enough certified copies to have sufficient on hand when needed. Keep all copies flat, crisp and clean; store them in a plastic cover.

- Finishing touches

If possible, use a cover with a hard board finish to give the CV a professional appearance and to prevent the pages from being bent and creased. Keep the CV and copies in a folder where dust and dirt cannot spoil the finish.

A nice touch to complete a CV is a passport-size photo of the applicant attached to the personal details section. This personalises the document and brings the applicant face-to face with the employer (so to speak) who is led to feel familiar with the applicant.

A school-leaver's CV will obviously not be as detailed as a working person's because the school leaver does not have a lot of previous working experience to record. This does not mean that a school leaver should not prepare a CV. There is still relevant information that can be provided for an employer, for example, hobbies, career goals, part-time or vacation work, clubs or organisations belonged to, subject awards, etc.

Compiling a covering letter

The covering letter should be short and business-like (one page maximum). This enables the employer to see at a glance the most relevant facts. The letter must be interesting and make the employer think you are genuinely interested and suitable to work for the company.

As this letter sets the tone of your application it must look professional; it must have no typing or grammatical errors, or obvious erasures. The covering letter must be tailored to suit the nature of the position applied for, leaving the prepared CV intact. This also helps to save time in getting your application to the next employer.

Tips for writing the covering letter

The following tips can help you draft the covering letter that makes your application stand out among many and make you the obvious choice for the job.

- Draft it first on a basic outline.
- Keep it neat (clearly legible handwriting or preferably typed).
- Keep it concise (short and brief but punchy on a single page) - don't waffle.
- Keep to the point. Remember the CV will cover all the necessary detail; the covering letter merely serves to introduce your CV to the reader. It refers to the post advertised and asks for consideration, highlighting your key qualifications and experience. It must make the reader *want* to read your full CV !
- Keep it relevant.
- Be sincere, business-like and clear.
- Pay attention to detail, that is, punctuation, spelling and format.
- Use the standard block letter format.
- Keep it clean - cover with plastic.
- Use blue or black ink, if writing.
- Take it with you when you go for an interview.
- Enclose the CV with your letter.
- As with the CV, the paper should be white, and the best quality possible.
- Try to address the letter to a particular person. If the person is not known, phone the personnel office of the company to find out.
- If responding to an advertisement, read the advertisement carefully. Underline key words and phone for more information if necessary.

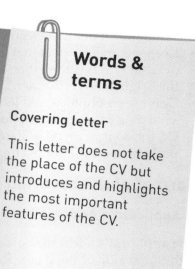

Words & terms

Covering letter

This letter does not take the place of the CV but introduces and highlights the most important features of the CV.

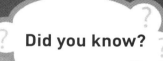

Did you know?

When and how to use a covering letter
You would use a covering letter in the following circumstances:
- in a general letter campaign (i.e. if canvassing jobs yourself the covering letter and CV should be sent to as many companies as possible)
- to gain employment information
- to answer and apply for a particular job advertised
- when applying for a bursary or scholarship

- Ask someone to read your letter and comment on it.
- Send your letter in a clean white envelope, clearly addressed.
- Keep a copy in a personal job-seeking file; this will serve as a record of what was written when asked to an interview. Clip the copy to the original advertisement you're replying to.
- Don't send photocopied letters to employers. Don't think you can save time by compiling one standard letter and photocopying it. On the contrary, you will be wasting money – your letter will most probably end up in the employer's waste paper bin!

Format of the covering letter

- ### Applicant's Address

The applicant's address should appear in block letters on the top right hand side of the page. The applicant's telephone number must be positioned directly below the address for easy reference. The date should also be included in the address.

- ### The Recipient's Address

The recipient's address should be placed on the left hand side below the applicant's address. The letter should be addressed to a specific person. (for example, the personnel manager).

- ### Headline

The headline gives the reason for the letter and should appear in block letters in the centre of the page after the recipient's address. The headline gives immediate structure to the letter and shows the reader that you are an organised person.

- ### First Paragraph

The first paragraph states the personal details, i.e. educational qualifications, skills, relevant experience, present salary.

- ### Second Paragraph

The second paragraph should explain why you are applying for the specific post and how suitable you are for the particular position.

- ### Follow-up Information.

In the follow-up information you indicate how you can be contacted and when you will be able to start. Mention the attachments, for example, CV, testimonial, references and certificates.

- ### Salutation (Ending)

Finish with 'Yours sincerely' or 'Yours faithfully'.

- ### Sign Your Name And Print It

It is important that the applicant's name be printed beneath the signature because signatures are hard to read.

It is not critical that the body of the letter follow the exact same sequence as proposed above. However, it is recommended that all the content be included as this is relevant information for the employer.

Assessment activity 1:

Divide into pairs and study the booklet or handout provided containing various examples of job opportunities, for example, adverts in a newspaper or a restaurant window, recruitment websites, articles on a new hotel development, etc.

Each group will be assigned a specific section of the booklet or handout and will be required to do the following:

- Identify the job opportunities presented.
- Determine whether you should apply (or not) for the position and give reasons.
- Identify what actions you would take to pursue the opportunity.
- Identify what methods you would choose to correspond with the prospective employer (for example, letter, email, fax, telephone).
- Select two of the jobs advertised in the booklet provided.
- Then select a suitable contact approach and prepare the appropriate correspondence. For telephone calls, prepare notes for questions or information required, etc. Document this approach and prepare the necessary documentation.

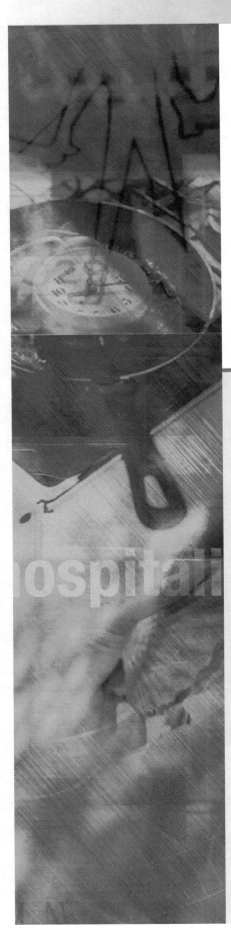

Module 2

Understanding the importance of personal presentation during an interview

Overview

The student should be able to ...

- prepare appropriately for an interview
- project a positive and appropriate personal image during an interview

An overview of recruitment techniques commonly employed in industry.

1. Psychometric Assessment

Psychometric assessment refers to the measurement of psychological characteristics. In particular, two types of characteristics are evaluated, namely cognitive (intellective processes, such as memory, thinking, judgement and reasoning) and affective (temperament, emotion, interests, attitudes and personality)

a. Cognitive Assessment
   Intelligence
   Intelligence is defined as the capacity to learn from experience, and is considered to involve the use of higher-level abstract thought processes.
   Ability
   Ability consists of two components – aptitude and achievement. Aptitude tests measure how well a person will perform a specific task in the future, given adequate training. Achievement tests, on the other hand, measure an individual's current level of subject knowledge or competence in a specific task.
   Potential
   Assessment of potential is included here as a counterpoint to the testing of ability and intelligence.

b. Affective Assessment
   Personality
   Personality has been defined as a unique combination of psychological qualities that cause an individual to behave in a fairly consistent manner in different situations and over time. Personality assessments are often utilised during recruitment and selection in order to maximise the fit between the individual and the work environment.

2. Behavioural assessment

a. Assessment Centres

Assessment centres are primarily used for the selection and evaluation of managerial-level employees. In an assessment centre, a small group of individuals are required to perform a variety of tasks.

b. Performance Tests

In these tests, the candidate is required to manipulate various physical objects. Such tests are used primarily for manual work, and consist of tasks that replicate those that will be done on the job.

The Employment Equity Act (1998) has attempted to eliminate many of the disadvantages of psychometric assessment by stating that such assessment is prohibited unless the following conditions have been met:

- The test must be scientifically validated and results must indicate that the test is appropriate for its intended purpose.
- The test must be able to be applied fairly to all employees regardless of their race or culture.
- The test must not be biased against members of designated groups (Black people, women and people with disabilities).

Unit 1 :

Preparing appropriately for an interview

The interview is by far the most frequently used selection procedure. The interview is usually conducted by a personnel officer as well as a person from the line management of the particular department or section the job is in. Sometimes another person from another department is also present to provide an outside evaluation of the candidate if it is a more senior position.

Interviews, like public speaking, can be nerve-wracking, but improve with practice and require thorough preparation. A lot depends on the interviewer. A skilled interviewer makes the applicant feel at ease and gets him/her to enjoy talking about him-/herself.

Researching the organisation and the prospective position

It is important to obtain information about the position and the organisation *before* the interview. This shows the interviewer that you are the type of individual that takes important issues seriously, has shown initiative by finding out more about the company – positive presentation of yourself.

Information about the position can be obtained by speaking to people working in similar positions, by reading the job specifications or by consulting career guides. More information about the company may be found, for example, by speaking to people working for that company, in libraries, newspapers, company pamphlets, handouts, the Internet and especially the company's website.

The following checklist may be helpful in the research process when you prepare for an interview:

The job

- Duties and responsibilities associated with the position
- Where the position fits in the company and various departments

The company

- Products and services
- Size of the organisation (number of sites, employees, departments, divisions, etc.)
- Types of customers, style of operation
- Culture of the organisation
- Mission statement
- Competitors
- Suppliers

Questions

- Questions they may possibly ask me
- Questions I can ask them

Confirming the interview

Missing an interview or being late is as good as losing the job - be absolutely sure of the date, time and place (building, floor and room number) of the appointment for the interview. Also confirm who the interviewer will be — have the contact person's name and title. Take all this information with you when you leave for the interview. When confirming the interview, ask for directions to the company offices and obtain a map if necessary. Arrange your transportation and accommodation in advance if you have to travel long distances; sometimes the company will arrange this for you at their cost.

Unit 2:

How to project a positive and appropriate personal image during an interview

Punctuality

Never be late for an interview. Arrive at least 10-15 minutes before the scheduled time for the interview. This will give you time to compose yourself and calm the butterflies in your stomach! Arriving late will create a negative impression and could alarm your interviewer as far as future punctuality is concerned. Estimate how long it will take to get there and add in time for emergencies. Allow for possible hold-ups such as traffic jams or battling to find parking.

Report to reception on arrival and give the name of the contact person for the interview.

Appearance

First impressions are said to be lasting. It is very important to project a professional and positive image when you go for an interview.

Depending on the company's image, it is important not to under-dress or over-dress. It is a good idea to visit the prospective company beforehand, as this will give you an idea of their image and dress code.

With the risk of sounding old-fashioned, a tailored dress or skirt for females and a tie for males (if not a suit) is recommended. Even though your prospective working environment may necessitate your wearing an overall or a pair of jeans, wearing neat clothing to the interview will indicate that you have respect for the interviewer and the company you intend to work for.

It is also very important not to create an image alien to you. Skilled interviewers will sense this as superficial or false and this could possibly cost you the job. Don't wear too much jewellery (six pieces of which your earrings are two, is an acceptable number). A wedding ring and wristwatch should be the only accessories for males. Females should be wary of adopting the 'sexy' approach in the hope of impressing the interviewer. It may make an impression, but not in the way you would want to impress him or her. Hair must be clean and well cut and shoes shining. A professional, efficient image will take you a long way in successful job hunting.

Body language

Poor body language can create a negative image during an interview.

Keep the following in mind when going for an interview:

- Stand up when meeting the interviewer and be ready to shake hands. Wait for the interviewer to extend his/her hand first. Although there are cultural differences, shaking hands firmly with your interviewer and looking him/her directly in the eye is generally favourably considered in a work situation.
- Smile when introduced.
- Take a seat and sit tidily – do not slump into a chair. Reception sections at personnel offices often have one-way windows and applicants are studied while kept waiting for the interview!
- Refuse a cup of something to drink politely if you feel you may be clumsy.
- Be modest and confident. Don't overdo it; there's a fine line between confidence and arrogance.
- Don't sit down before you are asked to do so.
- St up straight without slouching.
- Maintain good eye contact; look your interviewer(s) in the eye.
- Do not feel intimidated if you are placed on a single chair in front of an interview panel; it is part of the process to see whether you can handle stressful situations when attention is focused on you.

Listening during the interview

- Pay close attention to the questions the interviewer asks and listen carefully to ensure the information requested is exactly grasped. This will prevent you from giving irrelevant information.
- You may repeat the question asked to buy time to think and to confirm that you have understood the question correctly. Do not use this tactic too often as it makes the interview long and may frustrate the interviewer(s). If this tactic is used to often it may create a negative perception of you – this person is not suitable as we have to repeat every thing twice for him/her to understand. Asking for clarification now and then creates a positive perception: this person makes sure s/he understands before just jumping into a task – a positive attribute for any candidate.
- Do not smoke or chew gum!
- Don't ever accept a cigarette. It is usually considered rude or unprofessional to smoke in a public place, and even more so when going for an interview. Don't even smoke before the interview in the waiting room. If the prospective manager is a non-smoker, this could count against you.

Interview etiquette

The following are important points to remember for the interview:

- Be polite, friendly, enthusiastic and positive.
- Be pleasant to everyone you meet – remember to thank the person bringing the tea/coffee/water.
- Remember to thank the interviewer at the end of the interview.
- Also thank the person who shows you out and say goodbye.
- Do not criticise former employers during an interview. This is inappropriate, unprofessional behaviour that may be interpreted negatively and count against you.

Question time

Answering questions

- Try to express yourself as well as possible when answering questions and refrain from giving yes or no answers. Explain yourself - expand or follow-up with a relevant remark.
- When answering the questions, keep to the point and don't give irrelevant information that was not asked for. Ask the interviewer to repeat the question if you didn't understand it and if you don't know the answer, admit it. Your honesty will be appreciated. Don't give half-hearted replies such as 'maybe' or 'I don't mind'.

See example of Typical Interview Questions – Appendix N

Ask questions

During most interviews the applicant is given an opportunity to ask questions. It is important to ask questions about the job and the organisation as this shows your interest in the position and that you have done some research and preparation for the interview.

Prepare your questions beforehand in writing; do not to be dumbstruck when the opportunity arises for you to ask questions. Don't ask only self-centred questions that focus on own demands, for instance, about salary or fringe benefits, but also questions about the company and the position applied for, future prospects, training, etc. Leave the questions about salary etc. for the end of the interview.

In the workplace

The following are examples of questions to be asked:

- What exactly does the job entail?
  - What will be expected of me?
  - Whom will I be responsible to?
  - Where will I be working?
  - What kind of public transportation is available for getting to and from work?
  - Will I be given training?
  - What are the promotional possibilities?
  - What kind of fringe benefits does the company offer?
  - Why was this position created?
  - When may I expect to hear your decision on my application?

Concluding the interview

Before leaving after the interview, ask what follow-up action will take place and how long it will take before a final decision is made. Remember to take all your personal belongings with you when you leave the room. If you leave something behind, ask the receptionist to fetch it.

After the interview

Make notes on the interview or any other selection activity as soon as possible. Keep a record of what went well and what did not (pros and cons).

Even if the interview went well, don't relax your efforts and stop looking until a suitable job is found   Do not jump at the first offer that comes along.

Assessment activity 1:

Preparing for an interview

You will be given a job advertisement and some background information on the company (real or simulated), for example, Dros (a chain of pub-restaurants) is looking for a part-time food and beverage assistant. You are required to do the following;

- Prepare a CV and covering letter for application for the position.
- Describe how you would prepare for the interview according to the following checklist:
  - Confirmation of interview arrangements
  - Background information on company and post
  - Dress codes
  - Questions that the interviewer may ask and your replies
  - Body language and behaviour during the interview
  - Questions you will ask

Assessment activity 2:

Role play – interview

Plan, conduct and complete a simulated interview

- There must be at least two interviewers from the company side.
- Dress, body language, questions asked and answered, and levels of confidence will be assessed.
- If possible, record each interview on video for assessment feedback.

Summary

Preparing a curriculum vitae, comparing skills for available positions and submitting applications with appropriate correspondence

The most important aspect of finding a job is to realise that you are actually selling your personal skills to a prospective employer. Knowing your skills, capabilities and competencies is, therefore, necessary before you start the process of applying for a job.

To be able to compare and find more information on different jobs you need to know what sort of information to collect. Step one is to make a list of as many questions as possible for each career you are interested in. It is important to do proper research on careers in order to have enough quality information about different options available.

Sources of information on jobs and careers are newspapers, magazines, job mail, Department of Labour, companies and organisations, employment agencies, friends and relatives, vacancy boards, etc.

The next step is to develop appropriate contact strategies and activities in order to process opportunities that may be available including telephonic, written and electronic communication and personal contact. Once contact details have been secured, appropriate correspondence in accordance with the contact approach must be prepared. These are application forms, a CV and a covering letter.

The CV is the most essential document in obtaining a job. The CV creates the first impression of any applicant and must therefore be of high quality content and presentation format. The layout should be logical and easy to follow. There are standard layouts that can be used with good effect. A CV must contain personal and contact details, educational qualifications, employment history, leisure and personal interests, and an outline of career objectives. When needed, supporting documentation such as copy of ID and educational certificates must be attached.

A CV must be customised for the job application – a one-size-fits-all CV will not have the same effect and may even work against you in the application process.

Your CV must be presented in a professional manner – neatly typewritten on preferably white paper with black ink only. The length should not be more than 2-3 pages in total.

The covering letter is a 1-page document summarising why you are applying for the position and why you qualify – your key qualifications, skills and attributes are summarised in this letter – the reader must *want* to read your CV after reading the covering letter.

When you reach the stage when you are called for an interview there is more work to be done – any job interview requires special preparation — not only regarding your physical appearance, dress code, etc. It is also important to show interest in the company itself and not just in finding a job to earn money. If you do your homework and find out more about the company, the staff and the products or services that they render, you will be able to ask relevant questions and the interviewer will be able to see that you are a conscientious person who will show these same qualities in the work place.

Being on time for an interview and conducting yourself in a professional manner is of critical importance in being successful in securing a job. Body language and listening skills are keenly observed by interviewers and form part of the evaluation process. Your preparation for the interview will be demonstrated not only by the manner in which you answer questions but also by the questions you ask when given the opportunity during the interview.

References

Topic 1

Colleer, M. & Sussams, C. (1990): <u>Success in Principles of Catering</u>

Dalton, T. (2004): <u>The Food and Beverage Handbook</u>. Juta and Co Ltd.

Fuller, J.& Waller, K. (1991): <u>The Menu, Food and Profit</u>. Stanley Thomas (Publishers) Ltd.

Kinton, R., Ceserani, V., & Foskett, D. (1992): <u>The Theory of Catering. Seventh Edition</u>. Hodder & Stoughton. London.

Lotz, H.D. (1998): <u>Catering N6</u>

Powers, T. (1992): <u>Introduction to the Hospitality Industry. Second Ed.</u>, John Wiley & Sons, Inc. John Murray (publishers) Ltd.

Topic 2

Colleer, M.& Sussams, C. (1990): <u>Success in Principles of Catering</u>. John Murray (Publishers) Ltd

Kinton, R., Ceserani, V., & Foskett, D. (1992) <u>The Theory of Catering. Seventh Edition</u>. Hodder & Stoughton. London.

THETA, <u>Maintain Hygiene in Food Preparation, Cooking and Storage. Learner's Guide FP01</u>

Topic 3

Bulleid, A., Rabone, P., Rimmer, D., Ritchie, C., Roberts, T. & Wilson, N. (1994), <u>Serving Food and Drink: Table & Function</u>. Stanley Thomas (Publishers) Second Ed.

THETA, <u>Handle and Process Payments, Learner's Guide XX22</u>

Topic 4

Bulleid, A., Rabone, P., Rimmer, D., Ritchie, C., Roberts, T. & Wilson, N. (1994) <u>Serving Food and Drink: Table & Function</u>. Second Edition Stanley Thomas (Publishers).

THETA: <u>Maintain Practices and Procedures for Handling Cash / Cash Equivalents, Learner's Guide 7727</u>

Topic 5

Abbot, P. & Lewry, S. (199): <u>Front office: procedures, social skills, yield and management</u>. Second Edition, Butterworth-Heinemann.

Baker, S., Huyton, J. & Bradley, P. (2000): <u>Principles of Hotel Front Office Operations</u>. Fakeham Photosetting Ltd

THETA: <u>Provide Customer Service, Learner's Guide XX07</u>

Welgemoed, D., Erasmus, A. (1998): <u>Applied Management for Hospitality Services N5</u>. Future Managers (Pty) Ltd

Topic 6

Bulleid, A., Rabone, P., Rimmer, D., Ritchie, C., Roberts, T. & Wilson, N. (1994) <u>Serving Food and Drink: Table & Function</u> Second Edition. Stanley Thomas (Publishers)

Robbins, Stephen P (1996): <u>Organizational Behavior: Concepts, Controversies, Applications</u> 7th Ed Prentice HallInc. .

THETA: <u>Provide Customer Service, Learner's Guide XX07</u>

Wall, B. (1999): <u>Working Relationships – The simple truth about getting along with friends and foes at work</u>. Davies-Black Publishing.

Topic 7

THETA: <u>Identify Work Opportunities, Learner's Guide 7813</u>

Annexure A

Example of an à la carte menu

Starters

Soups:

Vegetable Soup	R30-00
Creamy Butternut Soup with a splash of Sour Cream	R35-00
Chicken Noodle Soup	R40-00

Salads:

Greek Salad - Lettuce, Cherry Tomatoes, Cucumber, Onions, Green Peppers, Olives & Feta Cheese	R35-00
Chicken Salad - Lettuce, Cherry Tomatoes, Chicken, Onions, Asparagus, Green Peppers & Pineapple	R40-00
St George Salad - Lettuce, Cherry Tomatoes, Chicken, Bean Sprouts, Apples and Nuts	R45-00

Fish:

Smoked Salmon Rolls with Feta filling topped with Caviar	R50-00
Prawn Cocktail - Shrimps in a Spicy Mayonnaise with Shredded Lettuce and a Prince Prawn	R60-00
Calamari Strips served with a Mushroom Sauce on a Bed of Rice	R40-00
Baby Sole served with Mussels	R55-00

Meat:

Beef Carpaccio with Rocket & Parmesan Shavings	R45-00
Chicken Livers served in a Bread Roll	R40-00

Vegetarian:

Asparagus served with a Bechamal Cheese Sauce	R35-00
Fruit Cocktail with Maraschino Cherries	R25-00
Avocado Dip served with Potatoe Croquettes	R25-00

Main Meals

Grilled Lamb Chops served with Boiled Baby Parsley Potatoes   R130-00
& Baby Carrots

Grilled Fillet served with a Mushroom or Pepper Sauce,   R130-00
Pan Fried Potatoes & French Beans

Oven Baked Baby Lamb Shanks served with Potatoe Croquettes   R130-00
& Baby Carrots

Grilled Chicken Breast (boneless) with a Cheese Sauce served   R110-00
with Savoury Rice & Pumpkin

Grilled Kingklip in a Lemon Butter Sauce topped with Baby   R130-00
Shrimps served with Savoury Rice & Baby Carrots

Desserts

Malva Pudding & Custard   R35-00

Chocolate Mousse   R30-00

Crème Caramel   R30-00

Ice Cream & Black Cherries   R45-00

Wine List

White Wine

Zonnebloem Blanc de Blanc:	R 55.00
Grunberger Stein	R 50.00
Three Rivers Sauvignon Blanc:	R 65.00
Nederburg Chardonnay:	R 65.00
Kupferberger Auslese	R 60.00
Theuniskraal Riesling:	R 60.00
Nederburg Stein:	R 60.00
Fleur de Cap Natural Light:	R 60.00
Two Oceans Sauvignon Blanc:	R 60.00
Nederburg Grand Cru:	R 55.00

Red Wine

Fleur De Cap Pinotage:	R 80.00
Zevenwacht Cabernet Sauvignon:	R 85.00
Fleur de Cap Merlot:	R 85.00
Nederburg Cabernet Sauvignon:	R 90.00
Nederburg Pinotage:	R 85.00
Nederburg Barron	R 70.00
Fleur du Cap Cabernet Sauvignon:	R 90.00
Drostdy Hof Merlot:	R 70.00
Zonnebloem Cabernet Sauvignon:	R 90.00
Chateau Libertas	R 70.00

Rosé Wine

Nederburg Rosè	R 60.00
Grunberger Rosenlese	R 60.00
JC Le Roux:	R 70.00
Sherry (per glass)	R 3.50
Juice (per jug)	R 26.00
Juice (per glass) at Arrival Drinks	R 4.00

Above rate is subject to change
Wines are subject to availability and management
reserves the right to substitute with similar wine.

Annexure B

Example of a Cocktail menu

COCKTAIL MENU

Hot Snacks

Cocktail Beef Souvlaki
Cocktail Marinated Ribs
Cocktail Lamb Sausages
Sweet Chilli Chicken Wings

Cold Snacks

Ham & Asparagus Rolls
Stuffed Eggs
Potato Cheese Balls
Salami & Mozzarella Kebab
Mini Fish Nuggets with Tartar Sauce
Fresh Vegetable Sticks Platter with Dip

Open Sandwiches

Smoked Salmon with sour cream & Black Pepper
Bread Fingers topped with smoked mussels
Chicken Mayonnaise
Sliced Beef with Mustard

Fresh Fruit Display

R165 per person

Annexure C

Typical Function Information Package including menu's

Menu 20

Roast Beef Burgundy
Roast Chicken with lemon & origanum
Roast Lamb in a mint flavoured herb sauce

Rice Pilaf , with fresh mint & black pepper
Roast Potatoes Coriander

Mixed Vegetables in olive oil & lemon
Cauliflower with a Béchamel Sauce
Pumpkin sprinkled with cinnamon

Pasta (Lasagne)

Traditional Greek Salad with feta cheese & olives
Beetroot Salad with Onion & Vinegar
Shredded Cabbage Salad with garlic , peppers & caraway seeds
Potato Salad with Parsley and Olive Oil
Bread rolls and butter

Desserts:
Ice Cream with Chocolate Sauce
Crème Caramel
Chocolate Mousse
Rainbow Jelly
Fridge Tart

Tea & Coffee

OPTIONAL EXTRAS

Bread Board display with 10 varieties of assorted bread and butter R6.00 per person
Cheese Board display with 8 varieties of cheese, crackers, small dried fruit and nuts R16.00 per person
Fresh fruit display with variety of fresh fruit R6.00 per person

R 165.00 per person (Starter not included)
Above rate is subject to change

SAINT GEORGE HOTEL

58 Old Pretoria-Kempton Park Road, Rietvleidam:
Tel: (011) 316 1254 Fax: (011) 316 5542 (Direct)

2007 PRICES

Thank you for your interest shown in our hotel. We take the pleasure in providing you with the menus & wine lists as requested.

The Menu Price includes the cost of the food, as well as tablecloths, cutlery, crockery, a podium, paper serviettes, tables for both cake & gifts. We do not charge a venue hire, but only a small set up fee, ranging between R300-00 & R2000-00, depending on the size of the venue being used.

Please note!!!
The menu price **does not** include the following extras:

(1) Any décor for the hall that you may need. The hotel can offer some items for hire (as below)

   (a) Coloured Overlays @ R 15.00 each
   (b) Material Napkins @ R 4.00 each
   (c) Chair Covers @ R 10.00 (plain) or R 15.00 (with coloured tie-back)
   (d) Candle stands R 120.00 (including four candles)
   (e) Silver Under plates @ R12.00 each
   (f) Waiters/Barmen @ R25.00 each per hour.
   (g) Nameboard R50-00 (Small) & R100-00 (Large)
   (h) Red Carpet @ R200-00

(2) Flowers can be arranged but are not included in the price. The hotel can provide you with many reputable references or alternatively, you are more than welcome to bring in your own florist.

(3) All alcohol must be purchased from the hotel. NO LIQUOR (OR FOOD) WILL BE ALLOWED FROM OUTSIDE.
It is your choice on whether you would like to have a CASH/OPEN/LIMIT Bar.

(4) The hotel offers two chapels on the premises. The smaller accommodates a MAXIMUM of 60 guests (@ R 500.00) and the larger can accommodate a MINIMUM of 70 guests up to approximately 180 guests (@ R 850.00). Marquee (@ R850.00 - when available).

(5) The hotel can make a provisional booking for you, under no obligation. This booking is kept for 2 weeks after which you can contact us to cancel or confirm.
Should you decide to confirm, a 50% deposit of expected costs is required to secure your booking. Information about the function can be given to the conference / function co-ordinators during the months leading up to the function. Ten - fourteen days prior to the function taking place, FINAL NUMBERS AND DETAILS are discussed AND THE BALANCE OF THE TOTAL IS PAYABLE.

For any further information, please do not hesitate to contact Jeannie/Judy/Robyn/Thobeka (On 011-316 1254) or alternatively, you can visit our website on www.stgeorge.co.za , for a better look at the hotel.

Menu 40

Roast Beef Lyonnaise , in a Red Wine & Onion Sauce
Roast Chicken with lemon & origanum
Roast Lamb with herb sauce
Roast Pork with Sweet and Sour Sauce
Madras Beef Curry OR Traditional Oxtail

Spanish Rice
Roast Potatoes Coriander , flavoured with wine

Mixed Vegetables in olive oil & lemon
Garden Peas
Cauliflower with a Béchamel Sauce & Cheese Topping
Pumpkin sprinkled with cinnamon
Baby marrows

Fish Display including Butterfish, Calamari, Hake and Mussels .
(this is part of the buffet and not a starter)

Lasagne Italiano
Penne Napolitano

Traditional Greek Salad with feta cheese & olives
Avocado Salad in Season OR Crab sticks Salad
Mixed Bean Salad with olive oil and onion
Shredded Cabbage Salad with garlic , black pepper and caraway seeds
Potato Salad with parsley and olive oil
Beetroot Salad with onions and vinegar
Copper Coin Salad

Desserts:

Baklava   Chicken's Nest
Crème Caramel   Ice Cream with Chocolate Sauce
Fridge Tart   Granadilla Cake
Chocolate Mousse   Malva Pudding
Red Pears with cream

Tea & Coffee

OPTIONAL EXTRAS

Bread Board display with 10 varieties of assorted bread and butter R6.00 per person
Cheese Board display with 8 varieties of cheese, crackers, small dried fruit and nuts R16.00 per person
Fresh fruit display with variety of fresh fruit R6.00 per person

R 200.00 per person (Starter not included)
Above rate is subject to change

Menu 30

Roast Beef Chasseur , in a red wine and mushroom sauce
Roast Chicken with lemon and origanum
Roast Lamb with mint sauce
Roast Pork

Rice Pilaf with mint & black pepper
Roast Potatoes Coriander flavoured with white wine

Lasagne Italiano
Macaroni Napolitano with fresh mint

Mixed Vegetables in olive oil and lemon
Cauliflower with Béchamel Sauce
Pumpkin sprinkled with cinnamon
Baby marrows

Fish Display including Butterfish, Calamari, Hake and Mussels (this is part of the buffet and is not
a starter)

Traditional Greek Salad with feta cheese & olives
Beetroot Salad with Onion & Vinegar
Potato Salad with Parsley and olive oil
Mixed bean salad with olive oil & onion
Copper Coin Salad

Desserts:

Greek Pastries
Ice Cream with Chocolate Sauce
Crème Caramel
Chocolate Mousse
Rainbow Jelly
Chocolate Cake
Carrot Cake
Malva Pudding

Tea & Coffee

OPTIONAL EXTRAS

Bread Board display with 10 varieties of assorted bread and butter R6.00 per person
Cheese Board display with 8 varieties of cheese, crackers, small dried fruit & nuts R16.00 per person
Fresh fruit display with variety of fresh fruit R6.00 per person

R 190.00 per person (Starter not included)
Above rate is subject to change

Menu 50 (A) : Greek Braai

Chicken portions on a Skewer (Prepared on hot coals)
Lamb chunks on a Skewer (Prepared on hot coals)
Souvlakia
Kleftico (lamb shanks) from the oven

Traditional Greek Salad with feta cheese and olives etc
Cucumber Salad with Fennel & Tomato
3 Bean Salad

Crispy Roast Potatoes with Coriander Flavouring
Savoury Rice
Cauliflower and Béchamel sauce

Desserts
Greek Pastries
Baklava
Chicken Nest
Red Pears with Cream
Crème Caramel
Finger Biscuits with Cream

Tea & Coffee

OPTIONAL EXTRAS

Bread Board display with 10 varieties of assorted bread and butter R6.00 per person
Cheese Board display with 8 varieties of cheese, crackers, small dried fruit & nuts R16.00 per person
Fresh fruit display with variety of fresh fruit R6.00 per person

R 190.00 per person (minimum of 30 persons)
Above rates are subject to change

Menu 50 (B) : Traditional South

African Braai

T-Bone Steaks
Boerewors
Chicken Pieces
Pap & Sauce
Lamb Chops
Spare Ribs

Coleslaw Salad
Potato Salad with Mayonnaise and Egg
Beetroot Salad with onion and vinegar
Traditional Greek Salad

Whole Roast Baby Potatoes
Baby Carrots & Peas
Pumpkin Fritters

Desserts

Ice Cream with Chocolate Sauce
Bread & Butter Pudding
Fridge Tart

Tea & Coffee

OPTIONAL EXTRAS

Bread Board display with 10 varieties of assorted bread and butter R6.00 per person
Cheese Board display with 8 varieties of cheese, crackers, small dried fruit and nuts R16.00 per person
Fresh fruit display with variety of fresh fruit R6.00 per person

R 190.00 per person (minimum of 30 persons)
Above rates are subject to change

Menu 60 : Fish Buffet

Main Course Buffet:

A variety of hot and cold dishes of fish prepared in the traditional way with their sauces and spices

Smoked Salmon
Prawns
Marinara Mix
Sole
Trout
Kingklip
Octopus (In Season)
Mussels
Sliced Crayfish
Calamari
Butterfish
Hake
Scallops
Baccalau (Cod Fish)

Coleslaw
Traditional Greek Salad with feta cheese and olives etc
Copper Coin Salad

Savoury Rice
Roast Potatoes Coriander, flavoured with wine

Desserts

Sago Pudding
Red Pears with Cream
Ice Cream with Chocolate Sauce
Greek Pastries

Tea & Coffee

OPTIONAL EXTRAS

Bread Board display with 10 varieties of assorted bread and butter R6.00 per person
Cheese Board display with 8 varieties of cheese, crackers, small dried fruit & nuts R16.00 per person
Fresh fruit display with variety of fresh fruit R6.00 per person

R 330.00 per person (Starter not included)
When a variety of the above is finished, it is not replaceable.
Above rate is subject to change

Menu 70 : Greek Menu

Starter:
2 Meze Platters per table (Finger Foods with Greek flavour)

Greek Buffet:
Souvlakia (Meat Kebabs)
Souvla Arni (Chunks of Meat on a Skewer)
Kotopoulla Rosto (Roast Chicken)
Arnisio (Roast Lamb)
Chirino (Roast Pork)
Vothino Rosto (Roast Beef)

A tray of fish including calamari , butterfish, mussels , hake and smoked salmon (this is part of the buffet and is not a starter)

Moussaka
Rice Pilaf with spices
Youvetsi (noodles with cubes of meat)

Dolmades (stuffed vine or spinach leaves)
Ntomates Gemistes (stuffed tomatoes)
Kolokithakia Gemista (stuffed baby marrows)
Bamies (okra in season)
3 Varieties of Vegetables
Mixed vegetable salad with tomato garnish
Potato Salad with Parsley and olive oil
Mushroom and Onion Salad with olive oil
Traditional Greek Salad with feta cheese and olives etc
Salata Horiatiko (Village Salad)

Desserts

Baklava   Kateifi
Chickens Nest   Crème Caramel
Chocolate Mousse   Black Forest Cake
Various Greek Pastries   Carrot Cake
Sago Pudding

Tea and Coffee

R 300.00 per person
(Some items may be out of season in which case there are substitutes) Above rate is subject to change

Menu 80 : Middle Eastern Menu

Starter: Meze on Buffet

(Including haloumi cheese, skordalia, tsakkistes, keftedes.)
Assorted Cold Meats and many more

Main Course Buffet:
Roast Lamb in garlic sauce and potatoes
Tavas (Lamb and cumin casserole)
Kleftiko
BBQ Sausage
Chicken Origanum
Souvlakia (Kebabs)

Youvetsi (noodles with cubed meat)

Yemista (dolmades, tomatoes and baby marrows)
Cous Cous
Rice Pilaf

Traditional Greek Salad with feta cheese & olives etc
Avocado Salad with lemon & pepper sauce
Mushroom Salad with olives
Asparagus Salad with Parmesan Cheese and olive oil
Chick pea Salad

Desserts:

Baklava   Black Forest Cake
Kataifi   Chocolate Cake
Chicken Nest

Tea & Coffee

OPTIONAL EXTRAS

Bread Board display with 10 varieties of assorted bread and butter R6.00 per person
Cheese Board display with 8 varieties of cheese, crackers, small dried fruit & nuts R16.00 per person
Fresh fruit display with variety of fresh fruit R6.00 per person

R 275.00 per person

Above rate is subject to change

Menu 90 : VIP Buffet

Main Course Buffet:
Beef, Pork and Mutton prepared and served with sauces
Chicken Fiorentina with parsley, onions and lemon sauce
Sliced Crayfish prepared with paprika, fresh cream and Tabasco
Kingklip Brazilian
Prawns (small) in lemon butter sauce
Madras Curry
Oxtail

Cannelloni with mushrooms, onion, parsley and peppers
Youvetsi (noodles with cubes of meat)
Spanish Rice with red pepper, spice and nuts
Spanish Paella (rice with chicken, variety of fish)
3 Varieties of Vegetables

Fish Display with mussels, smoked salmon, butterfish, kingklip, hake, fish fingers, marinara and shrimps. (This is not a starter)

Mixed Salad with capers and anchovies
Potato & Egg Salad
Traditional Greek Salad with feta cheese and olives etc
Mushroom and olive Salad
Asparagus with Parmesan Cheese
Avocado Salad with Tuna, peppers (in season)
Salad Nicoise

Dessert:

Carrot Cake   Black Forest Cake
Baklava   Kataifi
Malva Pudding   Chocolate Mousse
Berry Tart   Eclairs
Rum Balls   Petit Fours

And many more........

Tea & Coffee

OPTIONAL EXTRAS

Bread Board display with 10 varieties of assorted bread and butter R6.00 per person
Cheese Board display with 8 varieties of cheese, crackers, small dried fruit and nuts R16.00 per person
Fresh fruit display with variety of fresh fruit R6.00 per person

R 340.00 per person (Starter not included)

Above rate is subject to change

Portuguese Menu

Selection of Portuguese Rissoles with a variety of shrimp, chicken and tuna fillings

Plated Starter:

Calde Verde

Or

Chicken Soup

Salads:

Portuguese Salad
Potato Salad
Carrot Salad
Three Bean Salad

Buffet:

Espetada (Souvla using sirloin steak and course salt)
Pork Zebras (White wine, garlic with Peri-Peri)
Roast Chicken Peri-Peri
Bacalhau
Savoury Rice
Roast Baby Potatoes
Baked Cinnamon Pumpkin
Garden Vegetables

Dessert:

Fresh Fruit Salad
Ice Cream
Chocolate Mousse
Crème Caramel
Pastes de Nata
Baklava
Cheese Cake

R 200.00 per person
Above rate is subject to change

Menu 100 : Breakfast Menu

Varieties of Cereals
Variety of Yoghurts
Assorted Fresh Fruit in Season
Preserved Fruit (peaches , pears , guava)

Crispy Bacon
Grilled Lamb Sausages
Grilled Pork Sausages
Chicken Livers with Lemon & Onions
Poached Haddock

Potatoes and Fried Onions
Baked Beans in Tomato
Mushrooms in a Spring Sauce

Omelettes (cheese OR Tomato OR Mushroom)
Scrambled Eggs OR Fried Eggs

A variety of Cold Meats
Cheese Board and crackers

Scones
Croissants
Pancakes
Crumpets
Assorted bread, toast and butter

Desserts

A tray of Greek Sweets & Cakes

Tea and Coffee
Fresh Juices (Orange, Tropical Punch) on Buffet

R 165.00 per person (excluding Champagne)
Above rate is subject to change

Starter Menu

Cold Starter

Tuna Salad (tuna , onion , cucumber and tomato)	R 30.00
Greek Salad with feta and olives	R 20.00
Bacon Salad topped with nuts and garlic	R 30.00
Smoked Salmon with asparagus and tomato	R 35.00
Seafood Cocktail	
(Variety of fish in a garlic sauce served on a bed of lettuce)	R 45.00
Eggs Mayonnaise with Caviar	R 25.00
Shrimp Cocktail (with Tabasco sauce, mayonnaise, parsley, cabbage,	
black pepper served in a tall glass)	R 45.00
Ham Proscicutto with Melon in Season	R 40.00
Skordalia (mashed garlic potato spread with melba toast)	R 15.00
Fruit Cocktail with maraschino	R 20.00
Meze Platter for 5 (variety of greek finger foods)	R 100.00
Smoked Beef and Avocado (in season)	R 35.00
Cold meat platter (ham, salami, beef , asparagus , cucumber & tomato)	R 25.00

Hot Starter

Calamari Steak with mushrooms and tomato	R 30.00
Crayfish slices with olive oil and brandy	R 100.0
Kingklip Brazilian in wine and fresh cream sauce	R 45.00
Prawns shelled and fried in lemon butter)	R 100.0
Fish Platter Marinara	R 45.00
Asparagus Milanese with Cheese topping an d parsley	R 30.00
Snails (6 snails in parsley, garlic olive oil & brandy & brown bread)	R 30.00
Souvlakia (2xbbq fillet kebabs wit Greek Salad & lemon)	R 35.00
Chicken kebabs with potato salad	R 30.00
Soups (cape bean , tomato , spanish , chicken , vegetables , fish etc)	R 20.00
Chicken Livers with lemon and onion	R 25.00
Baby Sole with Rice & Mushrooms	R 35.00
2xChicken Drumsticks (with herbs and avocado OR asparagus)	R 30.00

All starters are priced PER PERSON

ALL ABOVE PRICES ARE SUBJECT TO CHANGE

Saint George Hotel Wine List

White Wine

Zonnebloem Blanc de Blanc:	R 55.00
Grunberger Stein	R 50.00
Three Rivers Sauvignon Blanc:	R 65.00
Nederburg Chardonnay:	R 65.00
Kupferberger Auslese	R 60.00
Theuniskraal Riesling:	R 60.00
Nederburg Stein:	R 60.00
Fleur de Cap Natural Light:	R 60.00
Two Oceans Sauvignon Blanc:	R 60.00
Nederburg Grand Cru:	R 55.00

Red Wine

Fleur De Cap Pinotage:	R 80.00
Zevenwacht Cabernet Sauvignon:	R 85.00
Fleur de Cap Merlot:	R 85.00
Nederburg Cabernet Sauvignon:	R 90.00
Nederburg Pinotage:	R 85.00
Nederburg Barron:	R 70.00
Fleur du Cap Cabernet Sauvignon:	R 90.00
Drostdy Hof Merlot:	R 70.00
Zonnebloem Cabernet Sauvignon:	R 90.00
Chateau Libertas	R 70.00

Rosé Wine

Nederburg Rosé	R 60.00
Grunberger Rosenlese	R 60.00
JC Le Roux:	R 70.00
Sherry (per glass)	R 3.50
Juice (per jug)	R 26.00
Juice (per glass) at Arrival Drinks	R 4.00

Above rate is subject to change

Wines are subject to availability and management
reserves the right to substitute with similar wine.

Saint George Hotel

DÉCOR

Unlimited Events	Rosemary/Alister	(012) 644 1114/5/6
Rose Bowl	Anna-Maria/ Salome	(012) 323 1767/ 082 452 2090
Draping	Jonathan	(011) 391 1051
Soft Light Décor	Theo	(012) 567 1512 / 082 837 9065
Via Functions & Flowers	George Sutherland	(012) 346 7641/082 655 5393
Silver Lining Functions	Zephne Gruar	(011) 967 1139/082 788 9603

CAKES

Miz Gooz Berry		(011) 422 1211
The Grape Vine		(012) 440 6910
Trou- en Geleentheidskoeke Mariana Scherman		(012) 667 5977 /083 309 3272
(After hours) Le Pâte à Choux – Jonathen Kershaw		(012) 734 1869 / 083 686 4163

DISCO'S

Reach Out Entertainment	Frank & Barbara	082 992 1092
Big Time Mobile Disco	Philippe	082 852 5783
Mobile Disco	Alex	082 884 8400
DJ Margarine	Werner van Heerden	083 767 4613
Musicians Unlimited	Maryanne Hodgskin	083 795 5588 / (011) 942 4919

OTHER

Rendezvous (String Quartet) Mitko Tasev		082 659 4061
El Bimbo Disco	Cesar (Latin music)	082 565 3099
Team-building	Affordable Adventures	(011) 465 9168
Marriage Officer/Priest	Jaco Venter	(011) 972 2096 / 083 414 5405

WEDDING DRESSES ETC

John B. Hockey	082 811 2709

PHOTOGRAPHERS

Freddy Cummings:		(011) 869 0186 / 083 760 2367
Frans du Plessis		083 263 2693
Adrian Hunter		(011) 782 0651
Basil Koufos		082 439 2022

VIDEOGRAPHERS

ICE Cool Video	Jeffery	082 449 1865
Michael Collet		(011) 640 4032
LM Video	Joe Godinho	(011) 467 1411/ 082 570 6295
Hookfish Design	Andrew Cartwright	082 333 7199

SAINT GEORGE HOTEL

58 Old Pretoria-Kempton Park Road, Rietvleidam:

Tel: (011) 316 1254 Fax: (011) 316 5542 (Direct)

BEVERAGE PRICES

Minerals
(Per Glass)

All Minerals	R 6.00
Fanta / Sprite Zero	R 9.00
Fruit Juice	R 7.00
Appletizer	R 11.00
Grapetizer	R 11.00
Mineral Water (Still / Sparkling)	R 7.00
Jugs of Juice	R 26.00

Beers & Ciders
(Per Glass)

Castle / Black Label etc	R 8.00
Millers	R 11.00
Windhoek / Castle Light	R 10.00
Hansa	R 8.00
Amstel	R 10.00
Heineken	R 12.00
Hunters Dry / Gold	R 11.00
Savannah Dry & Light	R 12.00
Smirnoff	R 11.00
Spin	R 12.00
Red Bull	R 18.00

Liquors
(Per Tot)

Whiskey	R 9.00
Rum	R 8.00
Gin	R 8.00
Cane	R 8.00
Brandy	R 8.00
Mix	R 6.00

*** Please note above rates are subject to change.**

SAINT GEORGE HOTEL

58 Old Pretoria-Kempton Park Road, Rietvleidam:
Tel: (011) 316 1254 Fax: (011) 316 5542 (Direct)

ACCOMMODATION RATES 2007

Standard Single	R390.00
Standard Sharing	R600.00 (R300.00pp)
Luxury Single	R440.00
Luxury Sharing	R660.00 (R330.00pp)
Suites Single	R660.00
Suite Sharing	R960.00 (R480.00pp)
Executive Single	R800.00
Executive Sharing	R1160.00 (R580.00pp)
Presidential Single	R1400.00
Presidential Sharing	R1600.00 (R800.00pp)

**All Accommodation includes a full English breakfast the following morning.
** Please note that all accommodation is subject to availability on a first confirm first serve basis.

FUNCTION CONTRACT

(Please read through carefully, sign and return on confirmation of booking)

CONDITIONS OF CONTRACT BETWEEN SAINT GEORGE HOTEL CC
(HEREAFTER REFERRED TO AS THE "HOTEL")

AND

_____
(PLEASE PRINT FULL NAME, NAME OF BUSINESS, ASSOCIATION ETC)

_____
(DATE OF FUNCTION)

VAT REGISTRATION NUMBER: _____

POSTAL ADDRESS TO WHERE   _____
ACCOUNT SHOULD BE SENT

_____

_____

_____

1. NO ALCOHOL WHATSOEVER, OTHER THAN THE HOTEL'S MAY BE BROUGHT ONTO THE PREMISES (including miniature bottles as gifts)
NO CORKAGE ARRANGEMENTS WILL BE MADE. ONLY HOTEL LIQUOR WILL BE ALLOWED.

2. Food provided by the Hotel for your Function **may not be taken off the premises.**

3. A.) GUESTS HAVE THE USE OF THE HALL UNTIL 01H00 (I.E. LAST GUESTS TO LEAVE BY 01H00 – NO EXCEPTIONS WILL BE MADE.

   B.) IN THE EVENT OF A WEDDING OR FUNCTION STARTING EARLIER IN THE DAY, THE HOURS WILL BE DISCUSSED ....MAXIMUM 8 HOURS......................................

4. MUSIC MAY NOT BE PLAYED TOO LOUD AND WILL BE AT THE MANAGEMENT'S DISCRETION. *Please refer to the DJ Contract.*

5. Breakages or damages to any of the Hotel's property will be charged for.

6. The Hotel cannot be held responsible for any loss or damage to a client's belongings or equipment whilst on the Hotel premises.

7. THIS SIGNED CONTRACT DOCUMENT AND A DEPOSIT OF 50% OF THE TOTAL QUOTED COST IS REQUIRED TO CONFIRM A RESERVATION.

   THE BALANCE OF THE FINAL CALCULATED AMOUNT DUE MUST BE PAID 7 DAYS BEFORE THE FUNCTION DATE.

   A limit bar will be included in the prepaid total amount. Should there be a credit owed to the client, the Hotel undertakes to refund this amount within two working days.

   An Open Bar must be settled in full on the night of the function either by Credit Card or a blank Cheque. Any other arrangements will be subject to the Management's approval.

8. Final numbers of guests will only be accepted **7 days** in advance. Thereafter, the quoted price will not be reduced for a lesser number of guests.

9. No drilling of holes or other alterations to the Hall walls for décor purposes will be permitted.

   Any decoration or fancy folding of serviettes etc. will be the responsibility of the client.

10. The cancellation of a Function 3 months prior to the date of the function will mean a forfeiture of 15% of the deposit paid; 2 months prior will be 30% and 1 month prior will be 50%. However, if the cancellation is made 14 days before the function date, the client will forfeit the full deposit.

11. This Contract is binding between the Client and SAINT GEORGE HOTEL CC.

12. Should the above conditions not be complied with, the Function will be cancelled.

I, ...hereby acknowledge, understand and agree to the terms and conditions as stated above.

Date signed: ....   Signature: ....

DJ CONTRACT

ATTENTION: **ALL DISC JOCKEYS ENGAGED FOR FUNCTIONS AT THE SAINT GEORGE HOTEL**

Please note that you are requested to co-operate if asked to lower the volume of your music to an acceptable tone.

The Management of the Saint George Hotel reserves the right to ask you to adjust the volume if necessary. You are assured that both discretion and integrity will always govern our request. Our priority is to please our clients and thus no unreasonable demands will be made.

We also wish to advise that the music is to end at **00H30**. Therefore 30 minutes are given to the DJ to pack his equipment and be out of the hall at **01H00** together with the other guests. Please note that weddings that are held earlier in the day will then have an earlier cut off time.

All DJ's are responsible for their own setup and breakdown, transport and the moving of their equipment.

Signed and accepted this .... day of ....20 ......

_____

Name of Disco

_____

Signature of DJ

_____

Signature of Client

Saint George Hotel

P.O. Box 27710, Sunnyside, 0132, RSA / Plot 58, Old Pretoria-Kempton Park Road,
Rietvleidam, Gauteng, RSA   Tel: (2711) 316 1254   Fax: (2711) 316 5542

CLIENT INFORMATION

(The completion of this information IN FULL is compulsory as it will eliminate any queries or a delay in receiving (or non-receipt) of our original Tax Invoice document issued to you for the services rendered by this establishment)

PLEASE FAX BACK TO: 011 – 316 5542 AS SOON AS POSSIBLE

FULL NAME OF ENTITY TO BE INVOICED: _____

TRADE NAME OF ENTITY: _____

VAT REGISTRATION NUMBER:
(This must be supplied if you are
a registered VAT Vendor) _____

POSTAL ADDRESS OF ENTITY: _____

_____

_____

PHYSICAL ADDRESS OF ENTITY: _____

_____

_____

_____

NAME OF PERSON RESPONSIBLE
FOR PAYING ACCOUNT: _____

TELEPHONE NUMBER OF ABOVE PERSON: _____ (CODE: ____)

FAX NUMBER OF ABOVE PERSON: _____ (CODE: ____)

IS OUR TAX INVOICE LINKED TO AN
ORDER NUMBER ??   YES: NO:

IF YES, ORDER NUMBER: _____

ORDER AMOUNT: R _____ _____

PLEASE NOTE THE FOLLOWING:
1.   Our Tax Invoice will be faxed to you merely for information purposes and not for payment purposes
2.   Our Tax Invoice will be posted to your Postal Address within 7 days after the service has been provided.
3.   All Tax Invoices are payable within 30 days of INVOICE DATE
4.   A Statement of your Account will be posted within 7 days after the last day of the month.
5.   Supporting documentation (eg: signed Refreshment bills, administrative charges etc. will only be supplied if requested)
6.   All payments should be made to: FIRST NATIONAL BANK
                                           CENTURION BRANCH (CODE: 261550)
                                           ACCOUNT NUMBER: 51060041328
                                           TYPE OF ACCOUNT: CHEQUE

58 Old Pretoria - Kempton Park Road

GPS co-ordinates
25 53 19'S
28 15 12'E

Directions

From Johannesburg (N1) - Olifantsfontein off-ramp

Travel North on the N1. Take the OLIFANTSFONTEIN off-ramp. Turn RIGHT at the traffic light into the R562. Continue STRAIGHT for 830 meters. Turn LEFT at the traffic light into OLD PRETORIA MAIN ROAD (R101). Continue Straight for 1.5 km. Turn RIGHT at the traffic light into the R562. Continue STRAIGHT for 11.3 km. You will cross the following in sequence: A 3-way stop street, a 4-way stop street, a second 4-way stop street and a traffic light. Turn LEFT at the next traffic light into GOEDE HOOP AVENUE (M57). Continue STRAIGHT for approximately 9.7 km. St. George Hotel and conference centre is on your right hand side.

From Johannesburg (N1) - Old Johannesburg off-ramp

Travel North on the N1. Pass the OLD JOHANNESBURG off-ramp (R101). Move over to the left and follow the N1 North to PRETORIA off-ramp. Follow the road as you turn RIGHT over the highway to stay on the N1. Continue straight on the N1 passing the JOHN VOSTER and BOTHA off-ramps. The next intersection is with the R21. Take the R21 (JHB Int. AIRPORT) off-ramp and keep RIGHT to follow the R21 back over the highway towards the Airport. Continue straight until you reach the first off-ramp (IRENE / RIETVLEIDAM). Turn LEFT to take the off-ramp. Keep LEFT to turn into NELLMAPIUS road. Continue straight and then turn RIGHT at the 4-way stop street into GOEDE HOOP ROAD (M57). Continue STRAIGHT for 2.7 km. St. George hotel and conference centre will be on your left hand side.

From Johannesburg International airport (R21) - Olifantsfontein off-ramp

Travel North on the R21. Take the OLIFANTSFONTEIN off-ramp (R562). Continue STRAIGHT up to a traffic light. Turn RIGHT at the traffic light into GOEDE HOOP AVENUE (M57). Continue STRAIGHT for 9.5 km. St. George hotel and conference centre will be on your right hand side.

From Pretoria (R21) - Irene / Rietvleidam off-ramp

Travel South on the R21. Take the IRENE / RIETVLEIDAM off ramp. Turn LEFT into NELLMAPIUS DRIVE (M31). Continue STRAIGHT up to a 4-way stop street. Turn RIGHT at the 4-way stop street into GOEDE HOOP ROAD (M57). Continue STRAIGHT for 2.8 km. St. George hotel and conference centre will be on your left hand side.

Created by: **MyMAP**™ 012 346 8443
www.mymap.co.za

Saint George Hotel

Tel: +27 11 316 1254/1166
Fax: +27 11 316 5541/2
e-mail: stgeorge@lantic.net
www.stgeorgehotel.co.za

P.O.Box 27710
Sunnyside, Pretoria, 0132
Portion 58
Old Pretoria-Kempton Park Road

PRETORIA
Orientation Map

Map No: 53

N

RIETVLEI DAM

DELMAS

TO PTA

HANS STRIJDOM

BOEING

N1

IRENE / RIETVLEIDAM OFF-RAMP

NELLMAPIUS

GOEDEHOOP

M57

R21

OLIFANTSFONTEIN
TEMBISA
OFF-RAMP

TO JHB INTERNATIONAL AIRPORT

MAIN

BOTHA

TRICHARDT

JOHN VOSTER

JEAN

N1

NELLMAPIUS
OLD JOHANNESBURG OFF-RAMP

M31

OLIFANTSFONTEIN ROAD

R562

TO PTA

WIERDA

OLD JHB ROAD

OLIFANTSFONTEIN OFF-RAMP

R101

N1

TO RANDBURG

TO JHB

Annexure D

Guidelines and Illustrations for lifting heavy objects

 **LIFTING TECHNIQUES**

Sponsored By:
U.S. ARMY CENTERFOR HEALTH PROMOTION
AND PREVENTIVE MEDICINE
ERGONOMICS PROGRAM

A USACHPPM INFORMATION BULLETIN PROMOTING BETTER HEALTH THROUGH PUBLIC AWARENESS

COMMON LIFTING PROBLEMS:	SOLUTIONS:
1. Lifting with back bent and legs straight.	Keep back straight and bend your knees!
2. Holding load too far from body.	Hold load as close to the body as possible.
3. Twisting while lifting.	Redesign the lift to avoid twisting. Turn your body using your feet. (See Pivot Technique.)

4. Losing balance during a lift because:
 	
• Your feet are too close together.
 	
• The load is uneven or unstable.
 	
• The load is too heavy.
	
	• Keep a wide, balanced stance with feet generally shoulder width apart, or wider.
	
	• Test the load before you lift. If the load is uneven, then
	   - Redistribute the load.
	   - Use the Tripod lift.
	   - Get help to lift the load.
	
	• If the load is too heavy, find:
	   - Another person to help.
	   - A mechanical lifting aid.

5. Contorting the body in order to lift and carry loads in cluttered areas.	Plan the move: inspect the pathways and destination to ensure that they are clear before you begin the lift.
6. Poor coordination between two or more people during the lift.	Communicate! Plan the lift together in order to coordinate your actions.

AS YOU LIFT, *Always...*

1. Keep the load as close to you as possible.

2. Keep your back straight.

3. Turn your feet outward and push your buttocks out. (Picture a professional weight lifter.)

4. Bend your knees.

5. Keep your head forward. Your lift will be more balanced and the curves in your spine will stay balanced and aligned.

6. Breathe out as you lift.

1

 # LIFTING TECHNIQUES

Sponsored By:
U.S. ARMY CENTERFOR HEALTH PROMOTION
AND PREVENTIVE MEDICINE
ERGONOMICS PROGRAM

A USACHPPM INFORMATION BULLETIN PROMOTING BETTER HEALTH THROUGH PUBLIC AWARENESS

Basic Lift (Diagonal Lift) - This lift is the most common method of good lifting technique. Use the basic lift for objects small enough to straddle where you have enough room to use a wide stance.

1. Get close to the object.

2. Stand with a wide stance: put one foot forward and to the side of the object.

3. Keep your back straight, push your buttocks out, and use your legs and hips to lower yourself down to the object.

4. Move the load as close to you as possible.

5. If the box has handles, grasp the handles firmly and go to step 9.

6. Put the hand (that is on the same side of your body as the forward foot) on the side of the object furthest from you.

7. Put the other hand on the side of the object closest to you. Your hands should be on opposite corners of the object.

8. Grasp the object firmly with both hands.

9. Prepare for the lift: look forward.

10. Lift upwards following your head and shoulders. Hold the load close to your body. Lift by extending your legs with your back straight, your buttocks out, and breathe out as you lift.

If you are doing this lift correctly, your head will lift up first, followed by your straight back. If your hips come up first and you must bend your back as you straighten up, you are doing this lift incorrectly.

2

LIFTING TECHNIQUES

Sponsored By:

U.S. ARMY CENTERFOR HEALTH PROMOTION
AND PREVENTIVE MEDICINE
ERGONOMICS PROGRAM

A USACHPPM INFORMATION BULLETIN PROMOTING BETTER HEALTH THROUGH PUBLIC AWARENESS

Power Lift - Use the power lift for objects too large for you to straddle. This lift is very similiar to the basic lift. In the power lift, the object shifts your center of gravity forward, and you must push your buttocks out to compensate. (Professional weight lifters lift using this position.)

1. Put one foot in front of the other using a wide stance.

2. Keep your back straight, push your buttocks out and use your legs and hips to lower yourself down to the object.

3. Move the load as close to you as possible.

4. Grasp the object firmly with both hands.

5. Prepare for the lift: look forward.

6. Lift upwards following your head and shoulders. Hold the load close to your body. Lift by extending your legs with your back straight, your buttocks out (exaggerate this position), and breathe out as you lift.

3

LIFTING TECHNIQUES

Sponsored By:
U.S. ARMY CENTERFOR HEALTH PROMOTION
AND PREVENTIVE MEDICINE
ERGONOMICS PROGRAM

A USACHPPM INFORMATION BULLETIN PROMOTING BETTER HEALTH THROUGH PUBLIC AWARENESS

Tripod Lift - Use the tripod lift for objects with uneven weight distribution (example: sacks of food).
Recommended for people with decreased arm strength. Not recommended for people with bad knees.

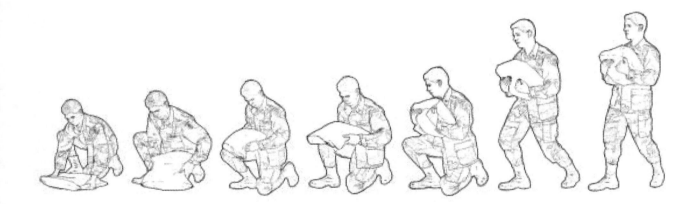

1. Put one foot next to the object. Keep your back straight, push your buttocks out and slowly lower yourself down onto one knee. (For support as you lower yourself down, put one hand on a stool or on your thigh for support.)

2. Position the object close to the knee on the ground.

3. Grasp the object firmly with both hands.

4. Slide the object from the knee on the ground to mid-thigh. Keep your head forward, your back straight, and your buttocks out, and lift the object onto the opposite thigh.

5. Put both of your forearms under the object (with your palms facing upward) and hug the object to your stomach and chest.

6. Prepare for the lift: look forward.

7. Lift upwards following your head and shoulders. Hold the load close to your body. Lift by extending your legs with your back straight, your buttocks out, and breathe out as you lift.

Copying and distribution of this pamphlet is authorized and encouraged

4

LIFTING TECHNIQUES

Sponsored By:
U.S. ARMY CENTERFOR HEALTH PROMOTION
AND PREVENTIVE MEDICINE
ERGONOMICS PROGRAM

A USACHPPM INFORMATION BULLETIN PROMOTING BETTER HEALTH THROUGH PUBLIC AWARENESS

Partial Squat Lift - Use the partial squat lift for small light objects with handles close to knee height.

1. Stand with the object close to your side.

2. Place your feet shoulder width apart, with one foot slightly ahead of the other.

3. Place one hand on a fixed surface (such as a table or stool) or on your thigh.

4. Keep your back straight, push your buttocks out and slowly lower yourself down to reach the object's handles.

5. Prepare for the lift: grasp the object and look forward.

6. For support as you lift, push down on the fixed surface (or on your thigh).

7. Lift upwards following your head and shoulders. Lift by extending your legs with your back straight, your buttocks out, and breathe out as you lift.

5

Sponsored By:
U.S. ARMY CENTERFOR HEALTH PROMOTION
AND PREVENTIVE MEDICINE
ERGONOMICS PROGRAM

A USACHPPM INFORMATION BULLETIN PROMOTING BETTER HEALTH THROUGH PUBLIC AWARENESS

The Golfers' Lift - Use the golfers' lift for small light objects in deep bins and to pick small objects off the floor. *Recommended for people with knee problems or decreased leg strength.*

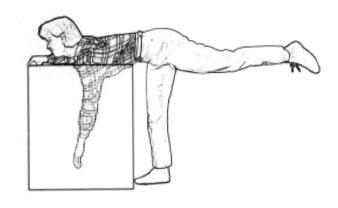

1. Place hand near the edge of a fixed surface (such as the edge of a table or bin). This hand will support your upper body during the lift.

2. Keep your back straight and raise one leg straight out behind you as you lean down to pick up the object. The weight of your leg will counterbalance the weight of your upper body.

3. Grasp the object firmly.

4. Prepare for the lift: look forward. Keep your leg raised as you initiate the lift.

5. To lift, push down on the fixed surface as you lower your leg. Keep your back straight and breathe out as you lift.

Copying and distribution of this pamphlet is authorized and encouraged

6

LIFTING TECHNIQUES

Sponsored By:

U.S. ARMY CENTER FOR HEALTH PROMOTION
AND PREVENTIVE MEDICINE
ERGONOMICS PROGRAM

A USACHPPM INFORMATION BULLETIN PROMOTING BETTER HEALTH THROUGH PUBLIC AWARENESS

Straight Leg Lift - Use the straight leg lift when obstacles prevent you from bending your knees. *Be careful! Lifts over obstacles that prevent you from bending your knees put you at increased risk for muscle strain. If possible, avoid this lift. Only use this lift when absolutely necessary (i.e. lifting out of a grocery cart, car trunk).*

1. Stand as close to the object as possible with knees slightly bent.

2. Do not bend your waist! Push your buttocks out.

3. If the obstacle (preventing you from bending your knees) is stable, lean your legs against the obstacle for support. Use your legs and hips to lower yourself down to the object.

5. Grasp the object firmly with both hands.

6. Prepare for the lift: look forward.

7. Lift upwards following your head and shoulders. Hold the load close to your body. Lift by extending your legs with your back straight, your buttocks out (exaggerate this position), and breathe out as you lift.

7

LIFTING TECHNIQUES

Sponsored By:

U.S. ARMY CENTERFOR HEALTH PROMOTION
AND PREVENTIVE MEDICINE
ERGONOMICS PROGRAM

A USACHPPM INFORMATION BULLETIN PROMOTING BETTER HEALTH THROUGH PUBLIC AWARENESS

Overhead Lift - Use the overhead lift to place objects on an overhead shelf. This lift begins with the object in your hands. *Be careful! Overhead lifts put you at increased risk for muscle strain. It can be difficult to maintain balance during the lift. If possible, avoid this lift. Only use this lift when absolutely necessary.*

1. Hold the object very close to your body.

2. Keep feet shoulder width apart, one foot slightly ahead of the other.

3. Prepare for the lift: look forward.

4. Raise the object to shelf height using the arm and shoulder muscles. Keep the object close to your body and breathe out as you lift.

5. As you reach the shelf, slowly shift your weight from your back foot to your forward foot. Keep your back straight.

6. When the load reaches the edge of the shelf, push the object onto the shelf.

8

 # LIFTING TECHNIQUES

Sponsored By:
U.S. ARMY CENTERFOR HEALTH PROMOTION
AND PREVENTIVE MEDICINE
ERGONOMICS PROGRAM

A USACHPPM INFORMATION BULLETIN PROMOTING BETTER HEALTH THROUGH PUBLIC AWARENESS

Pivot Technique - When you must lift an object and then turn to carry it away, it is common to twist the body. Twisting *while* lifting can cause serious damage to the tissues of the back. Use the pivot technique to avoid twisting while lifting.

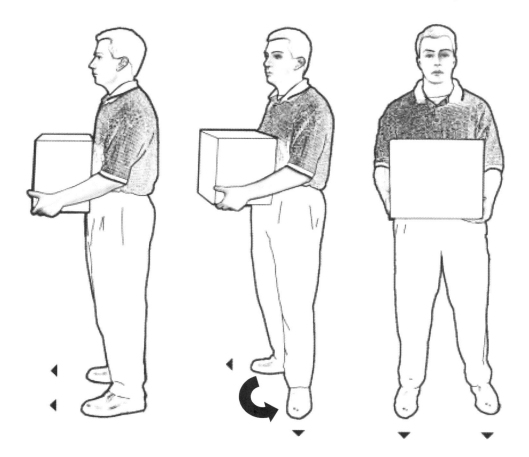

1. Lift the load using any of the previous techniques.

2. Hold the load very close to your body at waist level.

3. Turn the leading foot 90 degrees toward the direction you want to turn.

4. Bring the lagging foot next to the leading foot. Do not twist your body!

9

MOBILE PAY EXPRESS:

The smallest business can now accept credit cards

In its quest to empower small businesses, Absa introduced Mobile Pay Express, allowing traders to process credit card payments using any cellphone, fixed landline or web-enabled computer securely and within seconds.

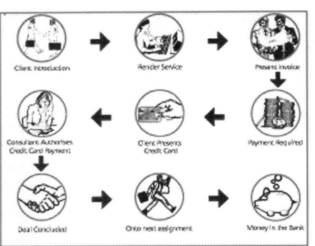

It reduces the need for traditional point-of-sale (POS) terminals as the infrastructure needed to effect mobile transactions is readily available. MasterCard, Visa, American Express and Diners Club cards can be used with this service.

Targeted mainly at small businesses, Mobile Pay Express is proof of Absa's ongoing efforts and commitment to empower small businesses in South Africa.

Christo Reynecke, Director: Absa Merchant Services, says: "We believe that all traders should have the opportunity to accept credit cards. By offering a secure and cost-effective alternative, more merchants can now enjoy the benefits of accepting credit cards."

The corporate market can also be serviced by offering tailor-made solutions.

Mobile traders do not require any additional software or hardware, are not dependent on specific networks and no SIM/handset upgrades are needed.

Any tone-enabled handset or telephone can support this service and it provides the ability to receive credit card payments and process refunds anywhere, any time.

Multiple handsets can also be linked to a single merchant, making it ideal for corporate and logistic companies. Multiple traders can also be linked to a single handset making it ideal for courier companies. Web maintenance of users and order tracking via the internet is possible.

Typical markets for business to consumers include consultants, home improvement providers (plumbers, electricians, etc), mobile mechanics, traders at flea markets, house doctors, fast food deliveries, roadside assistance, garden services, game lodges and home shopping delivery.

For more information, please contact 0860 111 222 or contactmerc@absa.co.za

Annexure F

Stepping up to quicker authorisations

The diagram below shows you step by step how to use Absa Card's IVR system to cut down on call duration for transaction authorisations.

The time taken to complete an authorisation call depends on how the caller responds to the IVR. If you wait to listen to each confirmation step, the call will take an average of 2 minutes and 51 seconds to complete. If you break out to a consultant right away (by pressing 9), the call will last about 2 minutes and 5 seconds.

However, if you skip the confirmation steps by using Quick Steps (QS) the call will take an average of only 50 seconds per transaction. Use Quick Steps only if you are sure that the correct information has been entered.

Vinniger magtigings – stap vir stap

Die diagram hier onder wys jou stap vir stap hoe om Absa Kaart se IVR-stelsel te gebruik om transaksiemagtigings vinniger te verkry.

Die oproeptyd vir 'n magtiging hang af van hoe die inbeller die IVR-stelsel gebruik. As jy wag om na elke bevestigingstap te luister, sal die oproep gemiddeld 2 minute en 51 sekondes duur. As jy direk na 'n konsultant deurskakel (deur 9 te druk) sal die oproep gemiddeld 2 minute en 5 sekondes duur.

As jy egter die bevestigingstappe oorslaan deur Quick Steps (QS) te gebruik, behoort die oproep gemiddeld net 50 sekondes per transaksie te duur. As jy Quick Steps gebruik, maak seker jy sleutel al die besonderhede korrek in.

| Number dialled | → | 086 010 0017 | ← | Nommer geskakel |

Welcome to Absa Card Authorisations. For instructions in English, press one. **If you are suspicious of the presenter of the card, press * (star) and ask for "Code 10 assistance".**
Welkom by Absa se 24-uur Magtigingsentrum. Vir aanwysings in Afrikaans, druk twee. As u agterdogtig is oor die aanbieder van die kaart, druk * (ster) en vra vir "Kode 10 bystand".

1 Please enter your merchant number, followed by the hash key (#)

e.g. 4712946328957362#

2 Please enter the sixteen-digit credit card number followed by the hash key (#)

QS   e.g. 0102#

3 Please enter the card expiry date. Enter the month first and then the year (mm/yy)

QS   e.g. 010#

4 Please enter the three-digit security number on the back of the credit card

QS   e.g. 100*00#

5 Please enter the transaction amount, using the star key (*) as a decimal point, followed by the hash key (#)

QS

6 For a straight purchase, press one.
For a budget purchase, press two.

7 Code readout, or request referred.
(The transaction has been authorised – your authorisation code is 123456789).
If your terminal does not accept a 9-digit code, enter only the first 6 digits of the code on your point-of-sale device.).
To repeat the authorisation code, please press 1.
For another authorisation, please press 2.
If you wish to speak to a consultant, please press 9.
Thank you for using this service. Goodbye!   QS

1 Sleutel asseblief u handelaarsnommer in, gevolg deur die hitsknoppie (#)

bv. 4712946328957362#

2 Sleutel asseblief die sestiensyfer-kredietkaartnommer in, gevolg deur die hitsknoppie (#)

QS   bv. 0102#

3 Sleutel asseblief die kaart se vervaldatum in, eers die maand en dan die jaar (mm/jj).

QS   bv. 010#

4 Sleutel asseblief die driesyfer-sekuriteitsnommer agterop die kaart in.

QS   bv. 100*00#

5 Sleutel asseblief die transaksiebedrag in, gevolg deur die hitsknoppie (#). Gebruik die ster-knoppie (*) as 'n desimale punt

QS

6 Vir gewone aankope, druk een.
Vir begrotingsaankope, druk twee.

7 Kode word verstrek, of versoek word verwys.
(Die transaksie is goedgekeur, die magtigingskode is 123456789).
As u terminaal nie 'n 9-syferkode aanvaar nie, sleutel net die eerste ses syfers van die kode in.
Om die magtigingskode te herhaal, druk asb 1.
Vir nog 'n magtiging, druk asb 2.
As u met 'n konsultant wil praat, druk asb 9.
Dankie dat u hierdie diens gebruik het. Tot siens!   QS

QS
Quick Step:
Press # to skip confirmation steps
Quick Step:
Druk # om bevestiging-stappe oor te slaan

QS
Quick Step:
Press # to end the call
Quick Step:
Druk # om die oproep te beëindig

2

Absa trader

DECEMBER   2006

Many things can go wrong with a card transaction if one does not follow the rules and safety precautions. To help you and your staff avoid the pitfalls, we list the most frequent problems and queries received from traders and cardholders, and how to handle them.

✔ Always compare the signature on the sales voucher with the one on the back of the card. Retain the signed voucher for at least 180 days from transaction date.

✔ Make a manual impression of the card on the imprinter (zip-zap) provided to you whenever a manual transaction takes place. A photo copy of the card is NOT acceptable.

✘ Don't accept cards for which you are not registered. Even if your terminal accepts any of the following cards, you MUST have a valid agreement with the card issuer to accept its cards. Contact the following numbers for registration:

- Diners Club – 011 358 8400
- American Express – 011 667 8173
- IEMAS – 012 674 7012
- Koopkrag – 012 348 5452
- Pretorium Trust – 012 321 2511
- Cape Consumers – 021 409 7600

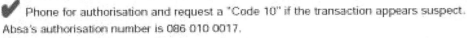

The ✔ and ✘ of card acceptance

✔ Phone for authorisation and request a "Code 10" if the transaction appears suspect. Absa's authorisation number is 086 010 0017.

✘ Don't leave your supervisor card lying around. Give it only to trusted staff members and don't write the PIN number on the back of the card. Remember, the principal merchant remains responsible for the actions of his staff members!

✔ Call our authorisations division for an authorisation code when you see the "please call" message on your terminal. Simply repeating the transaction will produce the same result.

✘ Don't break up a transaction into several smaller transactions to come under the floor limit in order to avoid obtaining authorisation.

✔ Contact our Merchant Help Desk on 0860 111 222 if any of your merchant details (address, telephone number, cheque account number, etc) have changed. Our Help Desk is equipped to solve most of your problems immediately. If a visit to your premises proves necessary to solve a problem or replace your terminal, the regional office nearest to you will be advised. The standard time required to solve any problem is 48 hours, although a visit to a

When and how to use the old 'zip-zap' – 2

Link

Win an XLink package worth R4 680! – 6

Making a manual imprint of a credit card is as old as the credit card itself. Although it has been superseded by generations of newer technology, the "zip-zap" method is still being used widely as a back-up.

Just what does this tried and trusted system involve? – Let's take a closer look and refresh your memory.

When to make a manual imprint

> *** An imprint is defined as the transfer of the embossed cardholder data from the front of a card to a transaction receipt, using a manual imprinter, in order to complete a transaction.**

• Card not read

When a credit card's magnetic stripe is damaged (or the POS terminal's card reader is faulty) the terminal will display the message "card not read". If this message is displayed, it is recommended to try swiping the card again. If the message is displayed again, you must then enter the credit card details by manually typing in the credit card number, expiry date, CVV and amount. However, this is a Supervisor function and can only be done using the Supervisor card and / or PIN.

• Terminal not working

Whenever a POS terminal is not working, a transaction may be done using a manual zip-zap machine. A valid imprint must be made and authorisation must be obtained, irrespective of the amount.

Once your POS terminal is working again, a "manual transaction" must be performed.

Don't try to deposit the zip-zap voucher over the counter at your bank. Zip-zap vouchers will not be accepted!

• Auth override

Certain transactions need to be authorised by the card issuer (the bank). Your POS terminal will automatically dial the bank in order to obtain an authorisation number. In certain instances the terminal would display the "Please call" message. This could be due to the bank wishing to obtain more information regarding the transaction in order to grant an authorisation. Another reason for a "Please call" is when the terminal could not reach the authorisation centre due to faulty communication links.

Absa's authorisation department must be contacted by phoning 086 010 0017.

Once the transaction was authorised, the bank will supply you with an authorisation code. This code must be written down and the transaction must be completed on the POS terminal by doing an "Authorisation override". This is a Supervisor function and can only be done using the Supervisor card and / or PIN.

Once the transaction was completed on the POS terminal you must make a valid imprint.

The authorisation code must also be recorded on the zip-zap voucher.

• Card not signed

When a cardholder presents a credit card with no signature on the back you must request the cardholder to present positive proof of identification.

Absa's authorisation department must be contacted and a "code 10" authorisation must be requested.

The authorisation official must be told that you are phoning for authorisation due to the fact that the credit card is not signed.

Once authorisation was granted you need to make a valid imprint of the credit card and complete the zip-zap voucher.

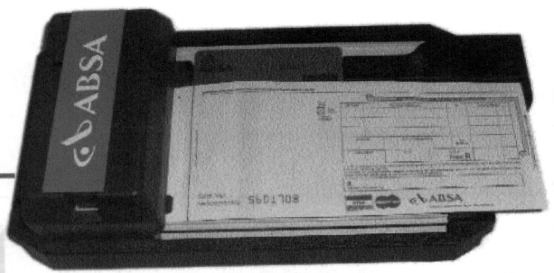

Left: Correct positioning of the credit card and the sales voucher on the zip-zap machine. Make sure the voucher is secured by the retaining edges to prevent the voucher from moving.

How to make a manual imprint

- Place the credit card on the designated area of the zip zap machine (see illustration above).

- Place a zip-zap voucher over the card and make sure the voucher is secured by the retaining edges to prevent the voucher from moving.

- Slide the zip-zap handle from left to right and back again.

- Check that all the credit card details as well as the merchant details are imprinted clearly (illustration below right).

- Complete the required information on the zip-zap voucher.

- Obtain and verify the cardholder signature.

- Supply the cardholder with the original copy (top copy).

- Retain the remaining copies for your records. All transaction vouchers must be kept for a minimum of 180 days (6 months) from transaction date.

- The following details must appear on all zip-zap vouchers:

- Transaction date.

- Total amount of the sale.

- Authorisation number obtained from the bank.

- Imprinted card details:
    - Credit card number
    - Expiry date
    - Cardholder name.

- Description of the goods and / or service.

- CVV number as printed on the tamper-proof signature strip on the reverse of the card.

- Cardholder signature.

- Merchant details on copper plate attached to the zip-zap machine:

- Merchant name

- Physical location.

And don't forget...

- When in doubt – make an imprint. It is better to make unnecessary imprints, rather that not making an imprint when required to do so. Remember, when you don't have an imprint when required, you will lose money as the transaction may be charged back!

- Imprints, together with other sales vouchers, must be kept for 180 days (six months) from transaction date.

- Manual imprints are never deposited at a bank. You must always keep the copies for your records. Should an imprint be made due to the POS terminal not working, you must perform a manual transaction on your POS terminal once it is fixed.

- "Scratching" or "rubbing" the card details with the back of a pen or any similar action on the printed POS slip or any other paper is not a valid imprint. The bank may institute a chargeback on the basis that it is not a valid imprint!

- Photo copies or faxes of the credit card are NOT valid imprints.

- Debit cards cannot be imprinted. In cases where a debit card cannot be processed on your POS terminal, you need to request alternative payment from the cardholder.

- Imprints MUST always be signed by the cardholder. It is not required to obtain a signature on the POS terminal slip in cases where an imprint was made.

Below: All the credit card details as well as the merchant details must be imprinted clearly on the voucher, and the merchant must fill in the required information.
Left: After the cardholder has signed the voucher, the signature must be compared with that on the credit card.

Some merchants must comply with
NEW CARD SECURITY PROGRAMME

The fight against credit card fraud has been taken a step further with the introduction of a new compliance standard for roleplayers in the card industry.

All merchants, payment services providers, data storage entities and acquirers, must now comply with the Payment Card Industry Data Security Standard (PCI DSS). This is a joint data security programme between Visa and MasterCard aimed at helping roleplayers in the industry to review their current systems and identify possible security weaknesses.

Any entity that stores, processes or transmits cardholder data must fully comply with the standard. However, merchants using Absa's point-of-sale terminals will not be required to demonstrate compliancy, provided that they do not capture or store cardholder details on any system.

If you capture any cardholder details such as the CVV number, expiry date and/or the card number on your cash register or swipe the client's card on a separate reader or any other device apart from the Absa stand-alone POS device, you are compelled to comply.

The PCI DSS resulted from the alignment of the Visa Account Information Security (AIS) programme and the MasterCard Site Data Protection (SDP) programme. The PCI DSS consists of a single set of security requirements and allows merchants and service providers to select a single vendor and implement a single process to comply with all payment card data security requirements.

The programme has been created in response to a growing number of successful hacks and the linked increase in credit card fraud leading to unforeseen expenses and fines, resulting in negative media reports. The PCI DSS programme was designed to help merchants, payment service providers and data storage entities to review their current systems and identify possible security weaknesses to be addressed.

Key requirements

The PCI Data Security Standard consists of 12 key requirements for protecting cardholder account and transaction information:

If you require further information and would like to review the standards, please log onto any of the following websites:

http://www.one-sec.com/
http://www.visacemea.com/ac/ais/data_security.jsp
https://sdp.mastercardintl.com/
https://www.pcisecuritystandards.org/

Further information will soon be provided to all merchants in this regard.

PCI Data Security Standard requirements

Build and maintain a secure network	1. Install and maintain a firewall configuration to protect data.
	2. Do not use vendor-supplied defaults for system passwords and other security parameters.
Protect cardholder data	3. Protect stored data.
	4. Encrypt transmission of cardholder data and sensitive information across public networks.
Maintain a vulnerability management programme	5. Use and regularly update anti-virus software.
	6. Develop and maintain secure systems and applications.
Implement strong access control measures	7. Restrict access to data by business need-to-know.
	8. Assign a unique ID to each person with computer access.
	9. Restrict physical access to cardholder data.
Regularly monitor and test networks	10. Track and monitor all access to network resources and cardholder data.
	11. Regularly test security systems and processes.
Maintain an information security policy	12. Maintain a policy that addresses information security.

5

COMBAT
Card Fraud

Don't be
A Victim!

Watch out
for the following suspicious behaviour...

While any of the following can occur in a perfectly legitimate transaction, these characteristics are frequently present during fraudulent transactions.

BE ALERT FOR CUSTOMERS WHO...

1 Make random purchases, selecting items with little regard to size, quality or value.

2 Cannot provide identification when asked.

3 Provide you with an authorisation number that they alleged to have obtained from the bank.

4 Purchase an unusual amount of expensive items - beware of transactional values above norm.

5 Make several small purchases to stay under the floor limit, or ask what the floor limit is - be aware of customers who insist that a transaction is split into more than one low value transaction.

 Standard Bank

 Investec Private Bank

 Diners Club International

 VISA

 AMERICAN EXPRESS Cards

 NEDBANK

 ABSA

 MasterCard

 FNB First National Bank

How can we help you?

Visa Card SECURITY FEATURES ⏬

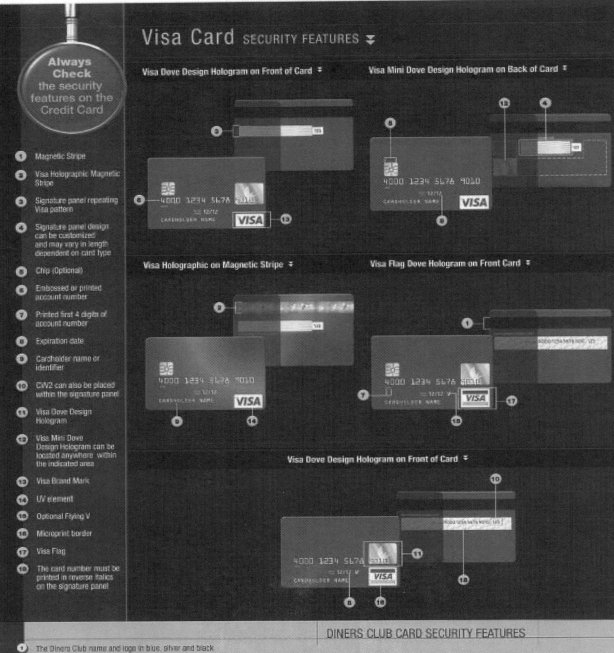

Visa Dove Design Hologram on Front of Card ⏬

Visa Mini Dove Design Hologram on Back of Card ⏬

Visa Holographic on Magnetic Stripe ⏬

Visa Flag Dove Hologram on Front Card ⏬

Visa Dove Design Hologram on Front of Card ⏬

Always Check the security features on the Credit Card

1. Magnetic Stripe
2. Visa Holographic Magnetic Stripe
3. Signature panel repeating Visa pattern
4. Signature panel design can be customized and may vary in length dependent on card type
5. Chip (Optional)
6. Embossed or printed account number
7. Printed first 4 digits of account number
8. Expiration date
9. Cardholder name or identifier
10. CVV2 can also be placed within the signature panel
11. Visa Dove Design Hologram
12. Visa Mini Dove Design Hologram can be located anywhere within the indicated area
13. Visa Brand Mark
14. UV element
15. Optional Flying V
16. Microprint border
17. Visa Flag
18. The card number must be printed in reverse italics on the signature panel

DINERS CLUB CARD SECURITY FEATURES

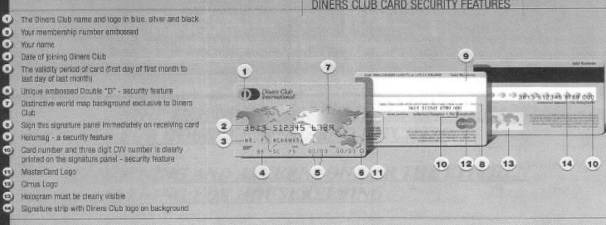

1. The Diners Club name and logo in blue, silver and black
2. Your membership number embossed
3. Your name
4. Date of joining Diners Club
5. The validity period of card (first day of first month to last day of last month)
6. Unique embossed Double "D" - security feature
7. Distinctive world map background exclusive to Diners Club
8. Sign this signature panel immediately on receiving card
9. Holomag - a security feature
10. Card number and three digit CVV number is clearly printed on the signature panel - security feature
11. MasterCard Logo
12. Cirrus Logo
13. Hologram must be clearly visible
14. Signature strip with Diners Club logo on background

MasterCard SECURITY FEATURES ⩤

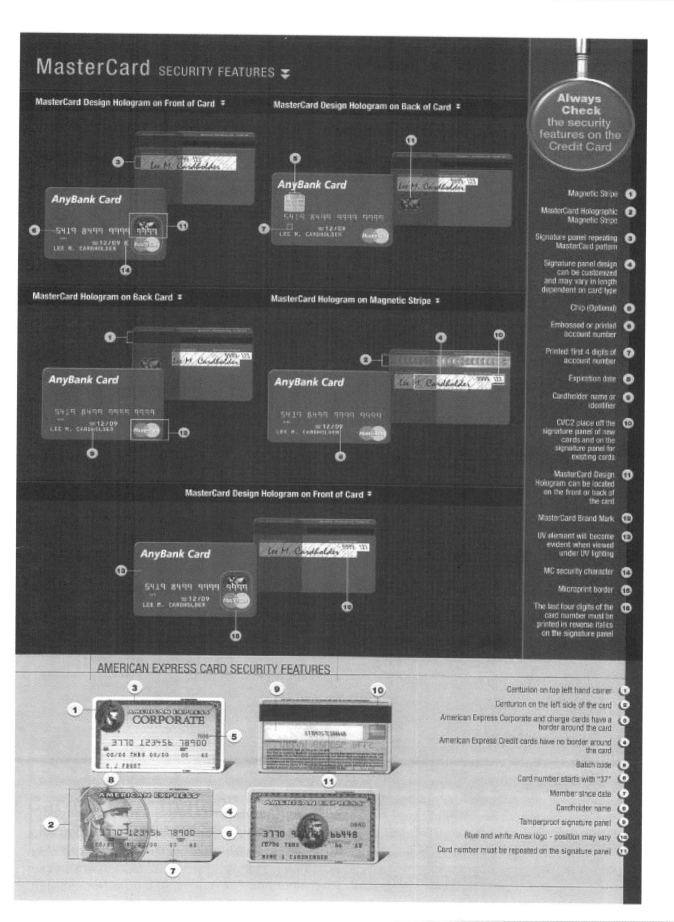

MasterCard Design Hologram on Front of Card ⩤

MasterCard Design Hologram on Back of Card ⩤

MasterCard Hologram on Back Card ⩤

MasterCard Hologram on Magnetic Stripe ⩤

MasterCard Design Hologram on Front of Card ⩤

Always Check the security features on the Credit Card

- Magnetic Stripe ❶
- MasterCard Holographic Magnetic Stripe ❷
- Signature panel repeating MasterCard pattern ❸
- Signature panel design can be customized and may vary in length dependent on card type ❹
- Chip (Optional) ❺
- Embossed or printed account number ❻
- Printed first 4 digits of account number ❼
- Expiration date ❽
- Cardholder name or identifier ❾
- CVC2 place off the signature panel of new cards and on the signature panel for existing cards ❿
- MasterCard Design Hologram can be located on the front or back of the card ⓫
- MasterCard Brand Mark ⓬
- UV element will become evident when viewed under UV lighting ⓭
- MC security character ⓮
- Microprint border ⓯
- The last four digits of the card number must be printed in reverse italics on the signature panel ⓰

AMERICAN EXPRESS CARD SECURITY FEATURES

- Centurion on top left hand corner ①
- Centurion on the left side of the card ②
- American Express Corporate and charge cards have a border around the card ③
- American Express Credit cards have no border around the card ④
- Batch code ⑤
- Card number starts with "37" ⑥
- Member since date ⑦
- Cardholder name ⑧
- Tamperproof signature panel ⑨
- Blue and white Amex logo - position may vary ⑩
- Card number must be repeated on the signature panel ⑪

tips to avoid chargeback's

1
Obtain a card imprint on manual (zip-zap machine) face-to-face transaction when the magnetic stripe cannot be read. Make an imprint of the card when a key entered (manual) transaction is done. It is your proof that the card was present during the transaction. A scanned, fax or photocopy is not regarded as an imprint.

2
The cardholder must sign the sales voucher.

3
Reconcile your daily settlement to ensure that transactions are processed correctly.

4
Obtain an authorisation for every transaction over your floor limit (when your electronic device does not provide you with one).

5
YOU must phone your authorisation centre for authorisation.
- Do not accept an authorisation code from the cardholder.
- Do not allow the customer to phone on your behalf.

6
Compare the signature on the card with the signature on the sales voucher.

7
Do not use your credit card at your own business to generate funds.

8
To avoid chargeback's you have to adhere to the rules and regulations as set out in your merchant agreement.

9
Provide copies of sales vouchers within the retrieval request timeframes.
- Don't delay!! Return copies of sales vouchers promptly!

Call for "CODE 10" authorisation

Call your authorisation centre immediately and ask for a Code 10 if:

- You believe you have a counterfeit or altered card.
- The presenter / transaction is suspicious.
- The signatures do not match.
- Account number of the printed sales voucher differs from that on the card.
- The customer does not have his card with him and insists on purchasing goods with a credit card number only.

Fraudulent Letter Authorising Card Use

In all instances, insist on both the credit card and the credit holder being present when payment is processed or call for an authorisation code.

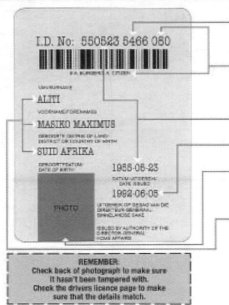

This indicates whether the I.D. belongs to a Male or Female.
0 - 4999 = Female
5000 - 9999 = Male

06 = S.A. Citizen
18 = Non S.A. Citizen
If issued subsequent to 1986.07.01. Prior issues reflect the Population Group Classification

Ensure that Date of Birth agress is holder that age?

Check to see when I.D. was issued Remember to age the photo.

Check photo to see:
1. If it is the holder
2. If it has been tampered with
3. If it is within the block

Ensure that names are:
1. Not completed with letraset
2. The same type of lettering
3. In a straight line
4. Contains no initials

REMEMBER:
Check back of photograph to make sure it hasn't been tampered with.
Check the drivers licence page to make sure that the details match.

Annexure J

Example of Reservation Form

Avuxeni Management Services CC t/a
THE ELEPHANT SPRINGS HOTEL 2003 / 110571 / 23
31 Sutter Road, Bela-Bela, 0480, Limpopo | P.O.Box 94, Bela-Bela, 0480, Limpopo
Tel: +27 14 736 2101 | Fax: +27 14 736 3586
E-mail: reservations@elephant-springs.co.za
Website: www.elephant-springs.co.za | Vat Reg. # 4960205609

Guest Registration

Personal Details

Surname		First Name	Title
Company		ID / Passport	
Vehicle reg.	A C	Nationality	Code

Address Details

Postal Address Street

Postal Address Area

Postal Address City

Postal Address Code

Postal Address Country

Contact Details

Telephone (Home)

Telephone (Fax)

Telephone (Work)

E-mail

Cell

Booking Details

Booking Number   Room Number

Arrival & Departure

Payment Method   Cash   Diners Club   American Express   Master Card   VISA   Other

Please complete the blank fields and sign

Please Note

Regrettably cheques are not accepted without prior arrangement. Our tariffs are subject to seasonal changes without prior notice. The value of the originally booked days remains payable even in the event of early departure. Cancellation costs applies as follows: 30 - 60 days 25% of total booked value, 15 - 29 days 50% of total booked value, 1 - 14 days 100% of total booked value are payable. For your own safety, no visitors are allowed in guest's rooms, kindly entertain your visitors in the public areas. Any additional guests in rooms will be charged for accordingly.

Disclaimer

I/we hereby agree that it is a condition of my/our occupation of the hotel premises that the owner shall not be responsible for loss or damage to any property brought by me/us upon the premises whether arising from fire, theft, or from any other cause and by whomsoever caused or arising from the negligence, whether gross or otherwise, or the wrongful act of any person in the employ of the owner. I/we, whether or not I/we occupy rooms in the hotel premises am/are deemed to contract with the owner on this basis.

Please consider your fellow guests, by not playing loud music after 23h00

_____
Signature

Annexure K

Example of Reservation Chart

Brief In-House Guests (Active)							
As on: 05 July 2007			**Restrictions:** Branches: EL Elephant Springs				
Code	Unit No	Booking	Guest Name	Address (City)	A	C	Departure
RAMD0005	HLTG08	14714	Ramdhani PraveshMr		1	0	7 Jul 2007
MABO0044	HLDG11	14719	Mabotja WMr		1	0	2 Aug 2007
MAGW0002	HLTG09	14730	Magwaye SSMr		1	0	6 Jul 2007

Note: Split bookings are indicated with an asterisk (*).
     Room list entries are indicated with a double asterisk (**).

Booking Count	Adults (A)	Children (C)
3	3	0

Annexure L

Example of Arrival List

Arrivals List (Brief)

Restrictions: From 5 Jul 2007 (00:00) until before 6 Jul 2007 (00:00) / Branches: EL Elephant Springs / Category: All Categories / Type: All / Status: All, except Cancelled, No-show & Faulty

Guest Code	Guest Name	Company	Occ.	Group Name	Booking	Ref.	Unit No	City	Arrival Date	Depart. Date	Status
MTHE0014	J Mthembu	n/a	2A3C	n/a	14644		CAG09		7/5/2007	7 Jul 2007	Prov
NYAT0008	Mr T Nyati	Lesedi Travel (Jhb) (Seekers	1A0C	n/a	14718	073538	HLTG16		7/5/2007	6 Jul 2007	Prov
MAWA0004	Mr & Mrs NN Mawasha	n/a	2A0C	n/a	14731		HLDG01		7/5/2007	6 Jul 2007	Prov

Booking Count: 3   Total Arrivals: 8 (5A 3C)

Note: Split bookings are indicated with an asterisk (*).

Room list entries are indicated with a double asterisk (**).

Status Key => Prov : Provisional , Conf : Confirmed or Deposit Partly Paid , Dep : Deposit Fully Paid , Full : Booking Fully Paid

Annexure M

Example of Training Manual:

How to make a booking

HOW TO MAKE A PRIVATE BOOKING

- Highlight on the Room number

- Click new

- Click guest and complete all the guest details

- Click Create new booking / select the existing one

- Add number of guests

- Click guest rate and complete

- Click due date

- Click accept

- Click Ignore the warnings

- Go to Reservations and refresh grid display

Questions: Do you want to add guest details now? (if you did, create the new clients Details and click accept.

NB. If you make a private booking you go to guest and Travel Agency, Company And Department, you go to Client/Company.

When the booking is done under Company name or Travel Agency?
This is how to add guest details

- Click on the booking

- Click View/Edit

- Click guest and enter guest details

                    OR

To add details

- Double click on booking nr.And complete all the details

HOW TO MAKE A TRAVEL AGENCY / COMPANY OR DEPARTMENT BOOKING

- Highlight on the room number

- Click new

- Click on Client / Company

- Click on the Company to add Company details

- Select Existing Client / Create new Client

- Click on Role and select Agent

- Complete the Agent and Guest rate

- Click Agent rate

- Click Due date

- Click Accept and click ignore warnings

NB. After the booking was done, click on the booking, click on View Edit to check whether the Voucher **AND** Agent rate is correct.

NB. After every booking you did; Please print the Registration form and the Booking Record, staple them together with the voucher or order and take everything to Rina for a signature.

NB. From there file these paper work in the files according to the date and month.

NB. If you do a Company Booking you add the extras automatic.

HOW TO LINK A BOOKING

- First of all you create a new booking

- Highlight on the Room Number you want to link

- Click on the previous booking

- Click View Edit and

- Click Yes and OK

- Click on the Previous Booking

- Click Folio

- Click on folio role and open select group master

- Click done

- Click on phone bill folio page and accept

- Click accept and Click Ignore Warnings

When the guest checking out you must have the complete records

1. Debtors check list
2. Statement x 3
3. Tax Invoice x 3
4. Registration form
5. Booking Record
6. Pro Forma Tax Invoice / Summary
7. The Voucher or Order

HOW TO PRINT THE REGISTRATION FORM

- Click on the Booking

- Click on the Status and select your Status (or the status you looking for)

- Click print

NB. You can only print the Tax Invoice and Statement for the booking which is checked Inn or Active booking

NB. If you are printing: Statement, Tax Invoice Booking Record, Registration Form Tax Summary and the Summary, you follow the very same procedure or method

BOOKINGS ON THE GRID

- Green - Provisional
- Brown - Deposit paid
- Orange - Confirmed
- Yellow - Confirmed
- Red   - Active
- Blue   - Left (Checked out)
- Light Blue – Left (but the booking is paid)
- Sky Blue - No Show
- Grey   - Cancelled

Function Sheet for Conferences, Click on the name and see the names:

Mafunyane	**R200.00 flat rate**	**30 Occupants**
Kambaku	**R200.00 flat rate**	**100 Occupants**
Shawu	**R200.00 flat rate**	**100 Occupants**
Shingwedzi	**R100.00 flat rate**	**12 Occupants**
CFSWI	**Cabana Pool Area**	**30 Occupants**

HOW TO MAKE A TRANSACTION / TO DO THE PAYMENT FOR THE BOOKING.

- Click on the booking

- Click on Transaction

- Open payment types and select the payment

- Click Post Transaction

- Click Post

- Click OK and close

TO CONFIRM A PROVISIONAL BOOKING

- **By Payment / Purchase Order**

- Click on Booking

- Click on View / Edit

- Click on Booking Reference, Type Account Nr. and expire date in

- Click on Except

- Click Booking

- Select Confirmed

- Click Except

- Click Ignore

- File in Confirmed File

HOW TO CHECK THE BOOKING INN
- Click on the Booking

- Click on Check-Inn

- Click on Check-Inn Selected Booking and Close

DON'T POST IT UNLESS OTHERWISE YOU GOT THE PAYMENT
HOW TO CHECK THE BOOKIN OUT

- Click on the Booking

- Click Check Out

From there you put the paper work in the Departure Basket, but everything is paid in full
If there is an account to pay, please write it in The City Ledger Book to hand the book
To Sanet, Debtors Department.

HOW TO ADD THE EXTRAS

- Click on the Booking

- Click View Edit and Click Extras

- Select the Extras and add Extras

HOW TO ADD A NOTE

- Click on the Booking

- Click View / Edit

- Click on Notes / Marketing and write you Noted

- Click Accept and Ignore

HOW TO PRINT A STATEMENT, TAX INVOICE AND DEBTORS CHECK LIST

- Click on Booking

- Go to status and Select Status

- Click Printer

- Click Print

HOW TO PRINT THE DEBTORS CHECK LIST

- Click Debtors

- Click Yes

- Click Debtors Check list

- Click Print

HOW TO PRINT THE IN-HOUSE, ARRIVALS AND DEPARTURE REPORTS FOR HOUSEKKEEPING AND KITCHEN

EVERY MORNING AND AFTERNOON FOR THE KITCHEN EVERY MORNING FOR HOUSEKEEPNG

A. – In-House Report. Report (Housekeeping & Kitchen)

- Click Report and Click Active In-House Guests

- Click Brief

- Click on Deposit Paid to open the Status

- Select the Active One

- Click Generate Report and Print

- Click Close

B – Arrival Report (housekeeping & Kitchen)

- Click Report and Arrival List

- Click Brief

- Go to Deposit paid Status and open it. Select (All except Cancelled,

No Show and Faulty)

- Click Generate Report and Print

C – Departure List (housekeeping & Kitchen)

- Click on Report

- Click Departure List

- Click Confidential

- Open the Status Deposit Paid and Select (All except Cancelled, No Show and Faulty)

- Click Generate Report and Print

HOW TO CHECK THE BOOKING INN

- Click on the Booking

- Click on Check-Inn

- Click on Check-Inn Selected Booking and Close

DON'T POST IT UNLESS OTHERWISE YOU GOT THE PAYMENT
HOW TO CHECK THE BOOKING OUT

- Click on the Booking

- Click Check Out

From there you put the paper work in the Departure Basket, but everything is Fully paid

If there is an account to pay, please write it in The City Ledger Book to hand The Book to Sanet. Debtors Department.

HOW TO ADD THE EXTRAS

- Click on the Booking

- Click View-Edit and Click Extras

- Select the Extras and add Extras

HOW TO ADD A NOTE

- Click on the Booking

- Click View / Edit

- Click on Notes/Marketing and write your Notes

- Accept and Ignore Warnings

HOW TO PRINT A STATEMENT, TAX INVOICE AND DEBTORS CHECK LIST

- Click on Booking

- Go to Status and Select Status

- Click Printer

- Click Print

HOW TO PRINT THE DEBTORS CHECK LIST

- Click Debtors

- Click Yes

- Click Debtors Check List

- Click Print

HOW TO PRINT THE IN-HOUSE, ARRIVALS AND DEPARTURE REPORTS FOR HOUSEKEEPING AND KITCHEN

EVERY MORNING AND AFTERNOON FOR THE KITCHEN EVERY MORNING FOR HOUSEKEEPING

A.- In-House Report. Report (Housekeeping & Kitchen)

- Click Report and Click Active In-house Guests

- Click Brief

- Click on Deposit paid to open the Status

- Select the Active One

- Click Generate Report and Print

- Click Close

B - Arrival Report (Housekeeping & Kitchen)

- Click Report and Arrival List

- Click Brief

- Go to Deposit paid status and open it, Select (All except Cancelled, No Show and Faulty.)

- Click Generate Report and Print

C - Departure List (Housekeeping & Kitchen)

- Click on Report

- Click Departure List

- Click Confidential

- Open the Status Deposit paid and Select (All except Cancelled, No Show & Faulty)

- Click Generate Report and Print

Annexure N

Example of Typical Interview Questions

General Interview Questions

Q: Tell me about yourself?
A: The best approach is to ask what the interviewer would like to know in particular. You might suggest going over your work experience or what you have accomplished during your career. This is a great opportunity to highlight your accomplishments.

Q: Why do you want to leave your current position? What's it like working for your current employer?
A: Always be positive when speaking about your current/former employer. Explain why/how increased responsibilities or opportunities will help you reach your career goals. Use the opportunity to explain what you've learned and what you contributed in your last position. Be sure to mention any activities that relate to the position under consideration.

Q: What are your strengths and weaknesses?
A: Be prepared to talk about what you've accomplished in your current/former position. Be specific and include examples of how you contributed to the company's success. This might include effects on sales, saved time, money, or resources, increased efficiency, or product development etc. When outlining any weaknesses, state whether you have been made aware of any weaknesses and how you have taken measures to address these issues. End with a positive spin on what you've learned and what you are doing to overcome any weaknesses.

Q: What do you require for a base salary?
A: Never quote a figure. If it were too high, you might exclude yourself from consideration; if it were too low the interviewer might question your qualifications. A better approach is to state your current salary and add that if the company decided to make you an offer, you are confident that the rate of pay would be in line with the responsibility of the position.

Q: Where do you want to be in five years?
A: Be prepared to answer this question. Your goals in the short term should be more general: gaining a greater understanding, developing new skills, etc. Your goals in the long term should reveal a desire to advance within your discipline or area of expertise.

Q: What is your philosophy on management/management style?
A: Be specific and site an example of how you supervise or expect to be supervised. This gives the employer a better idea of how you might fit into their organization.

More Interview Questions

Below are some more general questions that you can work through and prepare answers for in preparation for your interview:

- Why did you decide to get a degree in this field?
- What are the five biggest accomplishments in your life thus far?
- Tell us about a particularly difficult problem that you analyzed and what was your recommendation.
- Tell us about a situation where the analysis that you performed was incorrect. What would you have done differently?

- Your assignment is to assist the line organization to prepare the budget. A number of the line supervisors are new. What steps will you take to introduce the line supervisors to the process?
- What experience have you had in developing a budget?
- Tell us about a situation where you demonstrated good communication skills.
- Tell us about how you have handled a dissatisfied customer in the past.
- Here is a situation. How would you handle it? You discover your boss is cheating on his/her expense account. What should you do?
- What did you like most about your last job?